jim carrey

PAULA GUZZETTI

DILLON PRESS
Parsippany, New Jersey

Photo Credits
Front & back covers: Outline/Bonnie Schiffman.

Canapress: 19, 20, 21, 24, 26. The Globe & Mail/Tibor Kolley: 25. Globe Photos: 47; N.B.C.: 34, 35; N.B.C./Chris Haston: 30; S.N. 49, 51. Outline/Andrew Brusso: 5, 64; Stephen Danelian: 1; Steve Goldstein: 2–3; Pat Harbron: 6. Photofest: 8, 16, 17, 27, 36, 40, 44, 52; © 1995 Warner Bros.: 53. Retna/Fitzroy Barrett: 9; Steven Freeman: 56; Armando Gallo: 61; Steve Granitz: 57. Superstock: 12, 29.

Library of Congress Cataloging-in-Publication Data
Guzzetti, Paula.
      Jim Carrey / by Paula Guzzetti. — 1st ed.
             p. cm. — (Taking part books)
      Includes index.
      ISBN 0-382-39730-4 (LSB). — ISBN 0-382-39731-2 (pbk.)
      1. Carrey, Jim, 1962– —Juvenile literature. 2. Motion picture actors and actresses—
United States—Biography—Juvenile literature. 3. Comedians—United States—Biography—
Juvenile literature.
      [1. Carrey, Jim, 1962– . 2. Actors and actresses. 3. Comedians.]
      I. Title.
      PN2287.C278G88   1998
      791.43'028'092—dc20
      [B]   96-32008
Summary: A biography of talented comedian Jim Carrey, whose comic movies have made him a Hollywood superstar.

Cover and book design by Michelle Farinella

Published by Dillon Press
A Division of Simon & Schuster
299 Jefferson Road, Parsippany, NJ 07054

First Edition
Printed in the United States of America
10 9 8 7 6 5 4 3 2 1

CONTENTS

Jim loves to clown around.

CHAPTER

1

"America's Favorite Fool"

When Jim Carrey was about eight, he liked to stand in front of his bedroom mirror making faces. He would twist his features this way and that. He would roll his eyes, wriggle his nose, and stretch open his mouth as wide as he could.

Sometimes his mother, walking past his door, would see him and try to stop him. She told him that if he went on in that way, his face might freeze in a silly position forever. Then people would laugh at him for the rest of his life.

Those words made Jim go at it all the harder. He wanted people to laugh at him. More than anything else, he longed to be funny.

Today Jim Carrey is still making faces—as one of America's hottest comics. Known for his wild antics as well as his rubbery facade, he has been called America's favorite fool, a human cartoon, and the comic phenomenon of the 1990s. He has performed in comedy clubs; on television sitcoms, variety shows, and talk programs; and in films. His movie megahits—*Ace Ventura: Pet*

Jim in Dumb and Dumber

Detective, The Mask, Dumb and Dumber, and *Batman Forever*—alone have earned him millions of dollars and scores of devoted fans.

Now an acknowledged superstar, Jim has more than fulfilled his childhood dream. He is rich. He is famous.

Jim waves to the crowd at the premiere of The Mask.

And he has made countless numbers of people laugh.

But Jim's journey to the top was far from funny. He started out poor. He was often unhappy, and he attained stardom only after years of disappointment and struggle. Though his talent propelled him, it was hard work, determination, and a firm belief in his goal that got him where he is.

2

A Comic in the Making

Jim's story begins in Canada. He was born near Toronto on January 17, 1962, the youngest of four children. His father, Percy, was an accountant. Like Jim, Percy was also interested in show business. In fact, as a young boy, Percy had mastered the saxophone and the clarinet in hopes of becoming a professional musician. He had even managed to become the lead player in an orchestra by the time he was 16.

But Percy's career plans changed when he married. As a husband and potential father, Percy needed a more dependable line of work. Accounting seemed to offer the steady paycheck and regular hours required to support a family. So, unselfishly and with a tinge of regret, Percy gave up his dream of the stage for the routine of an office. But although he became an accountant by trade, he remained a performer at heart.

Jim's mother, Kathleen, had had a difficult childhood. The daughter of alcoholics, she had grown up with little attention or love. As a result, she was often lonely and

Toronto, Canada, as seen from the shores of Lake Ontario

depressed. During her marriage she suffered from bouts of real and imagined illness. Her husband stood by her, and her children did their best to cheer her up.

But despite difficulties, the Carrey household, during Jim's early years, was far from grim. It was filled with affection. Jim says, "We had problems like all families, but we had a lot of love. I was extremely loved. We always felt we had each other."

Also, the household often exploded with fun. The Carrey family had a wild sense of humor and could get very rambunctious. It wasn't unusual for family dinners to end in cherry-cheesecake fights or for guests to leave the Carrey table with butter smeared across their faces.

Jim's father, in particular, loved practical jokes and was usually the force behind the family's madness. He was Jim's first comic mentor and role model. "My father was really funny," Jim explains. "I wanted to be just like him."

Jim knew at an early age that he was destined for show business. "I can't imagine what it's like not to know what you want to do," he says. "It must be a horrible feeling. I knew what I wanted from the time I was a little kid."

His first comedic attempts took place at home. Jim discovered that running in slow motion or sliding down the stairs would make his sisters and brother giggle.

Later, as his talents developed, he put on shows for the entire family. His impersonations of annoying neighbors and relatives sent his parents into fits of laughter. His parents' encouragement was all he needed to go on. In a talk with television interviewer Barbara Walters in 1995, Jim said of his mother and father, "They didn't tell me I was being stupid. They told me I was being funny."

Yet, when Jim started school, he was reluctant to share his comic talents with his classmates. He was painfully shy. He was also self-conscious. As a first grader he was so tall and thin that the other children teased him. Shortening his full name, James Eugene, to Jimmy Gene, classmates called him Jimmy Gene the String Bean. Jim hadn't yet learned to put his physical traits to comedic use. And so the name stung.

School life brightened for Jim in the second grade. That's when he had his first experience on a stage.

It all started in music class during practice for a Christmas assembly. Jim began fooling around by mocking the musicians on a record. His teacher thought she would embarrass him by making him get up and do what he was doing in front of the whole class. Jim got up and did it. He was so funny that his teacher asked him to do the routine for the Christmas assembly.

Jim had gone from class joke to class clown. It was impossible to stop him after that.

In the next few years, Jim's zany sense of humor won him many friends. Children and teachers alike roared with laughter at his outrageous routines.

A particular favorite involved a pack of colored candles. Jim would put all the candles into his mouth, chew them up carefully, and then spit them out as if he were throwing up. The sight of all that colored goop spilling from his mouth left his audience in stitches.

Not even Jim's principal was immune to Jim's talents. Having spent hours studying the voices and movements of famous movie and television funnymen, Jim could do hilarious impersonations of comedy's biggest stars. His special favorites were Jerry Lewis, Dick Van Dyke, and the Three Stooges. When Jim's principal saw his Three Stooges routine, she laughed so hard she fell out of her chair!

By the time Jim was in seventh grade, he was performing for his classmates on a regular basis. His teacher even helped him to arrange a performance schedule. She told him that if he didn't fool around during class, he could have fifteen minutes at the end of the day to do a comedy routine. Jim would finish his work, then begin to plan what he would do. Just as his teacher promised,

Jerry Lewis one of Jim's favorite comedians

he got his allotted time each afternoon. Jim thought it was a very smart and fair arrangement. He now says that those daily sessions at school were an important part of his comedic development. He has stayed in touch with that teacher to this day.

But for all his fooling, Jim was an excellent student, who earned straight A's. He was also an impressive athlete,

Jim also enjoyed impersonating the Three Stooges.

excelling at hockey, Canada's national sport. His skill at the game won him additional admiration and praise.

By the time he was ready for high school, Jim was confident and hopeful. He had friends, his family seemed secure, and his career plans were set.

But then, without warning, his world came apart. The next six years would be a test of his courage and resolve.

17

CHAPTER

3

Hard Times

When Jim was 13, his father lost his job. It was a blow to the family from which they never recovered. Percy Carrey was 51 years old and had worked for the same company for more than 25 years. In fact, the company that let him go was the very one he had joined after giving up his plans for a show-business career. Suddenly the sacrifice he had made so many years before seemed pointless. He felt disillusioned and betrayed.

The loss of his father's job had a profound effect on Jim. It not only plunged his family into poverty, but it also left Jim bitter and angry. "It made me realize," Jim said in an August 8, 1994, article in *Time* magazine, "that life offers no assurances, so you might as well do what you're really passionate about." From then on he was determined never to give up on his show-business dream as his father had done.

At the same time that Percy was coping with the shame he felt because of unemployment, Jim's mother, Kathleen, was struggling through a period of illness. Jim

Jim's high school

was beside himself. The best he could offer was a bit of comic relief. When she was really in pain, he would go into her bedroom in his underwear and do his praying-mantis impression. Both of Jim's parents came to depend on his antics to get them through the tough times. In a March 1996 interview with the Arts & Entertainment Network, Jim joked about being called on to provide humor at the oddest hours. He said that his father would often creep into his room when he was asleep and whisper, "Jim. Jim. Sorry to wake you in the middle of the night, but your mother and I could use a good laugh.

The factory where the Carrey family worked

You're on in 5." In the case of Kathleen's illnesses, it was Jim's silliness, as much as medicine and tender care, that provided the cure.

Now almost destitute, the family pulled together to look for work. Eventually Percy, Kathleen, and the children found employment in a factory as security guards and janitors. The work was especially hard on Jim, who went from a full day of school to a full night cleaning the factory bathrooms. Too exhausted to concentrate on his

The Carreys lived in this factory-owned house for a time.

studies, he began to fall behind. He also avoided his friends. The last thing he wanted was to have to answer questions about his family's troubles.

Despite their efforts the Carreys still couldn't make ends meet. Eventually they were forced to move out of their home and into factory housing.

By the time Jim was 16, things had become so bad that he had to leave school and work full time. He resented having to earn a living at so early an age. He longed to complete his education and pursue his future plans. He could barely control his feelings of disappointment and anger.

Meanwhile, tensions were also increasing at home. Long hours of disagreeable work took their toll on the entire family. Where the Carreys had once been decent and fun-loving, they were becoming nasty and sullen. "The whole family was turning into monsters," Jim explained in the August 1994 issue of *Details* magazine. Not even Jim's half-hearted attempts at humor would help.

Realizing that the factory was the source of their unhappiness, the Carreys quit their jobs. It was a daring move, which left them without work and without income. Because the house they were occupying was factory-owned, quitting also meant that the family had no place to live. Desperate for shelter, they took refuge in a battered Volkswagen van, which became their temporary home. It was the lowest point in their lives.

4

The Road Back

The family's hopes now rested with Jim. The year before he left high school, Jim had had a brief chance to perform on the professional stage. A Toronto comedy club called Yuk Yuk's hosted an amateur night during which aspiring comedians could try out their acts in front of an audience. With the aid of his parents, Jim carefully prepared for his short time in the spotlight. His father helped him write a five-minute-long routine, and his mother put together his performance outfit. It was yellow polyester—"what all the nice young boy comics wear," she had said.

But the experience had been a disaster for Jim. His clothes were all wrong, and his routine simply didn't get laughs. Jim says: "First of all, the polyester suit didn't go over so well in the hip underground world. And then the owner of the club, Mark Breslin, liked to heckle young comics from the back on the microphone. He'd [say things like] 'Totally boring.'"

Jim was booed off the stage before his five minutes were up. He was devastated.

Jim first tried out his comedy routine at Yuk Yuk's, a comedy club in Toronto.

Two years later the family's plight gave Jim the courage to try the club again. But this time it was not just for fun. Now it was also for money. As a professional comic, Jim hoped to earn enough to help support his family. Having failed once before, he was aware of the risks. But, he says, "I felt like giving it a shot. Failure taught me that failure isn't the end unless you give up."

Jim was 17 when he returned to Yuk Yuk's. This time, to his great relief and delight, he was a hit. He began performing at the club several nights a week, doing comic impressions. His repertoire included practically every noted personality—from entertainer Sammy Davis, Jr., to movie legend James Stewart to the Amazing Kreskin, a popular magician of the day. Night after night

he worked on—
performing, per-
fecting his skills,
and finally begin-
ning to earn a
little money.

One night the
famous American
comedian Rodney
Dangerfield saw
Jim perform.
Rodney, who was
working at a nearby

*Mark Breslin at Yuk Yuk's, about the time
that Jim performed there*

club, was so impressed by Jim's ability that he invited
Jim to be his opening act. Rodney says, "He was really
sensational, an unusual talent. He could make his face
into anything."

It wasn't long before Jim was appearing in clubs
throughout Canada and on Canadian television. He also
began to be noticed by critics and to get glowing reviews.
A writer from the *Toronto Sun,* one of Canada's entertainment periodicals exclaimed, "I saw a genuine star coming
to life, and that happens so rarely that it's worth shouting
out the news to the world." Jim was on his way.

Jim began performing in comedy clubs in his teens.

Comedian Rodney Dangerfield

By the time he was 19, Jim had earned enough money to see his family settled in a new home. He had also established himself on the Canadian comedy circuit, and the doors to the best entertainment spots were open to him.

He now had a choice. He could play it safe, remain in Canada where he was known, and probably continue to earn a good living. Or he could try his luck in the United States, where no one had heard of him. Going to the United States would mean giving up what he had and starting all over. Competition would be tough. Audiences would be demanding. And American critics, who could make or break a performer's career, were known to be especially hard on young comics.

Eager to expand his comic horizons, Jim chose the more difficult course. Whatever the risks, however bumpy the road, Jim would press on.

CHAPTER

5

On to Hollywood

In 1981, Jim said goodbye to his family and set off for Los Angeles. With a thousand dollars in savings and a list of telephone contacts, he felt ready to begin the next phase of his professional life. But he soon discovered that neither the money nor the telephone numbers would do him much good. Decent lodgings proved to be more expensive than he had expected. In order to make his money last, he settled for a dingy room in a cheap motel.

Even more disappointing was the response he got from the people he telephoned. Jim explains: "Every L.A. comic or celebrity that came through Toronto, I asked if I could give a call when I finally got to L.A. And they'd [say], 'Sure, we'll paint the town red.' Then I'd call and [say] 'Remember me? We met in Canada. I just got into town.' And they'd say, 'Sorry, buddy. I just don't have room for you in my life.'"

Jim spent many lonely days, wondering whether his move to the United States had been a mistake.

Finally, in desperation, he took action. He had heard

Los Angeles, California, home to the movie studios of Hollywood

Jim in performance at the Comedy Store

that a struggling songwriter named Phil Roy had a room for rent in his home. On an impulse, Jim packed his things, checked out of the motel, and headed for Phil's house.

Phil says: "Jim just showed up at my door with a suitcase. I'd never met the guy before. He knocked on my door, and ever since that day we've been best friends." In one quick step, Jim had found both a companion and a home.

The first night that Jim and Phil were together, they composed a song. They called it the "Ha Ha Song" because they were both laughing so hard when they wrote it. The "Ha Ha Song" was one of many the two friends would write together.

Settled and happier, Jim now put all his energy into work. His efforts eventually won him spots in comedy clubs in Los Angeles. He also took his act on the road, traveling to Las Vegas to rejoin his friend Rodney Dangerfield and to New York for solo engagements. He quickly became a regular at the best-known nightclubs around the country, including Hollywood's famous Comedy Store.

The Comedy Store's master of ceremonies, Joey Gaynard, said of Jim: "I thought he was just really funny.

He had a very slick act for someone who came in from nowhere. He went over real big with the crowds right away. I don't know if I ever saw him bomb. He used his body like a rubber band. It was simply amazing."

Almost overnight Jim was a hit.

Now earning thousands of dollars for each appearance, Jim got an apartment and sent for his parents. Percy and Kathleen were thrilled to visit the United States and to share in Jim's success. For Percy, in particular, Jim's achievement was like the fulfillment of his own boyhood dream.

But although Jim was successful, he soon realized that he wasn't really happy. After a while he came to understand what was wrong.

"I wanted to be myself," Jim explains, "to create some things that had never been done before, rather than constantly sitting, waiting for the next famous person whom I could impersonate."

However, years of pretending to be other people had left him unsure of who he was. Although friends such as comedian Robin Williams and television talk-show host Arsenio Hall tried to talk him out of it, Jim left the stage for a period of self-exploration and discovery.

He spent the next months out of the public eye—

taking acting lessons, writing poetry, and learning to paint and sculpt. It was a difficult period during which he was sometimes confused and depressed. Unsure of his course, he sought the help of psychics and therapists. He also studied the teachings of various religions. Slowly, out of the struggle, came a new and more secure person, and a much more daring performer.

After a two-year absence, Jim returned to comedy with material that was wilder and more personal. He would go on stage with spiked hair and big red pants and just improvise. His innermost feelings and thoughts had become his professional focus.

It was about this time that Jim also got his first major television offer. Early in 1984, producers at NBC approached him about playing the lead role in a comedy series to be called *The Duck Factory*. Jim would play the part of an animator in a television studio who finds himself thrust into an executive position for which he is unprepared. Although the role would mean adhering to a prepared script, Jim decided to accept the offer. He hoped that the show would help him learn about television and gain a wider audience.

The Duck Factory aired that spring in an important prime-time slot. But despite its innovative mix of live action

Jim appeared as a cartoonist in The Duck Factory.

and cartoons, it didn't go over well with the public and was canceled after 13 episodes.

However, Jim had made his mark. Critics hailed his likability and charm. One reviewer for *Variety*, an important entertainment periodical, predicted that Jim Carrey would become a star.

The Duck Factory *mixed live action and cartoons.*

For a while that prediction seemed on the verge of coming true. Movie offers flowed in. Jim went from a small part in a 1984 film called *Finders Keepers* to a starring role a year later in a vampire spoof called *Once Bitten*. But once again Jim was disappointed. *Once Bitten* failed at the box office. It would be almost ten years before he would play another starring role.

Jim in vampire garb for his role in Once Bitten

Between 1986 and 1989, Jim did a series of small parts in films. He also continued to perform his comedy act in clubs. Because his club routines were now improvised, they were different every night. One night he would be a cockroach crawling around on all fours—the next, a snake stretched out along the rough wooden stage. "It was my expression; it was me," Jim says.

But his expression cost him dearly. Night after night of physical contortions left him black and blue and wracked with pain. One morning when he tried to get out of bed, he found that he couldn't stand. After a few days he went to a chiropractor, who gave him some exercises, which he did faithfully every day. At Jim's next visit the chiropractor was amazed at how well he had healed. Jim's determination had pulled him through. He was back to work in a flash, doing routines that were as strenuous as ever.

In the late 1980s, as Jim continued trying to establish himself in films, his personal life took a happy turn. While performing at the Comedy Store, he met an aspiring actress named Melissa Womer. Melissa was waiting tables at the Comedy Store. Jim and Melissa quickly fell in love and married. In 1987 they became the parents of a baby girl named Jane.

Now a devoted family man, Jim was torn between his new wife and daughter and his work. But he discovered, to his distress, that his performance schedule often had to take priority. Professional engagements in various parts of the country meant that he had to be away from Melissa and Jane for long periods of time. He was miserable without them. He says that only when he was actually on stage could he forget his unhappiness.

Now more than ever, Jim was desperate to make it big in films. Often, when he was home in Hollywood, he would slip out of the house and head up to the Hollywood hills. From his vantage point above the city, he would sit and dream about being a famous movie actor.

"By the time I'd drive down," he told television interviewer Barbara Walters in 1995, "I had convinced myself that I was a big star, that all the best directors wanted to do projects with me."

To make his dream seem even more real, he wrote a check to himself in the amount of $10 million "for acting services rendered," which he carried in his pocket.

Still, major movie offers did not come. However, in 1990, Jim did get another television offer, this time from the Fox Broadcasting Network. Producers at Fox invited him to join the cast of a new television show called *In Living Color*. He didn't want to do TV. But Fox's offer was too exciting to refuse.

Instead of playing the same character week after week as he had done in *The Duck Factory*, Jim would play a variety of characters during each show. He would have opportunities to improvise. He would be able to inter-weave original ideas with old and new comic impressions. And taping would be done in front of a live audience. In many ways the show would be similar to performing in a club. The difference was that Jim would be seen by millions of people each week.

In Living Color premiered in 1990 between *The Simpsons* and *Married with Children* and ran for five seasons. Over time it helped make Fox a major network and Jim Carrey a household name. During its run Jim also did two important television specials.

The first was a comedy show for a cable network. It was produced by Jim's own newly formed production company, which he called Jim-Gene, Inc., after his childhood nickname. The show was taped in Canada before a Canadian audience. Much of the material was drawn from Jim's childhood memories and from observations of people he had known. Jim had always been an acute observer of people and things. In an interview with the

The cast of In Living Color

Arts & Entertainment Network in March of 1996, his friend, actor Nicolas Cage, likened him to a sponge. "You have to be careful what you do around him," Cage explained, "because it *will* wind up in a movie. He just absorbs everything around him." The Canadian fans clearly loved everything Jim had absorbed, and they also loved the show. So did the cable viewers who saw it in 1991. But to Jim's profound sadness, his mother passed away before the program was televised. In tribute he dedicated it "to the memory of Kathleen Carrey aka 'Mommsie.'"

Then in 1992, Jim took on a dramatic role in a Fox made-for-TV movie. Entitled *Doing Time on Maple Drive*, the movie was his first real chance to do a serious part. Playing the unhappy son in a troubled family, he was so convincing that the film's director, who had never seen Jim's comic work, thought he had discovered a new dramatic talent. In a March 14, 1992, *TV Guide* interview, the director said of Jim, "I'd never imagined he was a comedic actor. He gave a very honest reading. It was so sad." Critics also praised Jim's performance, calling it both believable and touching.

Many who did know Jim's comedic work expressed surprise that someone that silly could be so serious. Jim explained that deep down, comedians are often the most serious people on earth.

By the early 1990s, Jim had become so well-known to the television-viewing public that he could hardly walk down the street without being recognized. This new fame both pleased and troubled him. He enjoyed the acclaim. However, there were times when he simply wanted to be left alone.

One such time was the Halloween he tried to take his daughter trick or treating. He was so bothered by fans that he complained, "I just gotta find a mask to cover my face up, so people don't go, 'It's the dude from *In Living Color!* Here's an extra candy—Do something!'" Because of the amount of attention being showered on him, Jim also had to give up his plans to take Jane to Disneyland. He was beginning to discover that fame has its price. And he hadn't yet even reached the top.

That final climb began in the summer of 1993, when he started work on a low-budget movie called *Ace Ventura: Pet Detective*. The Ace Ventura role had actually been turned down by at least five other actors before it found its way to Jim. No one, including Jim, liked the script as it was originally written. But the idea of a pet detective had so appealed to Jim that he decided to redo the screenplay and accept the part.

In both the script and the portrayal, Ace Ventura became pure Jim. More than a character, Ace was a comic showcase of Jim's most outrageous mannerisms and noises.

Ace is a detective hired by the Miami Dolphins to retrieve their missing mascot. Sporting a wild shirt, hiked-up pants, and a sky-high pompadour hairdo, he is the very image of over-coolness. Jim describes Ace as part James Bond, part Jerry Lewis. "He's cool, man," he says. "He's so cool it's ridiculous."

Jim took a big chance when he chose to make Ace so extreme. "I knew it was either going to be popular, or it was going to ruin my career," he explains. It almost did both.

The movie was released in February 1994. The critics panned it, including television reviewers Gene Siskel and Roger Ebert, who gave it a strong thumbs down. Fortunately for Jim, his fans ignored the bad reviews. Thousands flocked to movie theaters around the country and waited in long lines to see the film. Most loved what they saw. In its first weekend alone, *Ace Ventura* took in $12 million in box-office receipts.

Jim was in Atlanta, Georgia, the weekend that *Ace* opened. He and his friend, comic Wayne Flemming,

Ace Ventura shows his business card.

decided to take a tour of the city's movie theaters to look for his name on the theater marquees. When Jim spotted crowds of people beneath the marquees, he was stunned. If he had any doubt about what the crowds meant, his friend set him straight. "That's it," Wayne told him, "you're a big star now."

6

Carrey Mania

In the years since *Ace Ventura*'s release, Jim Carrey has gone from movie star to movie legend. In a string of hit films, he has continued to push silliness to the extreme, creating many zany characters that have won him worldwide fame. No one who has seen his work in *The Mask, Dumb and Dumber,* or *Batman Forever* can keep from marveling at his comic daring. It is clear that Jim will do anything for a laugh. And it is equally clear, from his phenomenal box-office success, that his fans are laughing at everything he does.

Jim began work on *The Mask* just after completing *Ace Ventura*. Based on a popular comic-book series, *The Mask* tells the story of a timid bank clerk named Stanley Ipkiss, who finds an ancient Nordic mask floating in the river. When Stanley puts the mask on, he is instantly transformed into a superconfident, superpowerful, super-strong superhero. As The Mask, Stanley can do all the things he could never do as himself. He can fight crime. He can punish villains. He can save a heroine and even

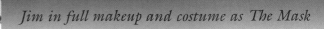

Jim in full makeup and costume as The Mask

win her heart. The world that The Mask inhabits is pure cartoon fantasy, in which anything can happen and does.

The dual Stanley Ipkiss/The Mask role was unusually demanding, even for Jim. Not only did he play both parts, but he also sang, danced, and performed many of The Mask's superhero feats. He was, in fact, so physically expressive and agile that he actually saved the studio thousands of dollars in special effects. The special effects finally used were simply devices to enhance Jim's talents.

As one special-effects technician said: "The beauty of Jim Carrey is that he can go pretty far, but there are things even he doesn't have the ability to do. So he goes as far as he can, and then we can take it that much further. For example, Jim Carrey can do weird and wild things with his mouth, but he can't take his jaw and drop it all the way down to the ground or have his tongue roll out on the table." That's where the technical magic filled in.

In addition to Jim's on-screen chores, the movie also required an unusual amount of off-screen preparation. Besides learning lines, mastering songs, and practicing elaborate dance routines and movements, Jim had to endure four grueling hours of makeup each day. "You just go insane," he says about the time he had to spend in the makeup chair, preparing to become the comic

Special effects make The Mask's tongue extra long.

hero. But he also says that the ordeal was worth it. The green skin, huge teeth, and leering grin helped him bring the character to life.

It is not surprising that *The Mask* went on to become an even bigger hit than *Ace Ventura,* grossing more than $300 million worldwide.

Jim took silliness to the other extreme in *Dumb and Dumber.* Where The Mask had been able to accomplish superhuman feats, Jim's character in *Dumb and Dumber* found the simplest tasks to be a challenge. Looking dumb was easy. Jim explains that he simply uncovered his own chipped front tooth and combed his hair forward as his childhood idol, Jerry Lewis, had sometimes done. Playing dumb was a bit harder. It required Jim to gear down, which he says he did by sitting glassy-eyed and imagining that he had just eaten lead paint.

Having carried the full weight of *The Mask* on his own, Jim was happy to have a *Dumb and Dumber* costar. Jeff Daniels, Jim's own choice for the costarring role, proved to be a strong comic partner. "It was like communication, rather than two separate clowns going at it," Jim says of the pairing. Some compared Jim and Jeff's on-screen relationship to that of Laurel and Hardy, a famous comedy team of the 1930s and 40s.

Jim in the makeup chair—the transformation begins.

*Jim and Jeff Daniels as "Dumb"
and "Dumber"*

As with *Ace Ventura*, most movie critics dismissed *Dumb and Dumber* as too silly to be taken seriously. But once again, Jim's fans took the film to their hearts. Like *Ace* and *The Mask*, *Dumb and Dumber* was a hit. It dominated the nation's movie screens for weeks and then went on to break records around the world.

Despite Jim's astonishing success, it wasn't until he was offered the role of the Riddler in *Batman Forever* that he felt he had truly made it. Jim explained, "Up to now, it's been 'Well, Jim's great, but no one wants to be in a Jim Carrey movie.'" The *Batman* offer proved that that had changed. Jim would be working with serious actors, including the classically trained Val Kilmer and the Oscar-winning Tommy Lee Jones.

In addition, Jim would also be seen by an even larger audience than usual. *Batman Forever* is the third film based on the popular comic-book series. Besides Jim's

Jim as the Riddler in Batman Forever

fans, the movie would also draw followers of the Batman saga, some of whom did not ordinarily go to Jim Carrey films. No wonder he found the offer so special.

Jim threw himself into the role of the Riddler with even more than his usual gusto. To get in shape for the Riddler's skintight bodysuit, he all but stopped eating, refusing to swallow even one tiny bit of food, according to his director, Joel Schumacher. Jim also had his hair dyed, cropped, and shaped into a copper-colored punk cut. And once again he donned a mask—this time, in the form of a green and black covering around his eyes. Giggling, cackling, and slithering his way across the movie screen, he was the very image of comic villainy. Many Hollywood insiders believe that it was Jim's presence in the film that made it such a hit. *Batman Forever* had the biggest weekend opening in Hollywood history, taking in $53.3 million.

While Jim's professional life was becoming "a fairy tale," to use Jim's own words, his personal life was sometimes less than happy. During the shooting of *Ace Ventura*, he and his wife, Melissa, separated. Jim blamed himself and his work for the split, saying, "It's hard for me to come down from what I do. It's like being an astronaut. You're on the moon all day, and then at night you go home and you don't want to take out the garbage. I can relax, but not at the prescribed times necessarily, and when you're married, you've got to have time for this and that, and it's just . . . impossible."

Although Jim's daughter, Jane, lives with her mother, Jim remains close to her and sees her several times a week.

Even more upsetting was the death of Jim's father. Percy Carrey passed away just as *Dumb and Dumber* was about to open. Jim found some comfort in the fact that Percy had at least lived long enough to see his son's success. "My father realized I reached my goal," he told Barbara Walters in 1995. "He saw that I had done the thing he had hoped to do and hoped his whole life for me to do."

That success, for which Jim had worked so hard and struggled so long, has now exceeded even his own dreams. In 1994 he was offered $10 million to film *The Mask II*. In 1995 he returned to the screen in a highly anticipated *Ace Ventura* sequel entitled *Ace Ventura: When Nature Calls*. Two recent films, *The Cable Guy* and *Liar, Liar*, will earn him more than $20 million each, making him the highest paid comedian in Hollywood history. In addition, all of his hit movies are now on videocassette for home viewing and are breaking sales records. There are even toys, games, and CD-ROMS related to Jim Carrey films. These items have become top sellers around the world.

The Riddler doll

It is not surprising that Jim's best-known movie characters have also found their way into the Saturday morning cartoons. During the 1995–96 television season, ABC and CBS created animated versions of *Dumb and Dumber, The Mask*, and *Ace Ventura* for young children. The head of programming at the Cartoon Network summed up Jim's appeal. "He's a big, exaggerated, dimwitted, slapstick personality," he says. "It's a natural to move that into cartoons."

The mid-1990s have also brought Jim many awards and honors. In 1994 he received the National Association of Theater Owners' Comedy Star of the Year Award. In 1995 he earned both a Golden Globe and a People's Choice Award nomination. In the same year he was also nominated for an MTV Movie Award for his work in *The Mask* and *Dumb and Dumber*. And also in 1995 he placed

Jim with his daughter, Jane, and actress Lauren Holly outside Mann's Chinese Theater. Jane and Lauren make sure that Jim's hands go deep into the wet cement.

his handprints and footprints in the cement outside Hollywood's famous Mann's Chinese Theater. Only the most legendary Hollywood performers are invited to do that.

With so much acclaim, Jim could easily become filled with a false sense of his own importance. But friends, including old pal Phil Roy, say that Jim remains the same kind and friendly guy he has always been. His sweet nature, which has been untarnished by his success, was one reason actress Lauren Holly was drawn to him. Introduced to Jim on the set of *Dumb and Dumber,* Lauren was charmed as much by Jim's gentleness as by his wacky sense of fun. It was an especially happy moment for her when, weeks after their meeting, Jim approached her about starting a serious relationship. "He said to me," Lauren revealed in the June 26, 1995, issue of *Newsweek* magazine, "'I would like you to be my girlfriend. Would you be my girlfriend?'" Lauren went on to ask, "What girl on the planet could refuse when someone says that?"

Jim and Lauren were married in September 1996 in a simple outdoor ceremony in the woods outside Los Angeles. There were no guests, no fans, and none of the extravagance or glamour of the usual Hollywood wedding. The only people in attendance were Jim's daughter, who was Lauren's maid of honor; Lauren's brother, who served as Jim's best man; and a few reporters, who, despite the couple's best efforts at secrecy, had somehow found out about the event. Jim is determined to make his second marriage a success.

Not even Jim's new wealth seems to have affected him. Refusing to splurge on fancy clothes, chauffeurs, and limousines, Jim prefers to put money away for Jane's future. His one indulgence is the $4 million house he recently bought in Los Angeles. In light of his homeless past, it seems a fitting purchase.

Jim has made it clear that he views his success not in terms of luxuries and cash, but in terms of opportunities. To him, reaching the top means the chance to collaborate "with the best people on the best material."

So with all of his achievements, where does Jim Carrey go from here? There will certainly be more films, both serious and silly. Jim knows that he can't do comedy forever and has already begun planning for more dramatic roles. His role in the 1997 comedy/drama *The Truman Show* is an example. By alternating comedy and drama, he hopes to wean his fans from his all out craziness to more serious performances. As he explained in *Newsweek*'s June 26, 1995 issue, "I might look like an absolute idiot doing this (meaning his brand of movie funny business) at 50." Like other highly successful actors, he may also want to try his hand at directing.

And of course, there will always be comedy clubs, Jim's true link to the past. He describes his work in clubs as a way to "keep connected to what's real." He says, "The stage is where you create. Standing up in front of 3,000 people, you're forced to come up with something. You force yourself out on a limb that way. It's like getting started over in show business every night."

But whatever Jim does, he will surely do it with all his heart and soul and with a firm conviction that he can succeed. And he undoubtedly will.

"My parents taught me to believe in miracles," he says. "My life is proof that they exist."

Jim is now enjoying the success for which he worked so hard.

INDEX

ABOUT THE AUTHOR

Paula Guzzetti spent the first part of her professional life teaching grades kindergarten through eight. Now a full-time writer, she has a special interest in history, literature, and the arts. In addition to *Jim Carrey*, Paula's books for children include *A Family Called Brontë*, *The White House*, and *The Last Hawaiian Queen*, a biography of Liliuokalani. Paula's next book for the TAKING PART series will be a biography of Hollywood actor Brad Pitt.

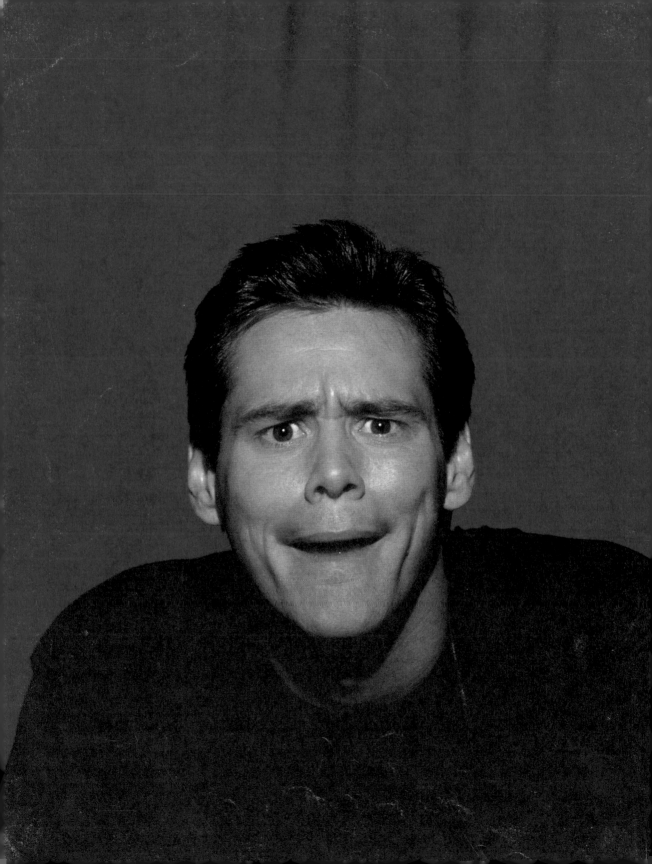

For Joss, Scott, Beau, and Sean

Text copyright © 1980 by Martha Alexander
New illustrations copyright © 2001 by Martha Alexander

Second edition 2001

Library of Congress Cataloging-in-Publication Data

Alexander, Martha.
We're in big trouble, Blackboard Bear / Martha Alexander. — 1st Candlewick Press ed.
p.   cm.
Summary: Anthony's bear learns a hard lesson about leaving other people's possessions alone.
ISBN 0-7636-0670-7
[1. Theft — Fiction. 2. Bears — Fiction.] I. Title.
PZ7.A3777 Wf2001
[E] — dc21   00-033677

2 4 6 8 10 9 7 5 3 1

Printed in Hong Kong

This book was typeset in Stempel Schneidler Roman.
The illustrations were done in colored pencil and watercolor.

Candlewick Press
2067 Massachusetts Avenue
Cambridge, Massachusetts 02140

We're in Big Trouble,
BLACKBOARD BEAR

Martha Alexander

CANDLEWICK PRESS
CAMBRIDGE, MASSACHUSETTS

Come on, sleepyhead! Let's go play.

Hi, everyone. What's the matter?

We're scared. There's a giant monster loose.

Last night it stole all the goldfish out of my pond.

And it took a big jar of my mom's honey right off the windowsill. It must have arms ten feet long!

And it took all the blueberries in our garden.
It left giant footprints all over.

Let's search for him. My bear can help, and he'll
protect us from the monster.

See, there are the prints. Maybe it's a dinosaur!
Or a lion! Or a gorilla!

Look, Anthony, they're as big as your bear's.

Yikes! They're just *like* your bear's.

Gosh! They *are* your bear's.

They are not! They couldn't be.
He was in my room with me all night.

Anthony, we're not playing with *you* anymore.
Your bear is just a robber! A thief!

Let's get the police and have him put in jail.

Those liars!

What? They're not lying?
You really took those things?

But why didn't you tell me?

Really? You thought I might not like you anymore?
I might even give you away?

I would *never* do that.
Don't you know I'm your *friend*?

But you're not in the woods, you know.

You can't just help yourself to other people's things.
Let's go return them.

We can't? You ate them *all*?

Oh, gosh, we're in trouble.

No money to pay them back.
What can we do?

You mean you want to draw?
Well, I'll get some chalk.

But, Anthony, I only had six fish.
There are eleven here.

Maybe one had babies.

I guess you're not so good at counting.
Well, nobody's good at everything.

"Whether you're craving a cookie that is chocolaty or savory, an easy recipe or one that is a bit more challenging, nothing will prepare you for the imaginative and sweet world Jesse Szewczyk creates in *Cookies: The New Classics*."
—Andy Baraghani, senior food editor at *Bon Appétit*

"This is the most beautiful book I have seen in a long tim[e] master baker and has a sense of style and sophistica[tion] evident in every recipe. I tore through each chapter saliva[ting] after page. The energy in the photography is electrifying and elevates an already scrumptious cookie to the level of art. I can't wait to eat my way through this book!"
—Rick Martínez, James Beard Award–nominated recipe developer, host, and cookbook author

"Jesse Szewczyk is as brilliantly creative as he is skilled in the kitchen—a killer combination that sets the stage for this unique and exciting collection of recipes. If you're looking to level-up, dress-up, and generally one-up standard cookies, this book is for you."
—Erin Jeanne McDowell, author of *The Book on Pie*

"Just when you think you've seen all the cookies, Jesse gives us these! What a magical, bright, unique, delicious collection of sweets. Jesse has pulled out all the stops here, and our bellies will be happier for it!"
—Molly Yeh, cookbook author and Food Network host

"A splendid treasure of a cookbook for cookie lovers. It will whet your appetite and also inspire your creativity."
—Nik Sharma, author of *The Flavor Equation*

"Jesse Szewczyk's approach to cookie-baking is innovative, tantalizing, and irresistible. This book does more than upgrade the quintessential cookie classics—it completely reinvents them. The avant-garde photography captures the edible ephemeral of the spirited recipes. Jesse transforms our kitchens into playgrounds—from malted to marbled to Mocha, there's a cookie for everyone."
—Vallery Lomas, author of *Life Is What You Bake It* and winner of *The Great American Baking Show*

"This book is a mood, and the recipes are destined to be on constant rotation in your kitchen. The biggest challenge is deciding what to bake first. For me, that's Bananas Foster Chocolate Chunk Cookies, then on to Red Wine Brownie Cookies because happy hour and baking were made for each other."
—Brian Hart Hoffman, editor-in-chief of *Bake from Scratch*

COOKIES

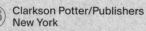

Photographs by Chelsea Kyle

Clarkson Potter/Publishers
New York

COOKIES
THE NEW CLASSICS

JESSE
SZEWCZYK

Published in the United States by Clarkson Potter/
Publishers, an imprint of Random House, a division of
Penguin Random House LLC, New York.
clarksonpotter.com

CLARKSON POTTER is a trademark and POTTER with
colophon is a registered trademark of Penguin Random
House LLC.

Library of Congress Cataloging-in-Publication Data
Names: Szewczyk, Jesse, author. | Kyle, Chelsea,
    photographer.
Title: Cookies: the new classics / Jesse Szewczyk.
Description: New York : Clarkson Potter/Publishers, [2021] |
    Includes bibliographical references and index.
Identifiers: LCCN 2021028567 (print) | LCCN 2021028568
    (ebook) | ISBN 9780593235669 (hardcover) |
    ISBN 9780593235676 (ebook)
Subjects: LCSH: Cookies. | LCGFT: Cookbooks.
Classification: LCC TX772 .S94 2021 (print) | LCC TX772
    (ebook) | DDC 641.86/54—dc23
LC record available at lccn.loc.gov/2021028567
LC ebook record available at lccn.loc.gov/2021028568

ISBN 978-0-593-23566-9
Ebook ISBN 978-0-593-23567-6

Printed in Canada

Photography assistant: Gabrielle Lakshmi
Prop stylist: Maeve Sheridan
Prop styling assistant: Ashleigh Sarbone
Food stylists: Drew Aichele and Jesse Szewczyk
Food styling assistant: Ben Weiner
Recipe cross-testing lead: Danielle DeLott

Editor: Raquel Pelzel
Editorial assistant: Bianca Cruz
Art director: Stephanie Huntwork
Designer: Robert Diaz
Production editor: Mark McCauslin
Copy editor: Carole Berglie
Production manager: Kelli Tokos
Compositors: Merri Ann Morrell and Hannah Hunt
Indexer: Elizabeth T. Parson

10 9 8 7 6 5 4 3 2 1

First Edition

Contents

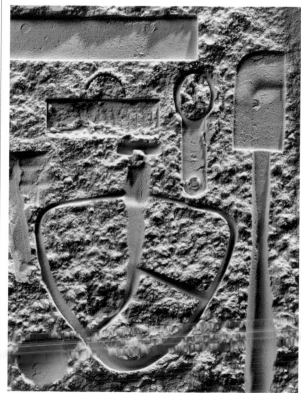

Tart

Spiced

Smoky

Savory

Introduction

When I first set out to write a cookie book, I struggled to figure out what I could add to the conversation that hadn't already been said. With so many chocolate chip cookies, snickerdoodles, and gingersnap recipes already out in the world, what was the point in creating more? If I wanted to bake snickerdoodles, I could easily track down an already perfected recipe. If a chocolate chip cookie was what I was after, a plethora of recipes were mine for the choosing. I realized that what I wanted to do was not to mimic what had already been done but, instead, to focus on creating a new set of recipes—a collection of cookies that pay homage to familiar favorites, but with a modern spin. I wanted to create a *new* set of classics.

This is how I approached writing *Cookies.* Within these pages you will find 100 unapologetically modern-yet-familiar recipes that promise to redefine your favorite go-to cookies, as well as introduce you to new ones to crave. Like spiced snickerdoodles made with the flesh of roasted sweet potatoes (page 180), or chocolate chunk cookies perfumed with fresh peppermint (page 37). From Cashew Caramel Cookies (page 132) to decadent Salt-and-Vinegar Potato Chip Cookies (page 169), these recipes move beyond the holy cookie trinity of chocolate chip, peanut butter, and oatmeal and add excitement to your baking repertoire. Everything from sugar cookies, blondies, thumbprint cookies, and no-bake bars are included, all complete with instructions that will guide you toward cookie-baking success. If like me you bake cookies for the excitement of trying something new, this is the perfect book for you.

The recipes are classified into eight chapters, each named after the dominant flavor of the cookies included: Chocolaty, Boozy, Fruity, Nutty, Tart, Spiced, Smoky, and Savory. This is exactly how I decide what I want to bake, allowing whatever flavor I'm craving to guide my decision. Within these chapters you will find familiar favorites updated with bold flavors. Take, for example, the Smoked Butter & Chocolate Chunk Cookies (page 206) in the Smoky chapter. At its core the recipe is a timeless classic, but adding a modern flourish (in this case, the alluring scent of applewood smoke) creates something that is equal parts comforting and fresh. For cookies that will awaken the senses, look no further than the Spiced chapter. Spiced Peanut Butter–Coconut Squares (page 203) demonstrate that you can make something bold and playful without even turning on your oven. Closing out the book is the Savory chapter, a collection of salty-leaning cookies perfect for serving at a cocktail party. As modern and inventive as the recipes are, they all evoke a sense of nostalgia and comfort as only a freshly made cookie can.

But if you're worried that the recipes sound complicated, don't be. Every recipe is developed to be easy to execute. I believe that baking cookies should be fun, stress-free, and rewarding. Everyone deserves to make cookies that are exciting and unique, and that's precisely what this book will help you do—in fact, I hope that as you bake a batch of Raspberry Chocolate Chunk Cookies (page 92) you feel like a friend is right there by your side, talking you through the recipe and passing on all the tips and tricks. So, say good-bye to cookies that leave you wanting—and hello to your new collection of classics.

Let's Make Cookies

I want bakers of all skill levels to feel confident enough to make beautiful, bakery-quality batches of cookies at home. For me, it wasn't enough for the cookies you make to simply taste great; I wanted them to be the kinds of cookies you feel accomplished making—the types of cookies you take photos of and proudly share online. To meet this goal, I've done my very best to distill every piece of advice I have to lead you to cookie success. Although some of the recipes might sound complicated, most of them are actually quite easy. That's what I think makes this book so special: The recipes are no more complicated than a standard chocolate chip cookie, but their flavors and textures are bold, exciting, and intriguing.

Each recipe includes make-ahead and storage instructions whenever applicable. For specialty ingredients, you'll find notes providing sourcing tips and substitution suggestions. For anyone looking for a recipe that can be made without an electric mixer, a "no mixer" symbol has been included at the top of the recipe. And for anyone who is avoiding turning on their oven, a "no bake" symbol has been added to recipes that don't require baking.

 No mixer   **No bake**

But before you jump into the kitchen, it's important to properly set yourself up. Baking should be fun and stress free, and taking the time to get organized makes all the difference.

Read the Recipe
Before you commit to making a recipe, I recommend reading it all the way through. Some cookie doughs require chilling times, and some call for specialty tools you might not have on hand, so it's important to know what you're getting into. Before jumping into a recipe, always give it a quick scan so there are no surprises.

Bring Ingredients to Room Temperature
Many of the recipes call for room-temperature ingredients, such as eggs, sour cream, and softened butter. I recommend leaving these ingredients out for one to two hours before baking. This will help all the ingredients combine easily and create a perfectly cohesive dough. But if you forget to plan ahead, don't fret. Butter can be softened in the microwave on 50 percent power for about 15 seconds, depending on your microwave; and eggs can be submerged in hot water for 5 minutes to bring them to room temperature.

Get Your Tools Ready
Pull out every bowl, whisk, sheet pan, cookie scoop, and other essentials needed to make your recipe before you get started. This will ensure you have the right tools at hand.

Measure Everything Ahead of Time
I suggest measuring out your ingredients before you start baking. This will help you move seamlessly through the steps. I have listed ingredients by both volume and weight and I suggest measuring by weight—especially for flour. A digital kitchen scale (page 21) comes in handy here.

Position Your Oven Racks
Every recipe includes directions for how to position your oven racks. This will help ensure your cookies bake evenly, so don't forget to do this before you preheat your oven.

Ingredients

Almost all the recipes in this book can be made with easy-to-find ingredients. Any cookies that call for ingredients that are a bit harder to find will include sourcing information in the Note sections.

From the Pantry

All-Purpose Flour: All the recipes in this book are made with all-purpose (plain) flour. This is the most common flour variety stocked in most pantries, with a protein content generally ranging between 9 and 12%. My go-to brand is King Arthur Baking Company's unbleached, all-purpose flour. Avoid flours labeled "self-rising," as they have added leaveners and salt in them. There is no need to stock up on cake, pastry, or bread flours.

A Note on Measuring Flour
I measure flour by spooning it into a measuring cup and leveling it off on the top with the flat spine of a knife. If you scoop out flour by dipping a measuring cup into a bin of flour, it packs the flour into the cup and results in a significantly more densely packed cup—meaning your cookies could turn out drier and not spread as much. A cup of flour that is spooned and leveled will weigh around 128 grams, whereas flour that is scooped and packed can weigh as much as 180 grams—that's an extra ⅓ cup of flour. For even greater accuracy, weigh your flour using a digital scale (see page 21).

Baking Powder and Soda are chemical leaveners that I use throughout this book. They help the cookies rise and expand in the oven, alter their texture, and contribute to their browning. Baking soda needs an acid such as molasses or lemon juice in order to start its reaction, while baking powder already has an acid. This is why many of the recipes in this book that contain large amounts of molasses (or brown sugar) rely on baking soda. Check the expiration dates of both leaveners before using them, as they can expire and become ineffective. I like to replace mine every six months (if I don't use it all up before then).

Brown Sugar: I tend to avoid using organic brown sugar when baking cookies because I've found that it often has much larger crystals that don't dissolve easily. Instead, I bake with refined, conventional light brown sugar. My go-to brand is Domino's. While you can use dark brown sugar in place of light, its higher concentration of molasses will change the texture and flavor of the cookies slightly. Another variety of brown sugar used

throughout this book is muscovado sugar. This is a type of unrefined cane sugar with a strong molasses flavor.

Chocolate: I call for both chocolate chips and chopped bars of chocolate in my cookie recipes. Semisweet and bittersweet chocolate can be used interchangeably, but you should not swap chips for chopped chocolate and vice versa. I bake with standard chocolate chips, and find that large baking discs and fèves (wide discs) change the way the cookies spread, so I don't recommend using them in place of chips. Chopped chocolate is listed as roughly or finely chopped throughout the book. Roughly chopped chocolate should be cut into large, irregular pieces that are approximately ¼ to ½ inch large and include the smaller, splinter-like pieces that break off, whereas finely chopped should be cut into tiny shards. How finely you chop your chocolate will affect how much your cookies spread, so don't ignore this detail. There are also a handful of recipes that call for white chocolate. My go-to brand to bake with is Ghirardelli.

Coarse Sugar: Throughout the book I refer to any sugars with large crystals as coarse sugar. This includes sanding sugar, turbinado sugar, and demerara sugar. I often save this type of sugar for rolling dough balls in before baking or for sprinkling on top as a final flourish. Any coarse sugar you have on hand can be used interchangeably unless specified in the recipe.

Cocoa Powder: This book uses natural, unsweetened cocoa powder—not Dutch-process cocoa powder. Natural cocoa powder is the variety most commonly sold in grocery stores and it is slightly acidic, causing it to react with leavening agents like baking soda. Popular brands such as Hershey's (not Special Dark) and Ghirardelli's Unsweetened Cocoa are good natural cocoa options.

Confectioners' Sugar: Any product labeled powdered sugar, icing sugar, or 10X can be used anytime a recipe calls for confectioners' sugar. They are all the same thing—essentially finely ground sugar mixed with cornstarch to prevent clumping.

Granulated Sugar, also known as white sugar, is the all-purpose sugar used throughout this book. This is the sugar that comes in big bags near the flour and is made from either sugar beets or sugarcane. Both varieties can be used interchangeably and oftentimes the bags will not even specify its source. Organic cane sugar will work in any recipe that calls for granulated sugar.

Kosher Salt: I always use Diamond Crystal kosher salt for baking. If you don't have Diamond Crystal on hand you can use any other salt in its place; just make sure to adjust the amount you use. Save your sea salts, rock salts, and flaky salts for other uses. Here is my general rule of thumb for swapping salt brands in recipes:

> 1 teaspoon Diamond Crystal kosher salt =
> ¾ teaspoon Morton's coarse kosher salt =
> ½ teaspoon table salt

Molasses: Unless otherwise noted, all molasses in this book is unsulphured light molasses (also called mild, sweet, or first molasses). I use Grandma's brand of molasses.

Vanilla: Throughout the book you will notice I use *a lot* of vanilla extract. Similar to how I use garlic in savory recipes, I believe it's difficult to overdo it with vanilla, and cookies often benefit from a generous glug. I use a relatively cheap vanilla extract for everyday baking and save the fancy stuff for uncooked components like frostings and glazes. There are a few recipes that call for vanilla seeds as well. In those cases, I slice the beans in half lengthwise and scrape the seeds out using the tip of a knife. The scraped pods can be used to infuse sugar or make homemade vanilla extract.

DIY Vanilla Extract

To make your own vanilla extract, add 1 cup of vodka, rum, or bourbon to an 8-ounce glass jar or bottle with an airtight lid. Split 8 vanilla beans in half lengthwise so their seeds are exposed, then add the beans and seeds to the jar with the spirit. (If you have leftover scraped pods from a recipe calling for the seeds, this is a good place to use them.) Secure the lid and give the jar a good shake. Let the extract steep for at least 2 months and up to a year. As you use the extract, continue to top it off with more spirit so you don't run out. I recommend you stop topping it off after 1 year, as the vanilla beans will have given up all their flavor.

From the Fridge

Butter: Unless noted, all the recipes in this book use uncultured, unsalted (sweet cream) butter. European-style butters are often cultured and have a higher fat content, resulting in cookies with a slightly different flavor and texture. If all you have on hand is European-style butter, however, you can use it as a substitute without worry.

Eggs: I use standard US-size large eggs, which is about 2 ounces/57 grams per egg. This is roughly equivalent to a EU/UK medium egg. Unless noted in the recipe, all eggs can be used cold straight from the fridge. To bring an egg to room temperature, submerge it in a bowl of hot water for 5 minutes.

Nuts and Seeds tend to go rancid rather quickly, so I recommend storing them in an airtight container in the fridge or freezer and letting them come to room temperature before baking with them. This includes poppy seeds, which are very high in fat and turn "off" quickly—if you have a jar that has been sitting in your cupboard for more than a year, I recommend buying a new bottle before baking the Lemon Poppy Seed Tea Cookies (page 151) or the Chewy Triple-Citrus Poppy Seed Cookies (page 173).

Toasting Nuts

The recipes in this book call for using toasted nuts. If your nuts are raw, scatter them on a rimmed baking sheet in a single layer and bake at 350°F until darkened in color slightly and very fragrant. It should take 15 to 20 minutes for peanuts, 7 to 10 minutes for pistachios and almonds, and 10 to 15 minutes for hazelnuts, cashews, and macadamia nuts.

Toasting Seeds

For most seeds (such as sesame) I find that toasting them on the stovetop is the most efficient method. To do so, add them to a dry skillet set over medium heat and cook, stirring constantly, until they darken in color slightly and are very fragrant. Immediately transfer them onto a plate to avoid burning. This method also works well for small amounts of shredded coconut.

Common Metric Conversions

Throughout the book I have listed both standard volume and metric weight measurements (see page 21 for advice on buying a scale). Depending on how a baker measures the ingredients, the weights of those ingredients can vary even though the volumes are the same. For example, most major food publications list 1 cup of flour as weighing anywhere between 120 to 142 grams. Throughout this book I have listed 1 cup of flour as weighing 128 grams, mimicking the *New York Times* standard. These are the standards I stick to in my kitchen:

1 cup all-purpose flour = 128 grams

1 cup granulated sugar = 200 grams

1 cup packed light or dark brown sugar = 200 grams

1 cup confectioners' sugar = 100 grams

1 cup unsweetened cocoa powder = 90 grams

1 stick butter = 113 grams (8 tablespoons)

1 cup old-fashioned rolled oats = 90 grams

1 cup creamy peanut butter, such as Jif or Skippy = 240 grams

1 cup standard-size chocolate chips (not discs) = 170 grams

1 large U.S. whole egg = 57 grams

1 large U.S. egg white = about 30 grams

1 cup liquid = 237 ml

Tools & Equipment

Most of the cookies in this book can be made with equipment you probably already have, but a few recipes call for specialty tools. These can be found in most kitchen supply stores or ordered online.

Measuring Tools

Digital Kitchen Scale: Throughout this book I have listed both weight and volume measurements for ingredients that tend to yield inconsistent amounts when measured by volume alone. I highly recommend buying a digital scale and measuring your ingredients by weight. Doing so is more accurate than measuring by volume and yields more consistent results.

Dry Measuring Cups and Spoons: If you do not own a digital kitchen scale, measuring cups are still a great option. For ingredients that are measured using measuring spoons, I have not listed their weights, as I found that many kitchen scales are unable to accurately capture weights less than 10 grams.

Liquid Measuring Cups: Liquid measuring cups are specifically designed to accurately measure liquids without spilling. I use Pyrex glass measuring cups, which have spouts for easy pouring. Any ingredients that are a liquid or syrup consistency at room temperature should be measured using a liquid measuring cup.

Portioning Tools

Cookie Cutters: For any recipe that calls for a specific shape cookie cutter, you can feel free to deviate slightly and use a similarly shaped cutter instead. For example, a 2-inch round cookie cutter can be used in place of a 2-inch square. Do note that if you use a much larger or smaller cutter, your baking time will be affected.

Cookie Scoops: Throughout this book I use two different sizes of cookie scoops: a #40 and a #16. A #40 scoop is about 1¾ inches wide and has a 1½ tablespoon capacity. This is what I use for most recipes and what I consider a medium scoop. If you don't have one, you can use a measuring spoon to portion out 2 tablespoons of dough instead. (The slight extra accounts for the excess dough that mounds on top of the scoop.) A #16 scoop is about 2⅓ inches wide and has a ¼ cup capacity. This is what I use for any of the large cookies in this book. If you don't have one, a ¼ cup measuring cup can be used instead.

Rolling Pin: I like to use a standard wooden rolling pin with handles when rolling out my dough. I have found that tapered, French-style rolling pins can be a bit difficult to use when trying to roll out chilled cookie dough.

Rulers are helpful when rolling out dough to a specific thickness or when cutting bars into perfect squares. I use a metal one in the kitchen because it's easy to clean.

Small Tools

Instant-Read and Candy Thermometers are essential for making caramels, marshmallows, and Italian meringues. By checking the temperature of cooked sugar, you ensure that your end products will have the right texture. A candy thermometer can be clipped onto the side of a pot and left on during cooking, which makes it super convenient; but instant-read thermometers should be left in hot mixtures only for a few seconds.

Microplane Zester is my preferred brand of zester and an essential tool for the Tart chapter, since so many of the cookies call for freshly zested citrus. If you don't have one, the small holes on a box grater would work, or you can use a vegetable peeler to peel off the skin of a citrus fruit, then mince it with a knife as finely as possible.

Offset Spatula: A tiny offset spatula can be used to spread dough in a baking pan and artfully swoosh frosting onto cookie tops. Its thin, flexible metal blade also makes it perfect for gently prying stubborn cookies out of baking pans.

Pastry Brushes come in handy when brushing the tops of cookies with egg wash or brushing excess flour off of rolled-out dough. Just be careful that none of the bristles fall out and stick to the cookies.

Piping Bags: Disposable piping bags can be purchased in bulk in rolls of 100, and they make filling sandwich cookies a breeze. You can also use large zip-top bags with one corner cut off.

Rubber Spatula: I prefer to use seamless one-piece spatulas versus the wooden-handled varieties; they are sturdier and easier to clean. My biggest piece of advice is to make sure they're well washed before using—savory flavors have a tendency to cling to them.

Whisk: Many of the recipes in this book do not use an electric mixer and instead rely on a whisk to incorporate the sugar into the butter. I also use my standard balloon whisk to combine my dry ingredients instead of sifting them.

Appliances

Conventional Oven: All the recipes in this book have been developed with a conventional oven (an oven without a fan), the most common type of oven most home bakers use. If you have a convection oven (an oven with a fan), keep an eye on your cookies during the last few minutes of baking. Cookies made in an oven with a fan will often bake slightly faster than those baked in a conventional oven. A good rule of thumb for those using a convection oven is to start checking them about 2 minutes before the recommended bake time.

A Note on Baking Times
You might notice that I often advise pulling your cookies out of the oven when they still look very soft and underbaked. One of the most common mistakes people make when baking cookies is that they bake them until they look firm. While the cookies cool (most cookies need at least 30 minutes to cool after baking—this is an essential step of the recipe), they continue to firm up on the baking sheet and completely change their texture. All the baking times throughout this book have taken this cooling into account. Even if your cookies come out of the oven looking soft and slightly underbaked, trust the process and be patient. You'll be rewarded with perfectly baked cookies.

Electric Mixer: Any recipe that calls for using a stand mixer can be made with an electric hand mixer instead. Just note that the mixing times might be slightly longer, as hand mixers are typically less powerful.

Food Processor: This will come in handy when making doughs that cut butter into the dry ingredients. Instead of having to pinch the butter cubes in the dry mixture by hand, you can quickly blitz it all together. This technique is utilized a lot in the Savory chapter to produce tender, pleasantly crumbly cookies.

Bakeware

Baking Pans: I use two sizes of baking pans throughout this book: an 8 × 8-inch square baking pan and a 9 × 13-inch rectangular one. I prefer using metal baking pans to glass so I can recklessly tap the pans on the countertop to remove any air bubbles in the batter and to deflate the bars after they come out of the oven. Metal pans also have squared-off edges (rather than a glass pan's rounded ones).

Baking Sheets: I prefer using a standard, 13 × 18-inch rimmed half-sheet pan versus a flat baking sheet. Sheet pans have rimmed edges that are easier to grip when you're wearing oven mitts, and the sides prevent the cookies from accidently sliding off. Baking sheets (the flat variety without raised edges) are more common; they allow the air to circulate more freely around the cookies, resulting in even coloring. Both types work well, so use whatever variety you have on hand. If you're using a smaller baking sheet, you will need to increase the number of batches you bake. In this case, I recommend keeping the cookie dough at room temperature while baking (unless noted in the recipe) and letting the baking sheets fully cool between each batch.

Cast-Iron Skillets: All of the skillet cookies in this book are baked in 10-inch cast-iron skillets, the most common size and what you most likely have on hand. Avoid using skillets that are smaller than 10 inches, as the dough might rise too high and spill out. Using ones that are larger than 10 inches will produce flatter, crisper skillet cookies.

Nonstick Baking Mats and Parchment Paper: I use both to line my baking sheets so my cookies don't stick. I always buy pre-cut sheets so they help fit perfectly on my sheets. I also use parchment paper to line baking pans when making bar cookies, leaving some overhang on the sides so I can easily lift the uncut bars out after baking. Of course, the benefit of nonstick baking mats is that they're infinitely reusable.

Oven Thermometer: I keep an oven thermometer hanging from my middle rack at all times. Many ovens (especially older models) are not properly calibrated and can run significantly hotter or cooler. To figure out exactly what temperature your oven is at, I suggest investing in a thermometer and then adjusting your baking temperature as needed. Also be aware that your oven might have hot spots—sections that run hot compared with other spots in the oven. If this is true for your oven, be sure to rotate the pans front to back while baking to ensure all the cookies bake evenly.

Tart Pans and Springform Pans: A few of the recipes in this book are made in round baking pans to create cookie wedges. Instead of rolling out the dough and cutting it into shapes, the dough gets pressed into a pan and sliced (like a pie) as soon as it comes out of the oven. Just make sure that your tart pans have removable bottoms so you can easily lift out the cookies after baking.

Online Resources

Bob's Red Mill Natural Foods
www.bobsredmill.com
Specialty flours, grains, and pantry items.

Kalustyan's
www.spiceandsweet.com
Hard-to-find ingredients and high-quality spices.

King Arthur Baking Company
www.kingarthurbaking.com
Premium baking supplies and ingredients.

Nielsen-Massey
www.nielsenmassey.com
High-quality vanilla and other extracts.

Nordic Ware
www.nordicware.com
Quality bakeware.

NY Cake
www.nycake.com
Professional baking supplies, such as sprinkles, food coloring, and cookie cutters.

Sur La Table
www.surlatable.com
All-purpose kitchen supplies and bakeware.

Valrhona
www.valrhona-chocolate.com
Premium chocolate and cocoa powder.

Webstaurant
www.webstaurant.com
Restaurant-quality tools, equipment, and appliances.

Wilton
www.wilton.com
Specialty baking supplies.

Chocolaty

Oatmeal Chocolate-Covered-Raisin Cookie

Black Cocoa Sandwich Cookies with Vanilla Bean Buttercream

Makes 18 sandwich cookies

What makes Oreos so dark? Black cocoa powder, a Dutch-process cocoa that has a bold, slightly smoky flavor. This recipe utilizes it to make faux Oreos that are exceptionally chocolaty. They get sandwiched together with a vanilla buttercream that is a tad less white than Oreo filling, but much richer in flavor.

Chocolate Cookies

1½ sticks (12 tablespoons/170 grams) unsalted butter, room temperature

1 cup (200 grams) granulated sugar

1 large egg, room temperature

2 teaspoons vanilla extract

1½ cups spooned and leveled all-purpose flour (192 grams), plus more for dusting

⅔ cup (60 grams) black cocoa powder, sifted (see Note)

¼ teaspoon kosher salt

Vanilla Bean Buttercream

1 stick (8 tablespoons/113 grams) unsalted butter, room temperature

½ teaspoon vanilla extract

1 vanilla bean, split lengthwise, seeds scraped out (reserve bean for another use)

Pinch of kosher salt

2⅓ cups (233 grams) confectioners' sugar

Note

Black cocoa powder can be found in specialty baking shops or can be easily ordered online. My favorite brand is from King Arthur Baking Company and comes in a large, resealable bag. Leftover black cocoa powder is delicious used in cakes or brownies. Just keep in mind that because black cocoa powder is stripped of its acid, it can't be used in place of natural cocoa powder in most recipes. Dutch-process cocoa powder is a better substitute and can be used interchangeably with black cocoa powder. It just won't give you the deep, dark color.

Make Ahead

If tightly wrapped in plastic, the dough can be kept in the refrigerator for up to 2 days before baking. If it's too cold to roll out, let it sit at room temperature for 15 minutes and try again.

Storage

The assembled cookies will keep in an airtight container in a single layer at room temperature for up to 1 week.

01 Make the cookies: In the bowl of a stand mixer fitted with the paddle attachment, combine the butter and sugar and beat on medium speed until smooth and fluffy, about 2 minutes. (Alternatively, use an electric hand mixer and large bowl.) Add the egg and vanilla extract and continue beating on medium speed just until combined, 1 to 2 minutes. Turn the mixer off and add the flour, black cocoa powder, and salt. Mix on low speed until combined and no pockets of dry flour remain, 2 to 3 minutes.

02 Transfer the dough to a lightly floured surface and press it together into a rough disc. Wrap in plastic and chill for 1 hour or up to 2 days.

03 Preheat the oven to 350°F and set 2 racks at the upper-middle and lower-middle positions. Line 2 baking sheets with parchment paper or nonstick baking mats.

04 Unwrap the dough and transfer it to a lightly floured work surface. Dust the top of the dough with flour and roll into a ¼-inch-thick sheet. Using a 2-inch round cookie cutter, cut out rounds and place them on the prepared baking sheets, spacing about 1 inch apart (18 per sheet). Press the dough scraps together and repeat the rolling and cutting process. Freeze the cookies on the baking sheets for 10 minutes.

05 Bake both sheets at the same time, swapping them midway, until the cookies have lost their sheen, are slightly puffed, and are very fragrant, 15 to 18 minutes. Let cool slightly on the baking sheets, then transfer to a wire rack to cool completely.

06 Make the buttercream: In the bowl of a stand mixer fitted with a paddle attachment, combine the butter, vanilla extract, vanilla seeds, and salt. (Alternatively, use a hand mixer and large bowl.) Mix on low speed until smooth, 1 to 2 minutes. With the mixer still running on low speed, slowly add the confectioners' sugar until completely incorporated, 3 to 4 minutes. If the filling is too dry to come together, add a teaspoon of water and continue mixing.

07 Dollop or pipe a tablespoon of the filling onto the flat side of half the cookies. Sandwich with the remaining cookies, flat side down.

Marbled Chocolate Sugar Cookies

Makes 18 cookies

These marbled sugar cookies get their swirling, two-toned pattern from smashing together vanilla and chocolate cookie doughs, then rolling that mixture in the palm of your hands to create their eye-catching design. The resulting cookies are chewy on the inside and crisp around the edges, and all the best parts of a classic sugar cookie are amped up with the chocolaty bite of cocoa powder.

01 Preheat the oven to 350°F and set 2 racks at the upper-middle and lower-middle positions. Line 2 baking sheets with parchment paper or nonstick baking mats.

02 In a medium bowl, whisk together the flour, baking powder, baking soda, and salt.

03 In the bowl of a stand mixer fitted with the paddle attachment, combine the butter, 1 cup (200 grams) of the granulated sugar, and the brown sugar. Beat on medium speed until smooth and fully combined, 2 to 3 minutes. (Alternatively, use a hand mixer and large bowl.) Turn the mixer off and add the egg and vanilla extract. Mix on medium speed until fluffy and lightened in color slightly, 2 to 3 minutes. With the mixer running on low speed, gradually add the flour mixture, beating until just combined.

04 Remove half the dough (about 2 cups/420 grams) and transfer to a medium bowl. Add the cocoa powder to the remaining dough in the mixer and mix on low speed until fully incorporated, 1 to 2 minutes. Cover both bowls of dough with plastic wrap and chill for 10 minutes

05 Take 1 tablespoon of each dough and roll them into rough 4-inch-long ropes. Press the ropes together, twirl them into a rough spiral shape, then roll into a ball using the palm of your hands to create the marble pattern. (It's okay to be a bit messy and imprecise.) Repeat with the remaining dough.

06 Roll the cookie dough balls in the remaining ½ cup (100 grams) of granulated sugar and place the dough balls at least 3 inches apart on the prepared baking sheets.

07 Bake both sheets at the same time, swapping the top sheet to the bottom rack and bottom sheet to the top rack midway through, until the cookies are lightly browned on the edges and puffed, 12 to 14 minutes. Immediately bang the baking sheet on the countertop to deflate the cookies slightly. Let cool slightly on the baking sheets, then transfer to a wire rack to let cool completely.

2½ **cups** spooned and leveled all-purpose flour (320 grams)

½ **teaspoon** baking powder

¼ **teaspoon** baking soda

¾ **teaspoon** kosher salt

2 sticks (16 tablespoons/226 grams) unsalted butter, room temperature

1½ cups (300 grams) granulated sugar, divided

⅓ cup (67 grams) packed light brown sugar

1 large egg, room temperature

1 tablespoon vanilla extract

2 tablespoons (14 grams) natural, unsweetened cocoa powder, sifted

Make Ahead

If wrapped tightly in plastic, both doughs can be stored in the refrigerator for several days before baking. When ready to bake, let sit at room temperature for about 30 minutes until you can easily form them into ropes and roll into balls.

Storage

The cookies will keep in an airtight container for up to 1 week.

Maple & Cinnamon Chocolate Moon Pies with Maple Marshmallow Crème

Makes 14 to 16 large moon pies

These chocolate moon pies are sandwiched together with a maple syrup–sweetened homemade marshmallow crème. The maple syrup lends the marshmallows a robust flavor that pairs wonderfully with the cinnamon-spiced cookies and dark chocolate. The cookies, crème, and coating combine to create a moon pie that is soft, chewy, and perfumed with warm baking spices. While not difficult to make, the recipe has three different components, so feel free to make the cookies up to a week before using. They can be sandwiched with the marshmallow crème a day before dipping in chocolate.

Maple and Cinnamon Cookies

1 sleeve graham crackers (9 full crackers/133 grams)

1½ cups spooned and leveled all-purpose flour (192 grams), plus more for dusting

1 teaspoon kosher salt

½ teaspoon baking powder

½ teaspoon baking soda

½ teaspoon ground cinnamon

1½ sticks (12 tablespoons/169 grams) cold unsalted butter, cut into ½-inch cubes

¼ cup (50 grams) packed light brown sugar

¼ cup (59 ml) maple syrup

2 teaspoons vanilla extract

Maple Marshmallow Crème

1 tablespoon unflavored powdered gelatin

1 cup (236 ml) maple syrup

2 teaspoons vanilla extract

Pinch of kosher salt

Chocolate Coating

1 pound (about 3 cups/453 grams) semisweet or bittersweet chocolate chips

1 tablespoon refined coconut oil

Flaky sea salt, for sprinkling (optional)

Make Ahead
If tightly wrapped in plastic, the dough can be kept in the refrigerator for up to 2 days before baking. If it's too cold to roll out, let sit at room temperature for 15 minutes and try again.

Storage
The assembled cookies will keep in an airtight container in a single layer at room temperature for several days.

(recipe continues)

01 Make the Maple and Cinnamon Cookies: In the bowl of a food processor fitted with the blade attachment, process the graham crackers until they are the texture of coarse sand, 15 to 20 seconds. Add the flour, salt, baking powder, baking soda, and cinnamon. Pulse 5 to 10 times, until well combined. Add the diced butter and process until no large pieces remain, about 30 seconds. Add the brown sugar, maple syrup, and vanilla extract and process until a smooth, soft dough forms that pulls away from the sides of the food processor, about 45 seconds. (The dough will have the texture of a soft sugar cookie dough.) Transfer the dough to a large piece of plastic wrap and press into a rough 1-inch-thick disc. Wrap tightly and let chill for 1 hour or up to 2 days.

02 Preheat the oven to 350°F and set 2 racks at the upper-middle and lower-middle positions. Line 2 baking sheets with parchment paper or nonstick baking mats.

03 Transfer the chilled dough to a lightly floured surface. Dust the top of the dough with flour and roll into a ¼-inch-thick sheet. Using a 2½-inch round cookie cutter, cut out circles and place them on the prepared baking sheets, spacing them about 1 inch apart (14 to 16 per sheet). Press the dough scraps together and repeat the rolling and cutting process. Freeze the cookies for 10 minutes. (If you can't fit both sheets in your freezer at once, feel free to consolidate them onto 1 sheet, then divide them again onto 2 sheets for baking.)

04 Bake both sheets at the same time, swapping the top sheet to the bottom rack and bottom sheet to the top midway through baking, until the cookies lose their sheen, are slightly puffed, and are lightly browned, 12 to 14 minutes. Let cool slightly on the baking sheets, then transfer to a wire rack to cool completely.

05 While the cookies are cooling, make the Maple Marshmallow Crème: In the bowl of a stand mixer fitted with a whisk attachment, stir together ¼ cup (59 ml) cold water and the gelatin until the gelatin dissolves. Set aside for 10 minutes to bloom. (Alternatively combine the water and gelatin in a large, deep, heatproof bowl.)

06 In a large pot fitted with a candy thermometer, combine the maple syrup, vanilla extract, and salt and set it over medium heat. (The syrup will bubble quite a bit while it cooks, so make sure to use a large enough pot so it does not overflow.) Without stirring, bring the mixture to a simmer and cook until the temperature reaches 240°F, about 10 minutes. If any sugar crystals form on the sides of the pot during cooking, use a wet pastry brush to dab the pot sides to dissolve them (let the water and sugar drip into the pot—don't disturb the simmering syrup with your pastry brush or the syrup might seize).

07 Immediately pour the hot syrup on top of the bloomed gelatin in the mixer bowl. To prevent splashing, gradually increase the mixer from low to high, then whip until the marshmallow is very sticky, glossy, and doubled in volume, 8 to 10 minutes. (Alternatively use an electric hand mixer.)

08 Immediately transfer the marshmallow crème to a large piping bag or a gallon-size zip-top baggie with a bottom corner snipped off. Working quickly, pipe about ¼ cup of the marshmallow crème onto the flat sides of half the cookies. Sandwich with the remaining cookies on top (flat side down) and let set for 30 minutes at room temperature to set up.

09 While the marshmallow is setting, make the Chocolate Coating: Bring a medium saucepan with 2 inches of water to a simmer over high heat. Place the chocolate and coconut oil in a medium heatproof bowl. Reduce the heat under the saucepan to medium and place the bowl with the chocolate on top of the pan of simmering water (make sure the bottom of the bowl doesn't touch the water) and melt the chocolate, stirring often, until completely smooth, 4 to 5 minutes. Turn off the heat and leave the bowl on top of the warm pot to keep the chocolate warm.

10 Using 2 forks to hold the moon pie, dip each one into the chocolate, flipping it over once to coat it on all sides. Allow excess chocolate to drip back into the bowl. Return the dipped moon pie to the baking sheet and repeat with the remaining moon pies. Sprinkle the tops with flaky sea salt (if using) and let them set for 4 hours before serving.

Double-Mint Chocolate Chunk Cookies

These double-mint cookies deliver all the comfort of the classic chocolate chip cookies you know and love, with the unexpected yet refreshing rush of mint, plus dark and white chocolate to mimic the beloved nostalgia of Andes mints. Unlike other mint-y baked goods that rely exclusively on mint extract to give them that requisite cool burst of flavor, this recipe uses both extract *and* fresh mint to elevate and deepen the flavor. The recipe is adapted from Tara O'Brady's *Basic, Great Chocolate Chip Cookies* recipe—my personal go-to and one I consider perfect. The influence of her no-mixer technique can be seen throughout this book.

01 In a medium saucepan over medium heat, melt the butter. Continue cooking, stirring often to prevent burning, just until the butter starts to sizzle but does not brown, 2 to 3 minutes. Remove from the heat, add the mint leaves, and let cool at room temperature for 30 minutes, stirring occasionally.

02 Preheat the oven to 350°F and set 2 racks at the upper-middle and lower-middle positions. Line 3 baking sheets (or as many as you have) with parchment paper or nonstick baking mats.

03 Strain the butter through a fine-mesh sieve and into a large bowl, pressing down on the mint with a spoon to squeeze out all the butter; discard the mint. Add the brown sugar and granulated sugar and whisk to combine. Add the eggs, vanilla, and peppermint extract and whisk until ribbony (meaning if you lift the whisk, thick ribbons fall from it) and smooth, about 1 minute.

04 Add the flour, baking powder, baking soda, and salt, and stir with a rubber spatula just until a dough forms. Mix in both chopped chocolates.

05 Using a large 2⅓-inch (#16) cookie scoop or ¼-cup measure, portion out the dough and roll into large balls, then place at least 3 inches apart on the prepared baking sheets (6 per sheet).

06 Bake 2 sheets at the same time, swapping them midway, until the tops of the cookies are lightly browned, 13 to 16 minutes, then bake the remaining sheet on either rack. (If reusing one of the baking sheets, allow it to cool for 15 minutes before baking another batch on it.) Immediately bang the baking sheets on the countertop as they come out of the oven to deflate the cookies slightly. Let cool slightly on the baking sheets, then transfer to a wire rack to cool completely.

2 sticks (16 tablespoons/226 grams) unsalted butter

½ cup (14 grams) packed fresh whole mint leaves

1⅓ cups (267 grams) packed light brown sugar

⅓ cup (67 grams) granulated sugar

2 large eggs, room temperature

1 teaspoon vanilla extract

¾ teaspoon peppermint extract

3¼ cups spooned and leveled all-purpose flour (416 grams)

1 teaspoon baking powder

1 teaspoon baking soda

1 teaspoon kosher salt

6 ounces (170 grams) white chocolate, roughly chopped (about 1¼ cups)

6 ounces (170 grams) semisweet or bittersweet chocolate, roughly chopped (about 1¼ cups)

Make Ahead

If wrapped tightly in plastic, the dough can be stored in the refrigerator for several days before baking. If too firm to scoop, let sit at room temperature for 15 minutes and try again.

Storage

The cookies will keep in an airtight container in a single layer for up to 1 week.

Fudgy Double-Dark Chocolate Skillet Cookie

1 stick (8 tablespoons/113 grams) unsalted butter, cut into ½-inch cubes

1 cup (200 grams) packed light brown sugar

1 tablespoon warm water

2 teaspoons vanilla extract

1 large egg, room temperature

¾ cup spooned and leveled all-purpose flour (96 grams)

3 tablespoons (21 grams) natural, unsweetened cocoa powder, sifted

¼ teaspoon kosher salt

¼ teaspoon baking soda

1 cup (6 ounces/170 grams) semisweet or bittersweet chocolate chips, divided

Ice cream, for serving (optional but highly recommended)

Note

The cookie will firm up and become sliceable once cooled. For a more decadent dessert, serve the cookie directly out of the skillet while still warm (and with vanilla ice cream); its texture will be gooey and fudgelike, so you're best off serving with a spoon.

Make Ahead

The cookie dough can be made several days in advance and stored in the fridge, tightly covered in plastic wrap. When ready to bake, press it into the bottom of a skillet coated with nonstick pan spray and bake as described in the recipe.

Storage

Remove any leftover cookie from the skillet and transfer to an airtight container. Store at room temperature for up to 1 week.

Makes one 10-inch skillet cookie

This skillet cookie is an easy baking project you can pull off with just one bowl and in under an hour—so, yes, that means you should keep the ingredients in your pantry at all times, because this is the cookie you'll turn to on *those* kinds of nights. It might look like a typical restaurant-style skillet cookie, but its unassuming appearance masks bold toffee-like flavors within. Nutty brown butter, dark brown sugar, and bittersweet chocolate combine to create a rich, intensely chocolaty skillet cookie that's crisp around the edges with a gooey, fudgy center. Top it with ice cream and you have a crowd-pleasing dessert that's practically impossible to dislike.

01 Position a rack in the middle of the oven and preheat to 350°F.

02 In a 10-inch cast-iron skillet set over medium heat, melt the butter. Continue cooking, stirring often to prevent the milk solids from burning and swirling so it coats the sides, until the butter foams and then darkens in color slightly and becomes very fragrant, 3 to 4 minutes. Transfer the butter to a large heatproof bowl, making sure to scrape it out with a rubber spatula and include any burnt bits stuck to the bottom. Let the brown butter cool at room temperature for 20 minutes. Do not wash the skillet; just set it aside to cool.

03 Add the brown sugar, warm water, and vanilla extract to the cooled (but still melted) butter and whisk to combine. Add the egg and continue whisking until the mixture is completely smooth, glossy, and lightened in color slightly, 1 to 2 minutes.

04 Add the flour, cocoa powder, salt, and baking soda. Stir with a rubber spatula until just combined. Stir in ¾ cup (4½ ounces /128 grams) of the chocolate chips.

05 Transfer the dough to the cooled skillet and spread it into an even layer by pushing down on it with a rubber spatula. Top with the remaining ¼ cup (1½ ounces/42 grams) chocolate chips, pressing them into the dough slightly. Bake until the edges are set, the cookie is slightly puffed, but the center is still soft, 16 to 18 minutes. (The cookie will continue cooking in the skillet after it comes out of the oven, so don't overbake.) Transfer the skillet to a wire rack and cool for 10 minutes before serving. The cookie will be soft and gooey when hot, but firm and sliceable once cooled. If you prefer your skillet cookies on the softer side, eat within 1 hour of baking.

Malted Chocolate Chip Cookie Bars

Makes 24 bars

I like to think of malted milk powder as my go-to ingredient for better baked goods. The flavor is a bit hard to describe, and its presence is not always known, but the addition of it reliably takes a cookie from good to great and adds a caramel-y taste. This recipe leans into that theory by taking classic chocolate chip cookie dough and amping it up with a generous amount of malted milk powder for a flavor that reminds me of buttered toast. So, although these bars might *look* rather simple, the flavor is quite complex. They're the perfect thing to serve alongside a glass of cold milk or a scoop of ice cream, or to stash in the freezer and quickly warm in the microwave for a comforting late-night treat.

Nonstick pan spray

2 cups spooned and leveled all-purpose flour (256 grams)

¾ cup (84 grams) malted milk powder (see Note)

¾ teaspoon kosher salt

¾ teaspoon baking soda

2 sticks (16 tablespoons/226 grams) unsalted butter, room temperature

1½ cups (300 grams) packed light brown sugar

2 large eggs, room temperature

1 tablespoon vanilla extract

1½ cups (about 9 ounces/255 grams) bittersweet or semisweet chocolate chips

2 teaspoons granulated sugar

Flaky sea salt, for sprinkling (optional)

Note

Malted milk powder can be found in the dried-milk section of most well-stocked grocery stores. If unavailable you can use Ovaltine as a substitute, although it will add a subtle chocolate flavor to the dough.

Make Ahead

If wrapped tightly in plastic, the dough can be made several days in advance and stored in the fridge. When ready to bake, let the dough sit at room temperature for 15 minutes, press into the baking pan, and bake as instructed.

Storage

The bars will keep in an airtight container in a single layer for up to 1 week.

01 Arrange a rack in the middle of the oven and preheat to 325°F. Grease a 9 × 13-inch baking pan with the nonstick pan spray. Line with parchment paper, leaving some overhang on all 4 sides so it's easy to lift out the cookies after baking, and coat once more with the pan spray.

02 In a medium bowl, whisk together the flour, malted milk powder, salt, and baking soda.

03 In the bowl of a stand mixer fitted with the paddle attachment, add the butter and brown sugar. (Alternatively, use a hand mixer and large bowl.) Beat on medium speed until light and fluffy, 2 to 3 minutes, scraping down the sides of the bowl halfway through. Turn the mixer off and add the eggs and vanilla extract. Mix on medium speed until fluffy, 1 to 2 minutes.

04 With the mixer running on low speed, gradually add the dry ingredients, beating until just combined. Turn off the mixer and remove the bowl. Stir in the chocolate chips with a rubber spatula.

05 Transfer the dough to the prepared baking pan, using a rubber spatula lightly coated with pan spray to spread it into an even layer. Sprinkle the top with the granulated sugar and flaky sea salt (if using).

06 Bake until the top is lightly browned and the edges are set but the center is still slightly soft, 40 to 45 minutes.

07 Let cool for at least 1 hour in the pan, then slice into 24 pieces (6 short rows and 4 long rows). The bars will be very soft when warm but firm up once cooled.

Brown Butter Brownie Cookies

Bittersweet chocolate, nutty brown butter, and molasses-y dark brown sugar meld together to create the ultimate brownie cookie that is fudgy, dense, chewy, and pleasantly bitter. The key to getting the dramatic cracks on top is to be patient and whip the eggs until they are pale and ribbony, and then to work quickly so the melted chocolate doesn't cool before the cookies go into the oven. This is a technique that Edd Kimber (a brilliant baker and cookbook author) popularized in his own brownie crinkle cookie recipe and is the source of inspiration for this adaptation.

1 cup (6 ounces/170 grams) bittersweet or semisweet chocolate chips

2 tablespoons (30 ml) warm water

1½ teaspoons vanilla extract

1 stick (8 tablespoons/113 grams) unsalted butter

2 large eggs, room temperature

¾ cup (150 grams) granulated sugar

½ cup (100 grams) packed light brown sugar

1 cup spooned and leveled all-purpose flour (128 grams)

2 tablespoons (14 grams) natural, unsweetened cocoa powder

1 teaspoon baking powder

1 teaspoon instant espresso powder (optional; see Note)

½ teaspoon kosher salt

Flaky sea salt, for sprinkling (optional)

Note
Instant espresso powder can be found in the coffee section of most well-stocked grocery stores. Its slight bitterness elevates the flavor of the chocolate and adds an extra layer of flavor, but you can leave it out if you prefer.

Storage
The cookies will keep in an airtight container in a single layer for up to 1 week.

01 Preheat the oven to 350°F and set 2 racks at the upper-middle and lower-middle positions. Line 2 baking sheets with parchment paper or nonstick baking mats.

02 In a medium heatproof bowl, add the chocolate chips, warm water, and vanilla extract.

03 In a small saucepan over medium heat, melt the butter. Continue cooking, stirring often, until the butter foams and then darkens in color slightly and is fragrant, 3 to 4 minutes. Slowly pour the hot butter over the chocolate chips. (Be careful—the mixture will sizzle.) Whisk until the chocolate is melted and the mixture is completely smooth. Set aside.

04 Add the eggs, granulated sugar, and brown sugar to the bowl of a stand mixer fitted with the whisk attachment. (Alternatively, use a hand mixer and large bowl.) Whip on high speed until the eggs are pale yellow, ribbony, and almost tripled in volume, about 6 minutes.

05 As the eggs are whipping, sift together the flour, cocoa powder, baking powder, espresso powder (if using), and salt in a medium bowl.

06 Reduce the mixer speed to low and slowly pour the melted chocolate mixture into the eggs. Mix until just combined, about 1 minute, then turn the mixer off and add the sifted flour mixture. Stir with a rubber spatula until just combined.

07 Using a large 2⅓-inch (#16) cookie scoop or ¼-cup measure, quickly portion out the dough onto the prepared baking sheets, spacing at least 2 inches apart. Sprinkle the tops with flaky sea salt (if using).

08 Bake both sheets at the same time, swapping them midway, until the tops of the cookies are cracked and shiny but they still appear slightly underdone, 9 to 11 minutes. Let cool slightly on the baking sheets, then transfer onto a wire rack to cool completely.

Chocolate Tahini Bars

If you're a fan of peanut butter and chocolate, chances are you're a fan of tahini and chocolate as well; you just might not know it. Tahini has the same rich, nutty qualities that peanut butter does, only bolder, with a subtle earthy flavor that adds a whole new dimension. This recipe tops a simple tahini and graham cracker base with silky chocolate ganache, creating savory-yet-sweet bars that are rich and fudge-like. They're easy to make and exciting to eat.

Graham Cracker–Tahini Crust

Nonstick pan spray

½ **stick (4 tablespoons/57 grams)** unsalted butter, melted and cooled slightly

1¼ **cups (316 grams)** tahini, room temperature (see Note)

2 **teaspoons** vanilla extract

½ **teaspoon** kosher salt

2 **cups (200 grams)** confectioners' sugar

1 **cup (113 grams)** graham cracker crumbs (from about 1 sleeve/9 full crackers)

Dark Chocolate Ganache

8 **ounces (about 1⅓ cups/227 grams)** semisweet or bittersweet chocolate, roughly chopped

½ **cup (118 ml)** heavy cream

1 **stick (8 tablespoons/113 grams)** unsalted butter, cut into ½-inch cubes

2 **teaspoons** vanilla extract

1 **tablespoon** toasted white or black sesame seeds, or a combination (see page 18)

Note

If your tahini is separated, stirring it with a butter knife will usually bring it back together. If it's being stubborn, pour it all (or use a spoon to dig it out of the container) into the bowl of a stand mixer fitted with a paddle attachment and mix on medium speed for 1 to 2 minutes, until emulsified. Letting tahini come to room temperature beforehand will help make this process easier. If you find your tahini is dry and crumbly no matter how much you mix it, it's best to purchase a fresh package.

Storage

The bars will keep in an airtight container in a single layer in the fridge for up to 1 week.

01 Make the Graham Cracker–Tahini Crust: Grease an 8 × 8-inch square baking pan with the nonstick pan spray. Line with parchment paper, leaving some overhang on all sides so it's easy to lift out the bars.

02 Whisk together the melted butter, tahini, vanilla extract, and salt in a large bowl until combined.

03 Add the confectioners' sugar and graham cracker crumbs. Stir with a rubber spatula until the confectioners' sugar is completely dissolved and the mixture is very thick. (It should be the texture of sticky Play-Doh.) Transfer to the prepared baking pan, spray your hands with pan spray, and press the mixture into an even layer in the bottom of the pan. Set aside.

04 Make the Dark Chocolate Ganache: Add the chocolate, heavy cream, butter, and vanilla extract to a medium, microwave-safe bowl. Microwave in 10-second increments, stirring between each, until the chocolate is completely melted and smooth, about 60 seconds total. Pour the chocolate mixture over the tahini base and use the back of a spoon to spread it into an even layer. Sprinkle the top with the sesame seeds and refrigerate for at least 6 hours or up to 2 days.

05 Take the bars out of the fridge. Run a large chef's knife under hot water, wipe with a paper towel, and slice into a 4 x 4 grid to make 16 pieces (the hot blade will help you make clean slices). Serve chilled.

Mocha Chocolate Chunk Cookies

These cookies have a decadent, fudgy center filled with pockets of molten dark chocolate. The batter is made with instant coffee, lending the cookies a subtle bitterness that enhances the chocolate and creates a mocha-like flavor. The beauty of the recipe is that you get to experience two different textures: fresh from the oven, the cookies are gooey with a lava cake interior thanks to the melted chocolate; but after an hour of cooling, the cookies firm up and become chewy and brownie-like. They're so good with a cup of hot coffee.

01 In a small saucepan over medium heat, melt the butter. Continue cooking, stirring often to prevent the milk solids from burning, until the butter foams and then darkens in color slightly and is very fragrant, 4 to 6 minutes. Immediately pour the butter into a large heatproof bowl and let cool at room temperature for 30 minutes.

02 As the butter is cooling, whisk together the flour, cocoa powder, baking powder, baking soda, and salt in a medium bowl. In a separate small bowl, combine the hot water, instant coffee, and vanilla extract and stir until completely dissolved.

03 Preheat the oven to 350°F and set 2 racks at the upper-middle and lower-middle positions. Line 3 baking sheets (or as many as you have) with parchment paper or nonstick baking mats.

04 Add both the brown and granulated sugars to the bowl of cooled butter and whisk to combine. Whisk in the instant coffee mixture until smooth, then add the flour mixture and stir with a rubber spatula until a soft dough forms. Stir in the chopped chocolate.

05 Using a large 2⅓-inch (#16) cookie scoop or ¼-cup measure, portion out the dough and roll into large balls. (If the dough is too sticky to work with, let it sit for 10 minutes and try again.) Place the dough balls at least 3 inches apart on the prepared baking sheets (about 6 per sheet).

06 Bake 2 sheets at the same time, swapping the top sheet to the bottom rack and bottom sheet to the top midway through, until the tops of the cookies lose their sheen but the cracks still appear slightly wet, 12 to 15 minutes, then bake the remaining sheet on either rack. (If reusing one of the baking sheets, allow it to cool for 15 minutes before baking another batch on it.) Let the cookies cool for at least 1 hour on the baking sheets. (They will be very soft when warm but firm up once cooled, so don't attempt to move them.)

2 sticks (16 tablespoons/226 grams) unsalted butter

3 cups spooned and leveled all-purpose flour (384 grams)

½ cup (45 grams) natural, unsweetened cocoa powder

1 teaspoon baking powder

1 teaspoon baking soda

1 teaspoon kosher salt

2 tablespoons (30 ml) hot water

1 tablespoon instant coffee granules

1 tablespoon vanilla extract

1½ cups (300 grams) packed light brown sugar

⅓ cup (67 grams) granulated sugar

2 large eggs, room temperature

8 ounces (227 grams) semisweet or bittersweet chocolate, roughly chopped (about 1⅓ cups)

Make Ahead
If wrapped tightly in plastic, the dough can be stored in the refrigerator for several days before baking. If too firm to scoop, let sit at room temperature for 15 minutes and try again.

Storage
The cookies will keep in an airtight container for up to 1 week.

Chocolate-Hazelnut Wedges

Makes 12 large wedges

These cookies are a riff on pecan sandies, a type of shortbread made with ground nuts that have a pleasantly sandy texture and rich buttery flavor, hence their name. This chocolate version uses toasted hazelnuts to create a rich, Nutella-like flavor. Instead of shaping the dough into a log, I press it into a springform pan, bake it, and cut it into wedges, giving the sandies a cakelike presentation that feels like a celebration. I like to shower the top with coarse sanding sugar to give them a bit of sparkle and crunch, but you can opt for chopped hazelnuts, or nothing at all, and still end up with wedges that impress.

01 Arrange a rack in the middle of the oven and preheat to 350°F. Spray a 9-inch springform pan or removable-bottom tart pan with the nonstick pan spray.

02 Add the hazelnuts to the bowl of a food processor fitted with the blade attachment and process until they're the texture of coarse sand, 15 to 20 seconds. Add the flour, cocoa powder, and salt and process until the mixture is thoroughly combined and the nuts have broken down even further into a fine sand-like texture, 20 to 25 seconds. Add the butter, brown sugar, and vanilla extract and process until a grainy dough forms that pulls away from the sides of the food processor, 25 to 30 seconds.

03 Transfer the dough to the prepared pan and press it into an even layer from edge to edge using a flat-bottomed measuring cup, taking care that the dough does not press up the sides. Prick the top of the dough in a decorative pattern with a fork and sprinkle the coarse sugar on top (if using). Using a thin, sharp knife, score the dough into 12 equal wedges, pressing the knife all the way through the dough (the marks will fill in somewhat during baking, but they do make slicing easier and cleaner).

04 Bake until the shortbread is fragrant, matte, and slightly puffed, 19 to 22 minutes. Let cool for 5 minutes, then carefully remove the side of the pan (or pop the base out from the ring if using a tart pan; the pan will still be hot, so use a kitchen towel or oven mitts and be careful). Immediately cut through the cookies with a thin, sharp knife along the marked lines (they're easier to cut while warm), but don't try to separate them—let them cool without moving for a full 2 hours. The cookies will be very soft and crumbly when warm but will firm up once cooled.

Nonstick pan spray

1 cup (130 grams) toasted unsalted hazelnuts (see Note)

1 cup spooned and leveled all-purpose flour (128 grams)

3 tablespoons (21 grams) natural, unsweetened cocoa powder

¼ teaspoon kosher salt

1 stick (½ cup/113 grams) cold unsalted butter, cut into ½-inch cubes

½ cup (100 grams) packed light brown sugar

2 teaspoons vanilla extract

2 teaspoons coarse sugar, such as turbinado or sanding sugar, or additional finely chopped hazelnuts (optional)

Note
See page 18 for instructions on toasting the hazelnuts. If using raw, skin-on hazelnuts (instead of blanched), immediately transfer them to a clean dish towel after toasting and rub vigorously to remove their skins. It's okay if some skin is still attached.

Storage
The shortbread will keep in an airtight container for up to 1 week.

Malted Brownie Biscotti

Makes 24 biscotti

If you're as big of a fan of corner-piece brownies as I am, then these biscotti are for you, perfect for dipping into coffee. A combination of cocoa powder and chopped bittersweet chocolate gives the biscotti a double hit of chocolaty flavor, while a generous amount of malted milk powder gives them a nuanced buttery undertone.

01 Position a rack in the middle of the oven and preheat to 350°F. Line a baking sheet with parchment paper or a nonstick baking mat.

02 In the bowl of a stand mixer fitted with the paddle attachment, combine the butter and sugar and beat on medium speed until smooth and fluffy, 2 to 3 minutes. (Alternatively, use an electric hand mixer and large bowl.) Add 2 of the eggs and the vanilla extract and continue beating on medium speed until combined, 2 to 3 minutes. Turn the mixer off and add the flour, malted milk powder, cocoa powder, baking soda, and salt. Mix on low speed until combined, about 1 minute. Stir in the chopped chocolate.

03 Transfer the dough to a generously floured surface and press together into one mass. (The dough will be very sticky, so feel free to use up to ¼ cup of flour to dust the surface.) Divide the dough into 2 equal pieces and form each into a 10-inch-long log that's 2 inches in diameter. Transfer both logs to the prepared baking sheet, leaving 3 inches of space between them. Flatten the logs with your hands until they are about 2½ inches wide and ¾ inch tall.

04 Crack the remaining egg into a small bowl and whisk with a fork until no streaks of yolk remain. Brush the tops and sides of the dough logs with the egg Transfer the baking sheet to the freezer and chill for 10 minutes, or up to 1 hour.

05 Bake until the tops have lost their sheen and the logs feel firm when touched, 28 to 30 minutes. Remove from the oven and reduce the temperature to 300°F. Let the logs cool on the baking sheet for 10 minutes, then carefully transfer them to a cutting board and cut each on a diagonal into ¾-inch-thick slices using a serrated knife. (If the biscotti start to crumble, lightly brush the tops with warm water.)

06 Transfer the slices, cut side down, onto 2 baking sheets lined with parchment paper or a nonstick baking mat (about 12 per sheet). Bake until they appear completely dry and crisp, 23 to 25 minutes, flipping them over halfway through baking. Let cool slightly on the baking sheet, then transfer to a wire rack and let cool completely.

1 stick (8 tablespoons/113 grams) unsalted butter, room temperature

¾ cup (150 grams) granulated sugar

3 large eggs, divided

1 tablespoon vanilla extract

1¾ cups spooned and leveled all-purpose flour (224 grams), plus more for dusting

¼ cup (28 grams) malted milk powder

¼ cup (23 grams) natural, unsweetened cocoa powder, sifted

1 teaspoon baking soda

½ teaspoon kosher salt

4 ounces (113 grams) semisweet or bittersweet chocolate, roughly chopped (about ¾ cup)

Storage

The biscotti will keep in an airtight container for up to 1 week.

Lavender Chocolate Chunk Cookies

Makes 18 large cookies

The unassuming look of these cookies masks their soft floral flavor. The surprising aroma hits your nose the moment you bring them to your lips. This is due to the infusion of dried lavender in warm melted butter, which lends the cookies a subtle lavender flavor that pairs beautifully with the rich, dark chocolate. If you're not typically a fan of strong floral flavors, you can cut the amount of dried lavender in half. This will still give the cookies a defined flavor, just a tad softer so even lavender skeptics will enjoy them. This is the cookie on the cover of this book—a cookie that is as beautiful as it is delicious.

2 sticks (16 tablespoons/226 grams) unsalted butter

3 tablespoons (6 grams) dried lavender, lightly crushed with your fingertips (see Note)

1⅓ cups (267 grams) packed light brown sugar

⅓ cup (67 grams) granulated sugar

2 large eggs, room temperature

1 tablespoon vanilla extract

3¼ cups spooned and leveled all-purpose flour (416 grams)

1 teaspoon baking powder

1 teaspoon baking soda

1 teaspoon kosher salt

8 ounces (227 grams) semisweet or bittersweet chocolate, roughly chopped (about 1½ cups)

Note
Dried lavender can be found in the spice section of specialty grocery stores or sold in bulk in the tea section. If ordering online, double check that the lavender you're purchasing is food-grade and meant for culinary use.

Make Ahead
If wrapped tightly in plastic, the dough can be stored in the refrigerator for several days before baking. If too firm to scoop, let sit at room temperature for 15 minutes and try again.

Storage
The cookies will keep in an airtight container for up to 1 week.

01 In a medium saucepan set over medium heat, melt the butter. Continue cooking, stirring often to prevent the bottom from burning, just until the butter starts to sizzle but does not brown, 2 to 3 minutes. Remove the pan from the heat, add the dried lavender, and let cool at room temperature for 30 minutes, stirring occasionally.

02 Preheat the oven to 350°F and set 2 racks at the upper-middle and lower-middle positions. Line 3 baking sheets (or as many as you have) with parchment paper or nonstick baking mats.

03 Strain the butter through a fine-mesh sieve into a large bowl, pressing down on the lavender with a spoon to extract all the butter, and discard the lavender. Add the brown sugar and the granulated sugar to the butter and whisk to combine. Add the eggs and vanilla extract and whisk until ribbony and smooth, about 1 minute.

04 Add the flour, baking powder, baking soda, and salt, and stir with a rubber spatula just until a dough forms. Mix in the chopped chocolate.

05 Using a large 2⅓-inch (#16) cookie scoop or ¼-cup measure, portion out the dough and roll into large balls. Place the dough balls at least 3 inches apart on the prepared baking sheets (6 per sheet).

06 Bake 2 sheets at the same time, swapping the top sheet to the bottom rack and bottom sheet to the top midway through, until the tops of the cookies are lightly browned, 13 to 16 minutes, then bake the remaining sheet on either rack. (If reusing one of the baking sheets, allow it to cool for 15 minutes before baking another batch on it.) Let the cookies cool slightly on the baking sheets, then transfer onto a wire rack to cool completely.

Minty Shortbread Sandwich Cookies

Makes 10 to 12 sandwich cookies

This recipe is inspired by one of my favorite cookies growing up: Mint Milanos. The classic store-bought version consists of two buttery biscuit cookies glued together with minty chocolate, but this version is made with shortbread cookies sandwiching chocolate ganache flavored with both mint and vanilla extract. I can't claim that they are better than the original, but they are pretty darn good.

Shortbread Cookies

2 sticks (16 tablespoons/226 grams) unsalted butter, room temperature

¾ cup (75 grams) confectioners' sugar

1 teaspoon vanilla extract

¼ teaspoon kosher salt

2½ cups spooned and leveled all-purpose flour (320 grams), plus more for dusting

¾ cup (150 grams) granulated sugar

Mint Chocolate Ganache

¼ cup (59 ml) whole milk

2 teaspoons mint extract

1½ teaspoons vanilla extract

Pinch of kosher salt

10 ounces (283 grams) bittersweet or semisweet chocolate, chopped (about 1¾ cups)

Note
Leftover ganache can be stored in the refrigerator for several weeks. To rewarm (for using to sandwich cookies), microwave in 10-second bursts, stirring between each, until softened but not melted; to remelt (to pour over cake, add to ice cream, drizzle over popcorn, or use as a base for hot chocolate) microwave in 10-second bursts, stirring between each until fully melted.

Make Ahead
Frozen, unbaked cookies can be kept in the freezer, tightly wrapped in plastic, for several months.

Storage
The assembled cookies will keep in an airtight container in a single layer at room temperature for up to 1 week.

01 Make the cookies: Position a rack in the middle of the oven and preheat to 350°F. Line a baking sheet with parchment paper or a nonstick baking mat.

02 In the bowl of a stand mixer fitted with the paddle attachment, beat the butter, confectioners' sugar, vanilla extract, and salt on medium speed until light and fluffy, 2 to 3 minutes. (Alternatively, use a hand mixer and large bowl.)

03 Add the flour and mix on low speed until a crumbly dough forms, about 1 minute.

04 Transfer the dough to a lightly floured surface and press together into a disk. Dust the top of the dough with flour and roll into a ¼-inch-thick sheet. Using a 2-inch round cookie cutter, cut out circles and place them on the prepared baking sheet, spacing them about 1 inch apart. Press the dough scraps together into a ball and repeat the rolling and cutting process. Freeze the cookies for 10 minutes.

05 Bake the cookies until the bottom edges are just starting to brown, 12 to 14 minutes. Remove from the oven and let the cookies cool on the pan just until they are no longer too hot to handle (about 5 minutes). Add the granulated sugar to a shallow, wide bowl and place the still-warm cookies in the sugar, turning them to coat on all sides. Return the cookies to the baking sheet and let them cool completely, about 30 minutes.

06 Make the ganache: In a medium pot over medium heat, combine the milk, mint and vanilla extracts, and salt. Cook, stirring constantly, until the mixture comes to a simmer. Reduce the heat to low, add the chopped chocolate, and stir until the ganache is completely smooth, about 1 minute. Pour into a medium heatproof bowl and let sit at room temperature, stirring occasionally, until thickened but still spoonable, about 30 minutes.

07 Dollop 1 heaping tablespoon of the ganache onto the flat undersides of half the cookies. Sandwich with the remaining cookies, flat side down. Let the cookies set at least 1 hour before serving to harden.

Chocolate Chunk Oatmeal Cookie Bars

If your favorite part of an oatmeal cookie is the chewy, soft interior, these bars are for you. The base is nutty with pockets of molten dark chocolate throughout; and instead of being overly oaty (or dry) like most oatmeal cookies, they are rich and chewy, like a pan of brownies. The bars are just as happy topped with a scoop of vanilla ice cream as they are packed into a baggie and enjoyed as a morning treat (they are made from oatmeal, after all). I recommend freezing any leftovers (or setting a few aside) for a decadent anytime treat. The dough has a generous amount of butter and chocolate, so you don't need to worry about two- or three-day-old bars drying out.

01 Position a rack in the middle of the oven and preheat to 325°F. Grease an 8 × 8-inch square baking pan with nonstick pan spray. Line with parchment paper, leaving some overhang on all sides so it's easy to lift out the bars.

02 In a large bowl, combine the melted butter, both sugars, the eggs, and vanilla extract. Whisk until the sugar is almost completely dissolved, 2 to 3 minutes. (Don't fret if the mixture appears broken at this stage.)

03 Add the flour, baking soda, salt, and cinnamon, and stir with a rubber spatula until a smooth dough forms, 1 minute. Mix in the oats and chopped chocolate with a rubber spatula.

04 Transfer the dough to the prepared baking pan and spread into an even layer using an offset spatula. Sprinkle with flaky sea salt (if using).

05 Bake for 35 to 40 minutes, until the top is lightly browned and the edges are set but the center is still slightly soft. A toothpick inserted into the center should have only a few moist crumbs stuck to it (a little melted chocolate stuck to it is normal!).

06 Let cool for at least 1 hour, then slice into a 4 x 4 grid to make 16 bars.

Nonstick pan spray

1½ **sticks (12 tablespoons/170 grams)** unsalted butter, melted and cooled slightly

¾ **cup (150 grams)** packed light brown sugar

⅓ **cup (67 grams)** granulated sugar

2 **large** eggs, room temperature

1 **tablespoon** vanilla extract

1¼ **cups** spooned and leveled all-purpose flour (160 grams)

¾ **teaspoon** baking soda

½ **teaspoon** kosher salt

1 **teaspoon** ground cinnamon

2 **cups (180 grams)** old-fashioned rolled oats

8 **ounces (about 1½ cups/227 grams)** chopped semisweet or bittersweet chocolate

Flaky sea salt, for sprinkling (optional)

Storage

The bars will keep in an airtight container in a single layer at room temperature for up to 1 week.

Chocolate-Dipped Mocha Madeleines

Makes 24 madeleines

Sea salt and chocolate turn classic French madeleines into every chocolate lovers' dream. The texture is light and airy, similar to a sponge cake, but the flavor is bold and deeply chocolaty. The batter is made with brewed coffee, giving them an intense, mocha-like flavor that elevates the chocolate and also tames its sweetness, making these the perfect breakfast treat.

01 Make the Chocolate Madeleines: In a medium bowl, whisk together the eggs, coffee, sugar, and vanilla extract until smooth.

02 In a second medium bowl, whisk together the flour, baking powder, salt, and cocoa. Add the wet ingredients to the dry and stir with a rubber spatula until smooth. Add the melted butter and mix with the spatula until fully incorporated. (It will look like too much butter at first, but just keep mixing.) Tightly cover the bowl with plastic wrap and refrigerate for 1 hour or up to overnight.

03 While the batter chills, brush the molds of a madeleine pan with a thin layer of melted butter and then refrigerate.

04 Position a rack in the middle of the oven and preheat to 375°F.

05 Remove the chilled madeleine pan from the fridge and immediately fill each well with 1 tablespoon of batter, then return the remaining batter to the fridge. Use a small spoon to evenly spread the batter into the molds and tap the pan on the countertop several times to evenly distribute it into the grooves. (The batter does not need to go all the way up the sides of the molds.) Bake until the madeleines pull away from the sides of the molds, 7 to 8 minutes. Transfer the pan to a wire rack and let the madeleines cool in the pan for 10 minutes.

06 Remove the madeleines from the pan and brush the pan with more melted butter. Chill the pan in the refrigerator for 10 minutes, then repeat the baking process until you run out of batter. Let the madeleines cool completely.

07 Make the coating: Add the chocolate and heavy cream to a medium, microwave-safe bowl. Microwave in 10-second increments, stirring between each, until the chocolate is completely melted and smooth, about 60 seconds total.

08 Dip the edges of the madeleines in the chocolate and set on parchment paper. Sprinkle with flaky sea salt, if using. Let set for 4 hours before serving.

Chocolate Madeleines

2 **large** eggs, room temperature

3 **tablespoons (45 ml)** brewed strong coffee, cooled

½ **cup (100 grams)** granulated sugar

1 **tablespoon** vanilla extract

1 **cup** spooned and leveled all-purpose flour (128 grams)

1 **teaspoon** baking powder

½ **teaspoon** kosher salt

3 **tablespoons (21 grams)** natural, unsweetened cocoa powder

1 **stick (8 tablespoons/113 grams)** unsalted butter, melted and cooled, plus more for brushing the pan

Chocolate Coating

6 **ounces (about 1 cup/170 grams)** semisweet or bittersweet chocolate, chopped

¼ **cup (59 ml)** heavy cream

Flaky sea salt, for sprinkling (optional)

Note
Madeleine pans can be found in specialty baking stores or are easily ordered online. I find that both metal and silicone molds work well.

Make Ahead
The madeleine batter can be made a day in advance and stored in the fridge before baking.

Storage
The madeleines will keep in an airtight container in a single layer at room temperature for up to 1 week.

Oatmeal Chocolate-Covered-Raisin Cookies

Makes 24 cookies

This recipe combines two of my all-time favorite treats: oatmeal cookies and movie theater–style chocolate-covered raisins. The candy coating melts into the cookie dough, giving it a soft, fudge-like texture and rich chocolate flavor (and prevents the oats from drying out the cookies). For even more insurance against dryness, a generous glug of maple syrup is added to the dough. A two-hour rest gives the dough time to absorb the moisture in the syrup, helping ensure your cookies are as moist as possible.

01 In a medium bowl, whisk together the flour, cinnamon, baking soda, and salt.

02 In the bowl of a stand mixer fitted with the paddle attachment, combine the butter, brown sugar, and granulated sugar. (Alternatively, use a hand mixer and large bowl.) Beat on medium speed until light and fluffy, 2 to 3 minutes. Turn the mixer off, scrape the sides and bottom, and add the eggs, maple syrup, and vanilla extract. Mix on medium speed until thoroughly combined and fluffy, 2 minutes. With the mixer running on low speed, gradually add the flour mixture, beating until just combined. Turn the mixer off, stir in the oats and chocolate-covered raisins with a rubber spatula, and cover with plastic wrap. Chill for at least 2 hours, preferably overnight.

03 Preheat the oven to 350°F and set 2 racks at the upper-middle and lower-middle positions. Line 4 baking sheets (or as many as you have) with parchment paper or nonstick baking mats.

04 Using a large 2½-inch (#10) cookie scoop or ¼-cup measure, portion out the dough and roll into large balls. Place 6 dough balls per baking sheet, spacing at least 3 inches apart.

05 Bake 2 sheets at the same time, swapping the top sheet to the bottom rack and bottom sheet to the top midway through, until the cookies are lightly browned but still soft, 12 to 14 minutes. (If reusing the baking sheets, allow them to cool for 15 minutes before baking another batch on them.) Let the cookies cool slightly on the baking sheets, then transfer to a wire rack to cool completely.

1¾ cups spooned and leveled all-purpose flour (224 grams)

2 teaspoons ground cinnamon

1 teaspoon baking soda

¾ teaspoon kosher salt

2 sticks (16 tablespoons/226 grams) unsalted butter, room temperature

1 cup (200 grams) packed light brown sugar

½ cup (100 grams) granulated sugar

2 large eggs

2 tablespoons (30 ml) maple syrup

1 tablespoon vanilla extract

3 cups (270 grams) old-fashioned rolled oats

2 cups (888 grams) chocolate-covered raisins, roughly chopped (see Note)

Note
Chocolate-covered raisins can be found in the candy section of most well-stocked grocery stores or pharmacies. My favorite brand is Raisinets. They have a creamy chocolate coating that becomes silky and fudge-like when baked—although any brand will work.

Make Ahead
If wrapped tightly in plastic, the dough can be stored in the refrigerator for several days before baking. If too firm to scoop, let sit at room temperature for 15 minutes and try again.

Storage
The cookies will keep in an airtight container for up to 1 week.

Boozy

Red Wine Brownie Cookie

Cinnamon-Rum Raisin Oatmeal Cookies

Makes 24 large cookies

This twist on chewy oatmeal-raisin cookies adds rum-soaked raisins to the mix, transforming the classic cookie into something bold and pleasantly boozy. Soaking the raisins in rum infuses them with flavor and adds an extra dose of moisture so the cookies stay soft for several days. These cookies make for a perfect nightcap.

1 cup (125 grams) dark or golden raisins

1 cup (237 ml) spiced dark rum (see Note)

3 teaspoons ground cinnamon, divided

½ cup plus 2 tablespoons (132 grams) granulated sugar, divided

2¼ cups spooned and leveled all-purpose flour (288 grams)

1 teaspoon baking soda

¾ teaspoon kosher salt

2 sticks (16 tablespoons/226 grams) unsalted butter, softened

1 cup (200 grams) packed light brown sugar

2 large eggs, room temperature

2 tablespoons (30 ml) maple syrup

2 teaspoons vanilla extract

3 cups (270 grams) old-fashioned rolled oats

Note
I like to use a strong, spiced dark rum to make these cookies. The flavor of the spirit perfumes the whole cookie, not just the raisins, so it lends the dough a subtle cinnamon-y flavor. If unavailable, any rum (including white rum) also works.

Make Ahead
The raisins can be cooked in the rum and stored in an airtight container in the fridge for several days before making the dough. If wrapped tightly in plastic, the finished dough can be stored in the refrigerator for several days before baking. If too firm to scoop, let sit at room temperature for 15 minutes and try again.

Storage
The cookies will keep in an airtight container for up to 1 week.

01   Combine the raisins, rum, 1 teaspoon of the cinnamon, and 2 tablespoons (32 grams) of the granulated sugar in a medium saucepan. Bring to a simmer over medium heat and cook, stirring occasionally, until all the rum has been absorbed by the raisins, 6 to 9 minutes. Remove the pan from the heat and let cool while you make the dough.

02   In a medium bowl, combine the flour, baking soda, salt, and remaining 2 teaspoons cinnamon.

03   In the bowl of a stand mixer fitted with the paddle attachment, combine the butter, brown sugar, and remaining ½ cup (100 grams) granulated sugar. (Alternatively, use a hand mixer and large bowl.) Beat on medium speed until light and fluffy, 2 to 3 minutes. Turn the mixer off, scrape down the sides and bottom, and add the eggs, maple syrup, and vanilla extract. Mix on medium speed until thoroughly combined and fluffy, 1 to 2 minutes. With the mixer running on low speed, gradually add the flour mixture, beating until just combined and no pockets of dry flour remain. Turn the mixer off and stir in the oats and cooled raisins with a rubber spatula. Cover the bowl with plastic wrap and chill for at least 3 hours or preferably overnight. (Do not skip the chilling step or else the cookies will spread too much.)

04   Preheat the oven to 350°F and set 2 racks at the upper-middle and lower-middle positions. Line 4 baking sheets (or as many as you have) with parchment paper or nonstick baking mats. Using a large 2⅓-inch (#16) cookie scoop or ¼-cup measure, portion out the dough and roll into large balls. Place 6 dough balls on each baking sheet, spacing them at least 3 inches apart.

05   Bake 2 sheets at the same time, swapping the top sheet to the bottom rack and bottom sheet to the top midway through baking, until the cookies are lightly browned but still soft in the center, 12 to 14 minutes. Repeat with the remaining baking sheets. (If reusing the baking sheets, allow them to cool for 15 minutes before baking another batch on them.) Let the cookies cool slightly on the baking sheets, then transfer to a wire rack to let cool completely.

Brown Butter–Bourbon Snickerdoodles

Makes 24 cookies

Many people think that snickerdoodles are just sugar cookies rolled in cinnamon sugar, but that's not necessarily true. The ingredient that makes a snickerdoodle the tender cookie equivalent of cinnamon toast is cream of tartar. Usually it's used to stiffen and stabilize egg whites when whipping them into meringue, but here it adds a distinctive tangy flavor and pleasant chew to the cookies. I also incorporate brown butter for a rich, nutty flavor and a splash of bourbon to bring out the toasty flavors of the brown sugar. I like using snickerdoodles to sandwich together a scoop of ice cream, but they are just as delicious on their own.

2 sticks (16 tablespoons/226 grams) unsalted butter

2½ cups spooned and leveled all-purpose flour (320 grams)

2 teaspoons cream of tartar

1 teaspoon baking soda

½ teaspoon kosher salt

1½ cups (300 grams) granulated sugar, divided

½ cup (100 grams) packed light brown sugar

2 large eggs, room temperature

2 tablespoons (30 ml) bourbon (see Note)

1 teaspoon vanilla extract

1 tablespoon ground cinnamon

Note
Feel free to use any whiskey in place of the bourbon; dark, spiced rum also works well and gives the dough a subtle cinnamon-y flavor.

Make Ahead
If wrapped tightly in plastic, the finished dough can be stored in the refrigerator for several days before baking. If too firm to scoop, let sit at room temperature for 15 minutes and try again.

Storage
The cookies will keep in an airtight container for up to 1 week.

01 In a small saucepan over medium heat, melt the butter. Continue cooking, stirring often to prevent the milk solids from burning, until the butter foams and then darkens in color slightly and is very fragrant, 3 to 4 minutes. Immediately pour the butter into a medium heatproof bowl and let it cool at room temperature for 20 minutes.

02 As the butter is cooling, combine the flour, cream of tartar, baking soda, and salt in a medium bowl. Preheat the oven to 350°F and set 2 racks at the upper-middle and lower-middle positions. Line 2 baking sheets with parchment paper or nonstick baking mats.

03 In the bowl of a stand mixer fitted with the paddle attachment, combine the cooled (but still melted) butter, 1 cup (200 grams) of the granulated sugar, and the brown sugar. Beat on medium speed until combined, 1 minute. (Alternatively, use a hand mixer and large bowl.) Turn the mixer off and add the eggs, bourbon, and vanilla extract. Mix on medium speed until pale yellow and ribbony, 2 to 3 minutes. With the mixer running on low speed, gradually add the dry ingredients, beating until just combined.

04 In a shallow dish, mix the remaining ½ cup (100 grams) granulated sugar and the cinnamon.

05 Using a medium 1¾-inch (#40) cookie scoop or 2 tablespoons, portion out the dough and roll into balls. Roll in the cinnamon sugar and place the dough balls at least 3 inches apart on the prepared baking sheets (12 per sheet).

06 Bake both sheets at the same time, swapping the top sheet to the bottom rack and bottom sheet to the top midway through baking, until the tops of the cookies are lightly browned, 8 to 11 minutes. Let cool slightly on the baking sheets, then transfer to a wire rack to cool completely.

Salted Absinthe Fudge Squares

Absinthe and chocolate might seem like an unlikely pairing, but their bold flavors perfectly complement one another. The bright, floral flavor of absinthe tames the richness of the dark chocolate, giving these fudge squares a surprisingly refreshing quality. The flavor is sweet and complex, with notes of anise rounding out the dark chocolate. It's a simple, no-bake recipe that is perfect for serving alongside cocktails, with after-dinner drinks, or even on a cheese board.

01 Grease an 8 × 8-inch square baking pan with the nonstick pan spray. Line with parchment paper, leaving some overhang on all sides so it's easy to lift out the fudge, and spray once more to lightly coat the paper.

02 Fill a medium saucepan halfway with water and bring to a simmer over medium heat, then reduce the heat to low to maintain a very gentle simmer.

03 In a large heatproof bowl slightly larger than the saucepan, add the chocolate chips, sweetened condensed milk, absinthe, vanilla extract, and salt. Stir so the chocolate is evenly coated with the sweetened condensed milk and place the bowl on top of the saucepan (the bottom of the bowl shouldn't touch the water). Melt the chocolate, stirring often, until it's completely smooth, 5 to 7 minutes. The mixture will be very thick.

04 Pour the fudge into the prepared pan and use an offset spatula to spread it into an even layer. Immediately sprinkle the top with flaky sea salt (if using). Let set at room temperature, uncovered, for 8 hours until firm, then slice into a 6 x 6 grid to make 36 squares.

Nonstick pan spray

3⅓ cups (20 ounces/567 grams) semisweet or bittersweet chocolate chips

1 14-ounce can (414 ml) sweetened condensed milk

3 tablespoons (44 ml) absinthe (see Note)

1 teaspoon vanilla extract

¼ teaspoon kosher salt

Flaky sea salt, for sprinkling (optional)

Note
Absinthe is an anise-flavored spirit that has a stunning chartreuse color and complex herbal flavor. If unavailable, Pastis or Herbsaint can be used in its place.

Storage
Fudge squares can be kept in an airtight container at room temperature for up to 1 week, or in the freezer for several months. (Bring them to room temperature before serving.)

Buttered Rum Sugar Cookies

Makes 24 cookies

Chewy, rich, and coated with crunchy sugar, this boozy take on sugar cookies borrows all the warm and luscious flavors of hot buttered rum. Browning the butter, swapping out granulated sugar for brown, and adding a generous amount of vanilla bring out the caramel flavors of the rum and give these cookies a bold, buttery flavor. They're crispy on the edges, chewy in the center, and an absolute treat to warm up a cold night.

01   In a small saucepan over medium heat, melt the butter. Continue cooking, stirring often to prevent the milk solids from burning, until the butter foams and then darkens in color slightly and is very fragrant, 3 to 4 minutes. Immediately pour the butter into a medium, heatproof bowl and let cool in the fridge for 1½ hours until it's mostly resolidified. (It's okay if the butter is still slightly soft.)

02   As the butter cools, in a medium bowl, combine the flour, salt, and baking soda. Set aside.

03   Preheat the oven to 350°F and set 2 racks at the upper-middle and lower-middle positions. Line 2 baking sheets with parchment paper or nonstick baking mats.

04   In the bowl of a stand mixer fitted with the paddle attachment, add the cooled butter and the brown sugar. Beat on medium speed, scraping down the sides and bottom of the bowl halfway through, until smooth and fully combined, 2 to 3 minutes. (Alternatively, use a hand mixer and large bowl.) Turn the mixer off and add the egg, molasses, rum, and vanilla extract. Mix on medium speed until very fluffy and lightened in color, 2 to 3 minutes. With the mixer running on low speed, gradually add the flour mixture, beating until just combined.

05   Place the granulated sugar in a shallow, wide bowl. Using a medium 1¾-inch (#40) cookie scoop or 2 tablespoons, portion out the dough and roll into balls. Roll the balls in the granulated sugar and place at least 3 inches apart on the prepared baking sheets, 12 per pan.

06   Bake both sheets at the same time, swapping the top sheet to the bottom rack and bottom sheet to the top midway through baking, until the cookies are lightly browned, 10 to 13 minutes. Let cool slightly on the baking sheets, then transfer to a wire rack and let cool completely.

2 sticks (16 tablespoons/226 grams) unsalted butter

2¾ cups spooned and leveled all-purpose flour (352 grams)

1½ teaspoons kosher salt

1 teaspoon baking soda

1⅔ cups (333 grams) packed light brown sugar

1 large egg, room temperature

2 tablespoons (30 ml) unsulphured molasses

2 tablespoons (30 ml) dark rum

1 tablespoon vanilla extract

⅔ cup (133 grams) granulated sugar

Make Ahead
If wrapped tightly in plastic, the finished dough can be stored in the refrigerator for several days before baking. If too firm to scoop, let sit at room temperature for 15 minutes and try again.

Storage
The cookies will keep in an airtight container for up to 1 week.

Campari Shortbread Cookies with Crunchy Orange Sugar

Makes 24 cookies

These Negroni-inspired shortbread cookies are coated with a hot pink glaze made with the slightly bitter aperitif Campari, giving the cookies a bold, orange-like flavor that balances the sweetness of the shortbread. A flourish of homemade orange sprinkles (which are surprisingly simple to make) gives them a bright, citrusy aroma reminiscent of the orange slice typically found in a Negroni.

Orange Sugar

2 tablespoons (30 grams) coarse sugar, such as turbinado or sanding sugar

1 teaspoon grated orange zest

Shortbread Cookies

3 sticks (24 tablespoons/339 grams) unsalted butter, softened

1 cup (100 grams) confectioners' sugar

1 teaspoon kosher salt

3 cups spooned and leveled all-purpose flour (384 grams), plus more for dusting

Campari Glaze

¼ cup plus 1 tablespoon (74 ml) Campari (see Note)

2¼ cups (225 grams) confectioners' sugar

1 teaspoon vanilla extract

Pinch of kosher salt

Note

Campari is a dark red liqueur with a fruity, intensely bitter flavor. Aperol, another less bitter and slightly sweeter apéritif, can be used in its place.

Make Ahead

For extra-crunchy orange sugar, make it the night before and leave it out, uncovered, at room temperature.

Storage

The cookies will keep in an airtight container in a single layer for up to 1 week. (Just make sure the glaze is completely dry first.)

01 Make the Orange Sugar: In a small bowl, combine the coarse sugar and orange zest. Use your fingertips to massage the zest into the sugar until very fragrant. Scatter the sugar in a single layer on a plate and let sit at room temperature, uncovered, to dry while you make the cookies.

02 Make the Shortbread Cookies: Line 2 baking sheets with parchment paper or nonstick baking mats.

03 In the bowl of a stand mixer fitted with the paddle attachment, combine the butter, confectioners' sugar, and salt. (Alternatively, use an electric hand mixer and large bowl.) Beat on medium speed until smooth and fluffy, 2 minutes. Turn the mixer off and add the flour. Mix on low speed until a dry dough forms, 2 to 3 minutes.

04 Transfer the dough to a piece of parchment paper lightly dusted with flour and press together into a ball. Dust the top of the dough with flour, place a second sheet of parchment paper on top, and roll the dough until it's ½ inch thick. Remove the top piece of parchment paper and use a 2½-inch round cutter to cut out rounds and place them on the prepared baking sheets, spacing about 1½ inches apart. Press the dough scraps together into a ball and repeat the rolling and cutting process. Freeze the cut cookies for 20 minutes.

05 Preheat the oven to 350°F and set 2 racks at the upper-middle and lower-middle positions. Bake both sheets at the same time, swapping them midway, until the tops of the cookies are light golden brown, 15 to 19 minutes. Let cool completely on the baking sheets.

06 Make the glaze: In a large bowl, whisk together the Campari, confectioners' sugar, vanilla extract, and salt until smooth. (If the glaze is too thick, add more Campari; if too thin, add additional confectioners' sugar.) Dip the tops of the cookies in the glaze, allowing the excess to drip back into the bowl. Sprinkle the cookies with the orange sprinkles and let set for 1 hour.

Bourbon Pecan Sandies

Makes 24 cookies

Classic pecan sandies are taken to the next level with cinnamon sugar and fiery bourbon. The simple shortbread base, made with pecans and a generous pinch of salt, makes the perfect understated cookie that is rich, nutty, and so good perfumed with smoky bourbon. The dough is formed into logs, rolled in crunchy cinnamon sugar, then sliced and baked until fragrant and golden brown. These sandies are delicate and crumbly, perfect to serve with coffee, tea, or an Old Fashioned for a sweet nightcap.

01 In the bowl of a stand mixer fitted with the paddle attachment, combine the butter, confectioners' sugar, and bourbon. (Alternatively, use a hand mixer and large bowl.) Beat on medium speed until light and fluffy, scraping down the sides and bottom of the bowl halfway through, 2 to 3 minutes. Add the flour, salt, and ½ teaspoon of the cinnamon, and mix on low speed until a crumbly dough forms, about 1 minute. Add the chopped pecans and mix on low speed just until combined. (It's okay if the mixer crushes the pecans slightly.)

02 Divide the dough in half (about 1½ cups/367 grams per half) and transfer each portion to a large sheet of plastic wrap. Roll each portion into 1½-inch-diameter logs and gently wrap each log in the plastic, twisting the ends tightly to help form a cylinder shape. Chill the logs in the freezer for 1 hour.

03 As the dough is chilling, place the granulated sugar and remaining 1 teaspoon cinnamon on a shallow plate and mix to combine. Line 2 baking sheets with parchment paper or nonstick baking mats.

04 Preheat the oven to 350°F and set 2 racks at the upper-middle and lower middle positions. Unwrap the chilled dough logs and transfer to the plate with the cinnamon sugar mixture. Roll the logs in the sugar, firmly pressing the sugar into the sides of the logs to help it stick. Use a sharp, thin knife to slice each log into ½-inch-thick slices, rotating the log between slices to help keep its shape (about 12 slices per log). Arrange the slices on the prepared baking sheets, spacing them about 2 inches apart.

05 Bake both sheets at the same time, swapping the top sheet to the bottom rack and bottom sheet to the top midway through baking, until the tops of the cookies are lightly browned, 19 to 23 minutes. Cool completely on the baking sheets before moving them. (The cookies will firm up as they cool.)

2 sticks (16 tablespoons/226 grams) unsalted butter, softened

¾ cup (75 grams) confectioners' sugar

2 tablespoons (30 ml) bourbon

2½ cups spooned and leveled all-purpose flour (320 grams)

1 teaspoon kosher salt

1½ teaspoons ground cinnamon, divided

1½ cups (150 grams) toasted unsalted pecans, finely chopped (see page 18)

½ cup (100 grams) granulated sugar

Make Ahead
The dough logs can be stored in the freezer, tightly wrapped in plastic, for several months before baking. If they are too cold to slice easily, let the logs sit out at room temperature for 15 minutes and try again.

Storage
The cookies will keep in an airtight container for up to 1 week.

Pretzels & Stout Cookie Bars

Makes 24 bars

Pretzels, dark chocolate, and hearty, bitter stout beer work together to create a chewy, blondie-like sweet-salty treat that you don't even need a mixer to make. Pockets of molten dark chocolate and crushed pretzels give the bars an array of textures; instead of being sweet and smooth like most cookie bars, they are complex and studded with contrasting textures. Serve them with a glass of milk, a pint of Guinness, or a scoop of vanilla ice cream.

2 sticks (16 tablespoons/226 grams) unsalted butter

Nonstick pan spray

2 cups (400 grams) packed light brown sugar

¼ cup (50 grams) granulated sugar

2 large eggs, room temperature

1 tablespoon vanilla extract

½ cup (118 ml) dry stout beer, such as Guinness (see Note)

3 cups spooned and leveled all-purpose flour (384 grams)

¾ teaspoon baking soda

1 teaspoon kosher salt

8 ounces (227 grams) semisweet or bittersweet chocolate, roughly chopped (about 1½ cups)

1½ cups (71 grams) salted mini pretzels, crushed into small, irregular pieces

Note
You can use other dark beer varieties such as porters or brown ales if stout isn't your thing; just avoid strong IPAs, as they can contribute an overly hoppy flavor.

Storage
The bars will keep in an airtight container for up to 1 week. The bars also freeze well when stored in an airtight container or zip-top bag. I like to heat individual frozen bars in the microwave for about 30 seconds for a quick treat.

01 In a small saucepan set over medium heat, melt the butter. Continue cooking, stirring often to prevent the milk solids from burning, until the butter foams and then darkens in color slightly and is very fragrant, 3 to 4 minutes. Immediately transfer the butter to a large heatproof bowl and let cool for 20 minutes until warm but no longer hot.

02 Arrange a rack in the middle of the oven and preheat to 325°F. Grease a 9 × 13-inch baking pan (preferably metal, since you'll be banging the bars on the countertop after baking) with nonstick pan spray. Line with parchment paper, leaving some overhang on all sides so it's easy to lift out the bars after baking. Lightly coat the parchment once more with the pan spray.

03 Add the brown sugar, granulated sugar, eggs, vanilla extract, and beer to the bowl of melted butter. Whisk until smooth, 1 to 2 minutes. Add the flour, baking soda, and salt and stir with a rubber spatula until a smooth dough forms. Stir in the chocolate and pretzels.

04 Transfer to the prepared pan and spread into an even layer using an offset spatula. Bake for 42 to 48 minutes, until the top is lightly browned, the edges are set, and a toothpick inserted into the center comes out with only a few moist crumbs attached. (Avoid inserting the toothpick into a pocket of melted chocolate.) Remove the pan from the oven and immediately bang it on the countertop several times to deflate the cookie base slightly.

05 The cookie base will be very gooey when hot but firm up once cooled, so set the pan aside for at least 2 hours before slicing the base into a 6 x 4 grid to make 24 pieces.

Spiced Honey Rum Balls

This version of old-school rum balls amps up the flavor with a few clever ingredient swaps, like graham crackers instead of traditional wafer cookies, honey to replace corn syrup, and warm spiced rum for white rum. A pinch of cinnamon brings out the rum's spices, while a toss in coarse sugar adds sparkle and crunch. Just think of them as a cross between cake balls and fudge: chewy, slightly soft, and *definitely* boozy. For a vegan version, feel free to swap out the honey for maple syrup—just make sure the graham crackers you use are also honey-free. I like to make these a day before serving to let the rum flavor intensify and the texture to become extra fudgy.

01 Add the walnuts to the bowl of a food processor fitted with the blade attachment. Process until the walnuts are finely ground and are the texture of coarse sand, 15 to 20 seconds.

02 To the ground walnuts add the graham crackers, cocoa powder, cinnamon, and salt. Process until the mixture is the texture of breadcrumbs, 30 to 45 seconds. Add the honey, rum, and vanilla extract and process until the mixture starts to pull away from the sides of the bowl, 20 to 25 seconds.

03 Portion out the dough using a rounded tablespoon and roll into balls. Immediately roll the balls in the coarse sugar and place them on a parchment-lined baking sheet. (Don't let them sit too long before rolling them in sugar or else they will dry out.) Let sit for 30 minutes before serving.

1 cup (92 grams) toasted unsalted walnuts
(see page 18)

3 sleeves graham crackers (27 full crackers/412 grams)

⅓ cup (30 grams) natural, unsweetened cocoa powder

¼ teaspoon ground cinnamon

½ teaspoon kosher salt

½ cup (118 ml) honey

¼ cup (59 ml) spiced dark rum

1 teaspoon vanilla extract

½ cup (125 grams) coarse sugar, such as turbinado or sanding sugar

Storage
The rum balls will keep in an airtight container in the fridge up to 1 week.

Black Forest "Salami" (Salami di Cioccolato)

Makes two 8-inch logs (about 24 slices)

Chocolate salami is a no-bake treat popular throughout Portugal and Italy. It consists of a chocolate log filled with all kinds of add-ins, like nuts and dried fruit. It gets coated with confectioners' sugar, then sliced into thin rounds that look just like salami. This version, made with dried tart cherries and fiery cherry brandy, borrows the beloved flavors of Black Forest cake. Serve this with coffee or tea, or shingled onto a cheese board for a sweet-and-savory pairing.

10 ounces (283 grams) semisweet or bittersweet chocolate chips or chopped chocolate (about 1¾ cups)

¾ cup (97 grams) dried tart cherries (preferably unsweetened)

1 cup (71 grams) crushed biscuit cookies, such as Digestive or Maria cookies

3 tablespoons (21 grams) natural, unsweetened cocoa powder, divided

1 stick (8 tablespoons/113 grams) unsalted butter

¾ cup (150 grams) granulated sugar

¼ teaspoon kosher salt

1 large pasteurized egg, room temperature (see Note)

1 teaspoon vanilla extract

2 tablespoons (30 ml) kirschwasser (cherry brandy, see Note)

Nonstick pan spray

½ cup (50 grams) confectioners' sugar

Note

Pasteurized eggs in the shell can be found in some grocery stores. If unavailable, substitute pasteurized eggs in a carton (which are easier to find) using the equivalent amount of 1 large egg as listed on the carton. I personally use standard eggs in the shell and assume the risk of eating raw eggs. Kirschwasser (also called kirsch) is a colorless brandy made from dark sour cherries. Cherry vodka can be used in its place or, for a nonalcoholic version, use 2 tablespoons maraschino cherry juice.

Storage

The unsliced logs can be stored in the fridge, tightly wrapped in plastic, for up to 1 week. I usually slice just what I want to eat and stash the rest of the log in the fridge until my next craving hits.

01 Add the chocolate to a medium, microwave-safe bowl. Microwave in 10-second increments, stirring between each, until the chocolate is completely melted and smooth, about 1 minute total. Set aside.

02 In a small bowl, toss the dried cherries and crushed cookies with 1 tablespoon (7 grams) of the cocoa powder until thoroughly coated. Set aside.

03 In the bowl of a stand mixer fitted with a paddle attachment, combine the butter, sugar, salt, and remaining 2 tablespoons (14 grams) cocoa powder. Mix on medium speed until fluffy, 2 to 3 minutes.

04 With the mixer running on medium speed, add the egg and continue mixing until combined, 1 to 2 minutes. Add the vanilla extract and kirschwasser and continue mixing until thoroughly combined, 1 to 2 minutes. (Don't fret if the mixture appears broken at this point.)

05 Reduce the mixer speed to low and slowly add the melted chocolate. Mix until smooth and glossy, 1 minute. Turn off the mixer and stir in the crushed cookies and cherries with a rubber spatula.

06 Transfer half (about 1½ cups/350 grams) of the mixture to the center of a 14-inch-long sheet of plastic wrap. Repeat with the remaining dough and a second sheet of plastic. Lightly coat your hands with nonstick pan spray and form each portion into a 1½-inch-diameter log that's about 8 inches long. Wrap each log in the plastic wrap, twisting the ends together to help form a tight cylinder. Transfer to the fridge and let set for at least 4 hours, rotating the logs every hour or so to prevent a flat bottom.

07 When ready to serve, place the confectioners' sugar on a large plate and unwrap each log. Roll each log in the confectioners' sugar to coat the outside. Using a thin, sharp knife, cut the logs into ½-inch-thick slices and serve immediately. (If the logs crumble while slicing, run your knife under hot water to warm it up and try again.)

Malted Mudslide Whoopie Pies

These whoopie pies take their flavor cues from the dessert-like cocktail the Mudslide. The cookies are made with a generous amount of Irish cream liqueur to give them a bold, boozy flavor, while the addition of malted milk powder mellows out their bite and gives them a buttery taste. Their texture lies somewhere between a cake and cookie, being both soft and brownie-like. A chocolate buttercream spiked with Kahlúa mimics the beloved flavor pairing of the cocktail and sandwiches them together.

Malted Irish Cream Cookies

1¾ cups spooned and leveled all-purpose flour (224 grams)

¾ teaspoon kosher salt

½ cup (45 grams) natural, unsweetened cocoa powder

¼ cup (28 grams) malted milk powder

1½ teaspoons baking soda

½ teaspoon baking powder

1 stick (8 tablespoons/113 grams) unsalted butter, room temperature

1 cup (200 grams) granulated sugar

1 large egg, room temperature

1 cup (237 ml) Irish cream liqueur, such as Baileys, room temperature

2 teaspoons vanilla extract

Chocolate-Kahlúa Buttercream

1 stick (8 tablespoons/113 grams) unsalted butter, room temperature

¼ cup (59 ml) coffee liqueur, such as Kahlúa

4 cups (400 grams) confectioners' sugar

¼ cup (28 grams) malted milk powder

3 tablespoons (21 grams) natural, unsweetened cocoa powder

½ teaspoon kosher salt

Make Ahead

Both the cookies and the buttercream can be made the day before assembling. Cookies can be stored at room temperature in an airtight container while the buttercream should be stored in the fridge, tightly wrapped in plastic. Before assembling, bring the buttercream to room temperature to make piping easier.

Storage

Leftover whoopie pies can be stored in an airtight container in the fridge for several days. I like to bring mine to room temperature before eating so the buttercream softens up, but they are just as delicious when cold.

01 Preheat the oven to 400°F and set 2 racks at the upper-middle and lower-middle positions. Line 2 baking sheets with parchment paper or nonstick baking mats.

02 Make the Malted Irish Cream Cookies: In a large bowl, whisk together the flour, salt, cocoa powder, malted milk powder, baking soda, and baking powder. Set aside.

03 In the bowl of a stand mixer fitted with the paddle attachment, combine the butter and sugar. (Alternatively, use a hand mixer and large bowl.) Beat on medium speed until smooth and fluffy, 2 to 3 minutes. Add the egg, Irish cream liqueur, and vanilla extract. Beat on medium speed until combined, 2 to 3 minutes. (Don't fret if the mixture appears broken at this point.) With the mixer running on low speed, gradually add the flour mixture, beating until just combined.

04 Using a large 2⅓-inch (#16) cookie scoop or ¼-cup measure, portion the batter into mounds on the prepared baking sheets, leaving at least 2 inches between each. Bake both sheets at the same time, swapping the top sheet to the bottom rack and bottom sheet to the top midway through baking, until the tops are domed but the cracks still appear moist, erring on the side of underbaking them, 8 to 11 minutes. Let cool completely on the baking sheets.

05 While the cookies are cooling, make the Chocolate-Kahlúa Buttercream: In the bowl of a stand mixer fitted with the paddle attachment, combine the butter, coffee liqueur, confectioners' sugar, malted milk powder, cocoa powder, and salt. (Alternatively, use a hand mixer and large bowl.) Mix on low speed until combined, 1 to 2 minutes, then increase to medium-high and beat until light and fluffy, 2 to 3 minutes.

06 Dollop or pipe about ¼ cup of the buttercream onto the undersides of half the cookies. Sandwich with the remaining cookies.

Red Wine Brownie Cookies

Red wine and chocolate combine to create a decadent brownie cookie that is rich, fudgy, and as full bodied as a cookie can be. Since the wine is reduced, you can use any type of dry red wine you have on hand, including the cheap stuff—or even mix a few varieties to use up your almost-empties. The cookies end up with a bold red-wine flavor and a super-satisfying chewy texture.

01 In a small saucepan over medium heat, melt the butter. Continue cooking, stirring often to prevent the milk solids from burning, until the butter foams and then darkens in color slightly and is very fragrant, 4 to 6 minutes. Immediately pour the butter into a large heatproof bowl. Do not wash the pan.

02 To the saucepan used to melt the butter, add the red wine and 2 tablespoons (32 grams) of the granulated sugar and bring to a simmer over high heat. (Be careful; the wine will sizzle when you pour it in the pan.) Reduce the heat to medium and simmer, stirring occasionally, until reduced to ⅓ cup (79 ml), 16 to 18 minutes. (The easiest way to test if the reduction is ready is to pour it into a heatproof measuring glass to see if it's at the ⅓-cup mark.) Pour the reduced wine into the bowl with the butter and let the mixture cool for 15 minutes.

03 As the butter/wine mixture cools, whisk together the flour, cocoa powder, baking powder, baking soda, and salt in a medium bowl. Preheat the oven to 350°F and set 2 racks at the upper-middle and lower-middle positions. Line 3 baking sheets (or as many as you have) with parchment paper or nonstick baking mats.

04 Whisk both the brown sugar and the remaining ⅓ cup (67 grams) granulated sugar into the butter/wine mixture, then whisk in the eggs and vanilla extract until smooth. Add the flour mixture and stir with a rubber spatula until a soft dough forms, then stir in the chopped chocolate.

05 Using a large 2⅓-inch (#16) cookie scoop or ¼-cup measure, portion out the dough and roll into large balls. Place the dough balls at least 3 inches apart on the prepared baking sheets (6 per sheet).

06 Bake 2 sheets at the same time, swapping the top sheet to the bottom rack and bottom sheet to the top midway through baking, until the tops lose their shine but their cracks still appear slightly wet (don't be tempted to overbake), 11 to 14 minutes, then bake the remaining baking sheet of cookies on either rack. Let the cookies cool completely on the baking sheets.

2 sticks (16 tablespoons/226 grams) unsalted butter

2 cups (473 ml) dry red wine, any variety

⅓ cup plus 2 tablespoons (99 grams) granulated sugar, divided

3¼ cups spooned and leveled all-purpose flour (416 grams)

½ cup (45 grams) natural, unsweetened cocoa powder, sifted

1 teaspoon baking powder

1 teaspoon baking soda

1 teaspoon kosher salt

1½ cups (300 grams) packed light brown sugar

2 large eggs, room temperature

2 teaspoons vanilla extract

8 ounces (227 grams) semisweet chocolate, roughly chopped (about 1⅓ cups)

Make Ahead

If wrapped tightly in plastic, the finished dough can be stored in the refrigerator for several days before baking. If too firm to scoop, let sit at room temperature for 15 minutes and try again.

Storage

The cookies will keep in an airtight container for up to 1 week.

Brown Butter & Guinness Chocolate Skillet Cookie

Although this might look like any other skillet cookie, the flavor is anything but that. A combination of nutty brown butter and Guinness lends the cookie an unexpected depth and hoppy flavor. It's everything you love about a skillet cookie—the pleasantly underbaked center contrasting with the crisp edges, *plus* a malty richness that makes it as decadent and stout as the beer itself.

01 In a 10-inch cast-iron skillet set over medium heat, melt the butter. Continue cooking, stirring often to prevent the milk solids from burning and swirling so it coats the sides of the skillet, until the butter foams and then darkens in color slightly and is very fragrant, 3 to 4 minutes. Transfer the butter to a large heatproof bowl, scraping any browned bits stuck to the bottom with a spatula into the bowl.

02 Add the stout and 2 tablespoons (30 grams) of brown sugar to the skillet and simmer over high heat. Reduce the heat to medium and simmer, stirring occasionally, until reduced to ¼ cup (59 ml), 7 to 10 minutes. The reduction will be thick and almost black. (The easiest way to test if the reduction is ready is to pour it into a heatproof measuring glass and see if it is at the ¼-cup mark. If you accidently over-reduce it, just add a splash of water.) Pour the reduced Guinness into the bowl with the butter and let cool for 30 minutes. Do not wash the skillet.

03 Arrange a rack in the middle of the oven and preheat to 350°F.

04 Add the remaining ½ cup (100 grams) brown sugar, the granulated sugar, and vanilla to the cooled (but still warm) butter mixture and whisk to combine. Add the egg and continue whisking until smooth, glossy, and lightened in color slightly, 1 to 2 minutes.

05 Add the flour, salt, and baking soda. Stir with a rubber spatula until just combined. Stir in the chopped chocolate.

06 Spray the empty skillet with nonstick pan spray. Transfer the dough to the skillet and spread into an even layer using an offset spatula. Bake until browned around the edges but still gooey in the center, 15 to 17 minutes. (The cookie will continue cooking in the skillet after it comes out of the oven—avoid overbaking.) Transfer the skillet to a wire rack and cool for 10 minutes before serving. The cookie will be soft and gooey when hot but firm and sliceable once cooled. If you prefer your skillet cookies on the softer side, eat within 1 hour of baking.

1 stick (8 tablespoons/113 grams) unsalted butter

¾ cup (177 ml) dry stout, preferably Guinness

½ cup plus 2 tablespoons (130 grams) packed light brown sugar, divided

¼ cup (50 grams) granulated sugar

1 teaspoon vanilla extract

1 large egg, room temperature

1½ cups spooned and leveled all-purpose flour (192 grams)

½ teaspoon kosher salt

½ teaspoon baking soda

6 ounces (170 grams) semisweet or bittersweet chocolate, roughly chopped (about 1 cup)

Nonstick pan spray

Ice cream, for serving (optional)

Make Ahead

The cookie dough can be made several days in advance and stored in the fridge, tightly covered in plastic wrap. When ready to bake, press it into the bottom of a skillet coated with nonstick pan spray and bake as instructed.

Storage

Remove any leftover cookie from the skillet and transfer to an airtight container. Store at room temperature for up to 1 week. I like to microwave leftovers for about 30 seconds to warm them up before eating.

Pineapple & Rum Macaroons

Makes about 24 small macaroons

Fresh pineapple and a splash of coconut rum give these macaroons a tropical, piña colada–inspired flavor. By cooking down the sweetened condensed milk with the pineapple, you will concentrate the flavor of the pineapple and cook out some of its moisture, helping ensure that the macaroons turn out crisp on the outside and perfectly chewy on the inside.

01 Preheat the oven to 300°F and set 2 racks at the upper-middle and lower-middle positions. Line 2 baking sheets with parchment paper or nonstick baking mats. Scatter the coconut in a single layer divided between the baking sheets. Bake, rotating the sheets halfway through and stirring so the coconut toasts evenly, just until the edges start to turn golden brown but the center shreds remain fairly white, 10 to 12 minutes. Let cool and increase the oven temperature to 350°F.

02 Combine the sweetened condensed milk, pineapple, rum, vanilla, and salt in a medium saucepan. Cook over medium-high heat, stirring frequently to prevent burning, until the mixture thickens and the pineapple is very soft, 7 to 9 minutes. Remove from the heat and let cool for 20 minutes.

03 In the bowl of a stand mixer fitted with the whisk attachment, add the egg whites. Whip on medium speed until foamy, 1 to 2 minutes, then increase the speed to high and whip until stiff peaks form, 3 to 4 minutes more. (Alternatively, use a hand mixer and large bowl.)

04 Add the cooled coconut (save the parchment paper for baking) and sweetened condensed milk mixture to the bowl of egg whites and stir with a rubber spatula until thoroughly combined.

05 Using a medium 1¾-inch (#40) cookie scoop or 2 tablespoons, place mounds of the coconut mixture on the prepared baking sheets, spacing them 2 inches apart. Bake both sheets at the same time, swapping them midway, until the macaroons no longer look wet and are dark golden brown on the bottom, 23 to 25 minutes. Let cool completely on the baking sheets.

06 If using, add the chocolate to a medium, microwave-safe bowl. Microwave in 10-second increments, stirring between each, until the chocolate is completely melted and smooth, about 60 seconds total. Dip the macaroons in the chocolate, drizzle the tops with any excess, and let set on parchment paper for 1 hour.

1 14-ounce bag (about 4 lightly packed cups/397 grams) sweetened shredded coconut

1 cup (237 ml) sweetened condensed milk (slightly less than 1 full 14-ounce can; see Note)

1 cup (200 grams) finely chopped fresh or canned pineapple (drained, if canned)

3 tablespoons (44 ml) coconut rum, such as Malibu

1 tablespoon vanilla extract

½ teaspoon kosher salt

2 large egg whites, room temperature

4 ounces (113 grams) semisweet or bittersweet chocolate chips (about ⅔ cup; optional)

Note

The small amount of sweetened condensed milk left over in the can is the perfect amount to add to an iced coffee or black tea. It's also delicious drizzled over sliced strawberries or kiwi.

Make Ahead

Coconut can be toasted several days in advance and stored in an airtight container at room temperature.

Storage

The macaroons will keep in an airtight container for up to 1 week.

Fruity

Berry Blast Marbled Sugar Cookie

Raspberry Chocolate Chunk Cookies

Makes 20 cookies

Sweet and tart, these raspberry and chocolate chunk cookies are a colorful upgrade of your typical chocolate chip cookie. I use freeze-dried raspberries here, not fresh, which contribute a surprisingly tart, concentrated berry flavor. By grinding them in a food processor with the flour, the berries break down and meld into the cookie dough, staining it a bright pinkish hue. The resulting flavor tastes almost like a pint of Graeter's black raspberry ice cream. I like the nostalgic flavor combination of raspberry and chocolate, but the recipe can be made with any freeze-dried berry of your liking.

2¼ **cups** spooned and leveled all-purpose flour (288 grams)

2 1.3-ounce packages (about 3 cups/74 grams/ 2.6 ounces total) freeze-dried raspberries (see Note)

¾ **teaspoon** baking soda

1 teaspoon kosher salt

2 sticks (16 tablespoons/226 grams) unsalted butter, room temperature

1¼ **cups (250 grams)** packed light brown sugar

½ **cup (100 grams)** granulated sugar

1 large egg, room temperature

1 tablespoon vanilla extract

8 ounces (227 grams) semisweet or bittersweet chocolate, roughly chopped (about 1⅓ cups)

Note
Freeze-dried raspberries can be found in the dried fruit and nuts section of most well-stocked grocery stores, such as Whole Foods and Trader Joe's. If unavailable, any freeze-dried berry, such as strawberries or blueberries, can work as a substitute.

Make Ahead
If wrapped tightly in plastic, the dough can be stored in the refrigerator for several days before baking. If too firm to scoop, let sit at room temperature for 15 minutes and try again.

Storage
The cookies will keep in an airtight container for up to 1 week.

01 Preheat the oven to 350°F and set 2 racks at the upper-middle and lower-middle positions. Line 2 baking sheets with parchment paper or nonstick baking mats.

02 Combine the flour, freeze-dried raspberries, baking soda, and salt in the bowl of a food processor fitted with the blade attachment. Process until the raspberries are completely broken down into a fine powder that mixes with the flour, 20 to 30 seconds. There should be no visible pieces of freeze-dried raspberries.

03 In the bowl of a stand mixer fitted with the paddle attachment, combined the butter, brown sugar, and granulated sugar. Beat on medium speed, scraping down the sides and bottom of the bowl halfway through, until smooth and fluffy, 2 to 3 minutes. (Alternatively, use a hand mixer and large bowl.) Turn the mixer off and add the egg and vanilla extract. Mix on medium speed until very fluffy and lightened in color slightly, 2 to 3 minutes. With the mixer running on low speed, gradually add the flour mixture, beating until just combined. Mix in the chopped chocolate with a rubber spatula.

04 Using a medium 1¾-inch (#40) cookie scoop or 2 tablespoons, portion out the dough and roll into balls. Place the dough balls at least 3 inches apart on the prepared baking sheets (about 10 per sheet).

05 Bake both sheets at the same time, swapping the top sheet to the bottom rack and bottom sheet to the top midway through baking, until the tops of the cookies crack and the bottoms are just starting to brown, 9 to 11 minutes. Remove from the oven and let cool slightly on the baking sheets, then transfer to a wire rack to cool completely.

Chewy Blueberry Muffin Sugar Cookies

Forget everything you know about sugar cookies. Forget everything you know about blueberry muffins. Now, dream of a cookie that combines the best attributes of both and you have this chewy, tart cookie with fresh blueberries in every bite. A unique rolling technique ensures that the blueberries don't burst open and leak while baking, so instead of mixing the blueberries directly into the cookie dough, they get stuffed into the dough, not unlike a dumpling.

01 In a small saucepan set over medium heat, melt the butter. Continue cooking, stirring often to prevent the milk solids from burning, until the butter foams and then darkens in color slightly and is very fragrant, 3 to 4 minutes. Immediately pour the butter into a large heatproof bowl and let cool at room temperature for 30 minutes.

02 Preheat the oven to 350°F and set 2 racks at the upper-middle and lower-middle positions. Line 3 baking sheets (or as many as you have) with parchment paper or nonstick baking mats. Toss the blueberries with 1 tablespoon (8 grams) of the flour in a medium bowl to coat them and set aside.

03 Add the brown sugar and granulated sugar to the bowl of cooled, melted butter and whisk to combine. Add the eggs, lemon zest, and vanilla extract and whisk until ribbony and smooth. Add the remaining 3¼ cups (416 grams) flour, the baking powder, baking soda, salt, and cinnamon, and stir with a rubber spatula just until a soft dough forms.

04 Add the coarse sugar to a large, shallow bowl. Using a large 2⅓-inch (#16) cookie scoop or ¼ cup measure, portion out the dough and roll into large balls. Flatten each dough ball into a rough ½-inch-thick disc using your hands. Make a small indentation in the middle of the disc using your finger and press 5 to 7 blueberries into the center. Gently fold the dough around the berries and reroll the dough between your hands into a tight ball, nestling the blueberries inside and taking care not to crush them. Roll the balls in the coarse sugar and place the balls at least 3 inches apart on the prepared baking sheets (6 per sheet).

05 Bake 2 sheets at the same time, swapping the top sheet to the bottom rack and bottom sheet to the top midway through baking, until the tops of the cookies are lightly browned, 14 to 17 minutes, then bake the last baking sheet on either rack. Let the cookies cool slightly on the baking sheets, then transfer to a wire rack to cool completely.

2 sticks (16 tablespoons/226 grams) unsalted butter

1 pint (about 320 grams) fresh medium blueberries (not frozen)

3¼ cups plus 1 tablespoon spooned and leveled all-purpose flour (424 grams), divided

1⅓ cups (267 grams) packed light brown sugar

⅓ cup (67 grams) granulated sugar

2 large eggs, room temperature

½ teaspoon grated fresh lemon zest

1 tablespoon vanilla extract

1 teaspoon baking powder

1 teaspoon baking soda

1 teaspoon kosher salt

2 teaspoons ground cinnamon

⅔ cup (134 grams) coarse sugar, such as turbinado, demerara (like Sugar in the Raw), or sanding sugar

Make Ahead

If wrapped tightly in plastic, the finished, unstuffed dough can be stored in the refrigerator for several days before baking. If too firm to scoop, let sit at room temperature for 15 minutes and try again. I find it easiest to stuff the cookies when the dough is not too cold.

Storage

The cookies will keep in an airtight container for up to 1 week.

Cornmeal Thumbprint Cookies with Quick Strawberry Jam

Makes 12 thumbprint cookies

These sweet-and-salty cornmeal cookies are filled with a quick homemade strawberry jam that takes less than 20 minutes to make. The result is a warm-weather version of holiday thumbprint cookies, highlighting two beloved summer flavors.

Cornmeal Cookies

1 stick (8 tablespoons/113 grams) unsalted butter, softened

⅔ cup (66 grams) confectioners' sugar

1 large egg yolk

1 tablespoon vanilla extract

1 cup spooned and leveled all-purpose flour (128 grams)

½ cup (87 grams) yellow cornmeal

¾ teaspoon kosher salt

½ cup (76 grams) coarse sugar, such as turbinado, demerara (like Sugar in the Raw), or sanding sugar

Quick Strawberry Jam

2 cups (300 grams) hulled and sliced fresh strawberries

½ cup (100 grams) granulated sugar

2 teaspoons vanilla extract

Pinch of kosher salt

½ teaspoon cornstarch

Note

Feel free to use your favorite store-bought preserves in place of the homemade strawberry jam to save time. Blueberry and peach preserves both go well with the cornmeal cookie base, too, and would be just as delicious.

Make Ahead

If wrapped tightly in plastic, the dough can be stored in the refrigerator for several days before baking. If too firm to scoop, let sit at room temperature for 15 minutes and try again.

Storage

The cookies will keep in an airtight container in a single layer for up to 1 week.

01 Make the cookies: In the bowl of a stand mixer fitted with the paddle attachment, combine the butter and confectioners' sugar. (Alternatively, use a hand mixer and large bowl.) Beat on medium speed until light and fluffy, scraping down the sides and bottom of the bowl halfway through, 2 to 3 minutes. Turn the mixer off and add the egg yolk and vanilla extract. Mix on medium speed until fluffy, 1 to 2 minutes. Turn the mixer off and add the flour, cornmeal, and salt. Mix on low speed just until a soft dough forms, 1 to 2 minutes. Wrap the bowl tightly in plastic wrap and chill for 2 hours.

02 Make the jam: Combine the strawberries, sugar, vanilla extract, salt, and ¼ cup water in a medium saucepan. Bring to a simmer over high heat, stirring constantly, then reduce the heat to medium and cook, stirring often to prevent the bottom from burning, until the strawberries are completely broken down and the jam is thick enough to coat the back of a spoon, 12 to 14 minutes. Dissolve the cornstarch in 1 tablespoon cold water and stir it into the jam mixture. Continue cooking until the mixture is very thick and a few bubbles have popped at the surface, 2 to 3 minutes more. Remove from the heat and let cool for at least 20 minutes (or refrigerate up to 1 week).

03 Arrange a rack in the middle of the oven and preheat to 375°F. Line a baking sheet with parchment paper or a nonstick baking mat. Place the coarse sugar for the cornmeal cookies in a shallow, wide bowl.

04 Using a medium 1¾-inch (#40) cookie scoop or 2 tablespoons, portion out the dough and roll into balls. Roll the cookie dough balls in the coarse sugar and place at least 3 inches apart on the prepared baking sheet. Using your thumb, press in the center of each cookie dough ball to create an indentation.

05 Bake until the cookies are just starting to brown on the top, 8 to 10 minutes. Remove from the oven and immediately press down on the indentations, this time using a spoon. Fill each indentation with about 1½ teaspoons of the strawberry jam, then bake once more until the cookies are deep golden brown, 10 to 12 minutes more. Let the cookies cool for at least 1 hour on the baking sheet before serving to allow time for the jam to set.

Grape Jam Bars with Salted Peanut Streusel

Makes 12 bars

This recipe crams all the nostalgic flavors of a PB&J sandwich into chewy, streusel-topped cookie bars. An oatmeal-cookie base made with creamy peanut butter is spread with a generous amount of Concord grape jelly, then topped with a salty peanut streusel made with oats and brown sugar. The resulting bars are sweet, salty, and perfect for throwing into a brown paper bag to tote to school or work.

Cookie Base

Nonstick pan spray

1 stick (8 tablespoons/113 grams) unsalted butter, room temperature

⅓ cup (67 grams) packed light brown sugar

⅓ cup (88 grams) creamy peanut butter, such as Skippy or Jif (see Note)

1 large egg

2 teaspoons vanilla extract

1⅓ cups spooned and leveled all-purpose flour (171 grams)

¼ teaspoon kosher salt

⅔ cup (60 grams) old-fashioned rolled oats

1 cup (290 grams) grape jam or jelly (preferably Concord)

Salted Peanut Streusel

½ cup spooned and leveled all-purpose flour (64 grams)

¼ cup (50 grams) packed light brown sugar

½ cup (45 grams) old-fashioned rolled oats

⅓ cup (43 grams) roasted salted peanuts, coarsely chopped (see page 18)

½ stick (4 tablespoons/57 grams) cold unsalted butter, cut into ½-inch cubes

Note

Avoid using natural varieties of peanut butter in this recipe, as they can make the cookie base oily or dry. Instead, use a conventional peanut butter such as Skippy or Jif.

Storage

The bars will keep in an airtight container for up to 1 week.

01 Arrange a rack in the middle of the oven and preheat to 350°F. Grease an 8 × 8-inch square baking pan with nonstick pan spray. Line with parchment paper, leaving some overhang on all sides so it's easy to lift the bars out of the pan after baking. Lightly coat the paper with pan spray.

02 Make the Cookie Base: In the bowl of a stand mixer fitted with the paddle attachment, combine the butter and brown sugar. (Alternatively, use a hand mixer and large bowl.) Beat on medium speed until light and fluffy, scraping down the sides and bottom of the bowl halfway through, 2 to 3 minutes. Turn the mixer off and add the peanut butter, egg, and vanilla extract. Mix on medium speed until smooth and fluffy, 1 to 2 minutes. Turn the mixer off and add the flour and salt and mix on low speed just until a soft dough forms. Remove the bowl from the stand and stir in the oats with a rubber spatula.

03 Transfer the dough to the prepared pan and press into an even layer from edge to edge using a flat-bottomed measuring cup or clean hands. Bake until the edges are lightly browned and the base is just barely set, 13 to 15 minutes. Remove from the oven and let cool for 20 minutes.

04 As the cookie base is cooling, make the Salted Peanut Streusel: In a medium bowl, combine the flour, brown sugar, oats, and peanuts. Add the butter cubes and press them into the dry ingredients with your fingertips until small, pea-sized pebbles form. Continue working the butter in with your fingers until no pockets of dry flour remain. Set aside.

05 Transfer the jam into a small bowl and stir vigorously with a spoon to break up any chunks. Spread over the top of the cooled cookie base, then scatter the streusel over the top and gently press it in using your hands. Bake until the streusel is a deep golden brown and the jam is bubbling up on the sides, 20 to 25 minutes. Let cool for 3 hours. Slice in half, then slice each half into 6 long planks to make 12 bars. (The bars will be very soft and fall apart if you attempt to cut them sooner.)

Cherry Chocolate Chunk Cookie Bars

Makes 24 bars

Cherry and chocolate were made to be together—and this recipe proves it. Lying somewhere between a brownie and a cookie, these bars are filled with pockets of molten dark chocolate and sweet maraschino cherries. The flavor is similar to a cherry cordial, thanks to a splash of fragrant maraschino liqueur. I recommend splurging on high-quality jarred cherries and avoiding the heavily dyed ones often used to top sundaes.

Nonstick pan spray

1 cup (220 grams) high-quality maraschino cherries, drained, stemmed, and roughly chopped

¼ cup (23 grams) natural, unsweetened cocoa powder

3 cups spooned and leveled all-purpose flour (384 grams)

1 teaspoon kosher salt

¾ teaspoon baking soda

2 sticks (16 tablespoons/226 grams) unsalted butter, softened

2 cups (400 grams) packed light brown sugar

2 large eggs, room temperature

1 teaspoon vanilla extract

1 tablespoon maraschino liqueur or the reserved juice from the cherries (see Note)

8 ounces (227 grams) semisweet or bittersweet chocolate, roughly chopped (about 1⅓ cups)

Note

Maraschino liqueur will give the brownies a boozy, cherry cordial-like flavor. If you don't have it on hand, you can just use 1 tablespoon of the liquid the cherries are packed in. Any leftover liquid can be used in cocktails or other baked goods.

Storage

The bars will keep in an airtight container for up to 1 week.

01 Arrange a rack in the middle of the oven and preheat to 325°F. Grease a 9 × 13-inch baking pan with the nonstick pan spray. Line with parchment paper, leaving some overhang on all sides so it's easy to lift the bars out of the pan after baking. Lightly coat the paper with pan spray.

02 Place the chopped cherries in a colander set over a large bowl or in the sink. Squeeze the cherries and press them against the side of the colander to remove some of their excess moisture, then pat them dry with paper towels several times. Let the cherries sit in the colander to drain as you make the batter.

03 In a medium bowl, combine the cocoa powder, flour, salt, and baking soda and whisk to combine.

04 In the bowl of a stand mixer fitted with the paddle attachment, combine the butter and brown sugar. (Alternatively, use a hand mixer and large bowl.) Beat on medium speed until light and fluffy, 2 to 3 minutes. Turn the mixer off and add the eggs, vanilla extract, and maraschino liqueur. Mix on medium speed until very fluffy and lightened in color, 3 to 4 minutes. The mixture should have the texture of frosting.

05 With the mixer running on low speed, gradually add the dry ingredients, beating until just combined. Gently stir in the chopped chocolate and the cherries. (The dough will be very thick.)

06 Transfer the dough to the prepared baking pan and spread into an even layer using a spatula coated with pan spray. (If you're having trouble spreading the dough in the pan, lightly wet your hands and use them to press it down.) Bake for 40 to 45 minutes, until the edges are set but the center is still slightly soft and a knife inserted into the center comes out with only a few moist crumbs attached. (Just be careful not to insert the knife into a melted chocolate piece.) Let cool for at least 2 hours in the pan, carefully lift out of the pan, then slice into 6 long rows by 4 short rows (24 pieces). The bars will be very soft when warm but firm up once cooled.

White Chocolate Chunk Cookies with Mango & Coconut

Makes 18 large cookies

Mango isn't typically thought of as a go-to cookie ingredient, but it's one of my favorite flavors to pair with creamy white chocolate. In this recipe, fresh mango is cooked in melted butter, giving these chewy white chocolate chunk cookies a bold floral flavor. The resulting hint of tropical sweetness perfectly complements the nutty coconut. They are chewy in the center and crispy around the edges, with pockets of tender, ripe mango throughout.

01 In a medium saucepan set over medium-high heat, melt the butter. Add the mango and cook, stirring occasionally, until the mango is very soft and just starting to turn golden brown, 12 to 14 minutes. The mango should be so soft that you can easily smash it against the side of the pan without any resistance. Immediately pour the butter and mango into a large heatproof bowl and let cool for 20 minutes.

02 Add the brown sugar and ⅓ cup (67 grams) of the granulated sugar to the bowl with the butter and stir vigorously with a rubber spatula until smooth. Add the eggs and vanilla extract and stir until glossy.

03 Add the flour, baking powder, baking soda, and salt, and stir with a rubber spatula just until a soft dough forms. Mix in the chopped white chocolate and coconut. Cover the bowl with plastic wrap and refrigerate the dough for 1½ hours. (Don't skip this step or the cookies will spread too much.)

04 Preheat the oven to 350°F and set 2 racks at the upper-middle and lower-middle positions. Line 3 baking sheets (or as many as you have) with parchment paper or nonstick baking mats. Place the remaining ⅔ cup (133 grams) granulated sugar in a shallow, wide bowl.

05 Using a large 2⅓-inch (#16) cookie scoop or ¼-cup measure, portion out the dough and roll into large balls. Roll the balls in the sugar to coat them and place at least 3 inches apart on the prepared baking sheets. (About 6 per sheet; the cookies spread quite a bit while baking.)

06 Bake 2 sheets at the same time, swapping the top sheet to the bottom rack and bottom sheet to the top midway through baking, until the tops of the cookies are lightly browned, 14 to 17 minutes, then bake the last sheet on either rack. (If reusing one of the baking sheets, allow it to cool for 15 minutes before baking another batch on it.) Let the cookies cool slightly on the baking sheets, then transfer to a wire rack to cool completely.

2 sticks (16 tablespoons/226 grams) unsalted butter

2 cups (280 grams) diced fresh mango

1⅓ cups (267 grams) packed light brown sugar

1 cup (200 grams) granulated sugar, divided

2 large eggs, room temperature

1 tablespoon vanilla extract

3 cups spooned and leveled all-purpose flour (301 grams)

1 teaspoon baking powder

1 teaspoon baking soda

1 teaspoon kosher salt

8 ounces (227 grams) white chocolate, roughly chopped (about 1½ cups)

1 cup (105 grams) sweetened shredded coconut

Make Ahead

If wrapped tightly in plastic, the dough can be stored in the refrigerator for several days before baking. If too firm to scoop, let sit at room temperature for 15 minutes and try again.

Storage

The cookies will keep in an airtight container for up to 1 week.

Strawberry Shortcake Cookies

Makes 12 large cookies

Think of these cookies as big, buttery shortcakes in cookie form. The dough is made with cold butter that has been grated on a box grater, mimicking the technique used to make perfectly flaky biscuits. The fresh strawberries bleed their juices into the cookies as they bake, creating sweet, jamlike pockets of fruit throughout. The tops get sprinkled with coarse sugar, forming a crunchy, caramelized exterior that provides a contrasting texture against the tender, cakelike cookies. It's all the best parts of strawberry shortcake combined into a single bite. I like to serve them while still warm with a dollop of whipped cream or crème fraîche, or a scoop of vanilla ice cream.

01 Preheat the oven to 375°F and set 2 racks at the upper-middle and lower-middle positions. Line 2 baking sheets with parchment paper or nonstick baking mats.

02 In a large bowl, whisk together the flour, baking powder, granulated sugar, and salt. In a separate large bowl, combine the Greek yogurt, vanilla extract, lemon zest, and chopped strawberries and stir with a rubber spatula.

03 Using the largest holes of a box grater, grate the stick of butter into the bowl of dry ingredients. Using your hands, toss the butter shreds into the flour and pinch them into small, pea-sized pieces. (It's okay if there are still a few shreds of butter that have not been broken up completely.)

04 Add the yogurt mixture to the flour mixture and stir with a rubber spatula until a shaggy dough forms. (The dough will be more of a biscuit texture than a traditional cookie dough.)

05 Using a large 2⅓-inch (#16) cookie scoop or ¼-cup measure, portion out the dough and roll into large balls (again, don't expect the dough to be super smooth—a rough-textured dough is okay). Place the coarse sugar in a shallow, wide bowl and press the tops of the dough balls in the sugar. Place the balls at least 3 inches apart on the prepared baking sheets, sugar side up (about 6 per pan).

06 Bake both sheets at the same time, swapping the top sheet to the bottom rack and bottom sheet to the top midway through baking, until the tops of the cookies are deep golden brown, 25 to 30 minutes. (Don't fret if the strawberries bleed some of their juices onto the baking sheet as they bake.) Let cool slightly on the baking sheets before serving. The cookies are best served warm.

1¼ cups spooned and leveled all-purpose flour (192 grams)

2 teaspoons baking powder

3 tablespoons (32 grams) granulated sugar

½ teaspoon kosher salt

¾ cup (170 grams) plain full-fat Greek yogurt

1 tablespoon vanilla extract

½ teaspoon grated fresh lemon zest

8 ounces (227 grams) fresh strawberries, hulled and cut into ½-inch pieces (1⅓ cups)

1 stick (8 tablespoons/113 grams) cold unsalted butter

⅓ cup (67 grams) coarse sugar, such as turbinado, demerara (like Sugar in the Raw), or sanding sugar

Storage

The cookies will keep in an airtight container for several days. When ready to eat, I suggest briefly heating them in the microwave.

Berry Blast Marbled Sugar Cookies

Makes 14 large cookies

Three different types of freeze-dried berries give these swirling sugar cookies their vibrant color and sweet-tart, bold berry flavor that reminds me of my fruity Trix and Froot Loops cereal days. While the recipe calls for using a mixture of freeze-dried berries, you can use a combination of any freeze-dried fruits you have on hand. Freeze-dried pineapple and apples work great, giving the cookies a pop of fruity flavor outside of the berry profile.

1 1.3-ounce package (about 1½ cups/37 grams) freeze-dried strawberries

1 1.3-ounce package (about 1½ cups/37 grams) freeze-dried raspberries

1 1.3-ounce package (about 1½ cups/37 grams) freeze-dried blueberries

2 sticks (16 tablespoons/226 grams) unsalted butter, softened

1½ cups (300 grams) granulated sugar, divided

⅓ cup (67 grams) packed light brown sugar

1 large egg, room temperature

1 tablespoon vanilla extract

1¾ cups spooned and leveled all-purpose flour (224 grams)

½ teaspoon baking powder

¼ teaspoon baking soda

¾ teaspoon kosher salt

Storage
The cookies will keep in an airtight container for up to 1 week.

(recipe continues)

01 Preheat the oven to 350°F and set 2 racks at the upper-middle and lower-middle positions. Line 2 baking sheets with parchment paper or nonstick baking mats.

02 In the bowl of a food processor fitted with the blade attachment (or in a blender), add the freeze-dried strawberries. Process until they are the texture of fine flour, with no visible chunks of berries. Transfer to a medium bowl. Repeat the process with the freeze-dried raspberries and then the blueberries, placing them into separate bowls. Set aside. (If your food processor or blender is unable to break the berries down completely, pass the powders through a fine-mesh sieve to remove any large pieces.)

03 In the bowl of a stand mixer fitted with the paddle attachment, combine the butter, 1 cup (200 grams) of the granulated sugar, and the brown sugar. Beat on medium speed, scraping down the sides and bottom of the bowl halfway through, until smooth and fully combined, 2 to 3 minutes. (Alternatively, use a hand mixer and large bowl.) Turn the mixer off and add the egg and vanilla extract. Mix on medium speed until fluffy and lightened in color slightly, 2 to 3 minutes. Turn the mixer off and add the flour, baking powder, baking soda, and salt. Mix on low speed until a soft dough forms.

04 Divide the dough into thirds (about 1 cup/240 grams per third) and add each portion to one of the bowls of freeze-dried berry powder. Mix the berry powders into the dough using a rubber spatula until completely combined. (Feel free to use clean hands to knead the berry powder into the dough if it's giving you trouble.)

05 Take 1 tablespoon of each dough and roll each into a rough 4-inch rope. Press the ropes together lengthwise so all three flavors are combined, twirl them into a rough spiral shape, then roll into a ball using the palm of your hands to create the marble pattern. (It's okay to be a bit messy and imprecise.) Repeat with the remaining dough.

06 Add the remaining ½ cup (50 grams) granulated sugar to a shallow, wide bowl and roll the dough balls in the sugar. Place 6 to 8 balls on each baking sheet, spacing them 3 inches apart. Bake both baking sheets at the same time, swapping the top sheet to the bottom rack and bottom sheet to the top midway through baking, until the tops of the cookies crack and the bottoms are just starting to brown, 13 to 15 minutes. Immediately bang the baking sheets on the countertop to deflate the cookies slightly and then let them cool completely on the baking sheets.

Bananas Foster Chocolate Chunk Cookies

2 sticks (16 tablespoons/226 grams) unsalted butter

2 large semi-ripe bananas (about 1¼ cups/300 grams), peeled and roughly chopped

¾ teaspoon ground cinnamon

2¾ cups spooned and leveled all-purpose flour (352 grams)

¾ teaspoon baking soda

¼ teaspoon baking powder

¾ teaspoon kosher salt

¼ cup (48 grams) vegetable shortening

¾ cup (150 grams) packed light brown sugar

1¼ cups (250 grams) granulated sugar, divided

2 large eggs, room temperature

2 teaspoons vanilla extract

6 ounces (170 grams) bittersweet or semisweet chocolate, roughly chopped (about 1 cup)

Make Ahead
If wrapped tightly in plastic, the dough balls can be stored in the refrigerator for several days before baking.

Storage
The cookies will keep in an airtight container for up to 1 week.

Makes 24 cookies

If chocolate chip cookies and bananas Foster had a baby, it would be these unassuming treats. They have a flavor reminiscent of bananas Foster—a classic dessert that combines the richness of cooked bananas with melted butter. The trick to unleashing their bold flavor is to cook the bananas in butter until they are golden brown and falling apart. This helps caramelize the fruit's sugar and concentrates the flavor, so don't rush it.

01 Melt the butter in a medium saucepan over medium heat. Add the bananas and cook, stirring frequently, until they begin to fall apart, darken in color to a light golden-brown, and are very fragrant, 8 to 10 minutes total. Remove the pan from the heat, stir in the cinnamon, and let cool for 30 minutes.

02 Combine the flour, baking soda, baking powder, and salt in a medium bowl and whisk to combine. Line 3 baking sheets (or as many as you have) with parchment paper or nonstick baking mats.

03 In the bowl of a stand mixer fitted with the paddle attachment, combine the cooled (but still melted) banana mixture, the vegetable shortening, brown sugar, and ¾ cup (150 grams) of the granulated sugar. (Alternatively, use a hand mixer and large bowl.) Beat on medium speed until fully combined, 1 to 2 minutes. Turn the mixer off and add the eggs and vanilla extract. Mix on medium speed until light and ribbony, 2 to 3 minutes. With the mixer running on low speed, gradually add the dry ingredients, beating until just combined. Stir in the chopped chocolate with a rubber spatula.

04 Add the remaining ½ cup (100 grams) granulated sugar to a wide bowl. Using a medium 1¾-inch (#40) cookie scoop or 2 tablespoons, portion out the dough and roll into balls. Roll the balls in the sugar and place them 3 inches apart on the baking sheets (about 8 per sheet). Chill in the refrigerator, uncovered, for 30 minutes. (If you can't fit all 3 sheets in your fridge at once, consolidate the balls on 1 sheet, then divide them again for baking.)

05 As the dough balls are chilling, preheat the oven to 350°F and set 2 racks at the upper-middle and lower-middle positions.

06 Bake 2 sheets at the same time, swapping them midway, until the tops are lightly browned, 12 to 14 minutes, then bake the remaining tray on either rack. Let the cookies cool slightly on the baking sheets, then transfer to a wire rack to cool completely, and bake the remaining sheet of dough balls.

Blackberry Streusel Blondies

These bars are a cross between chewy classic blondies and a crunchy, summery cobbler. Fresh blackberries get tossed in cornstarch to prevent their juices from making the bars soggy, scattered over a cinnamon-y blondie dough, then covered in a blanket of crunchy streusel. As the bars bake, the blackberries soften and bleed their sweet juices into the bottom crust, giving it a tart, fruity flavor. Try serving them warm with a scoop of vanilla ice cream or let them cool completely and eat them as a quick on-the-go breakfast.

Blackberry Blondies

Nonstick pan spray

2 cups (241 grams) fresh blackberries (see Note)

2 teaspoons cornstarch

1½ sticks (12 tablespoons/170 grams) unsalted butter, melted and cooled slightly

1¼ cups (250 grams) packed light brown sugar

2 large eggs, room temperature

1 tablespoon vanilla extract

½ teaspoon grated fresh lemon zest

1⅔ cups spooned and leveled all-purpose flour (213 grams)

1 teaspoon baking powder

1 teaspoon kosher salt

1 teaspoon ground cinnamon

Cinnamon Streusel Topping

1¼ cups spooned and leveled all-purpose flour (160 grams)

⅓ cup (67 grams) packed light brown sugar

1 teaspoon ground cinnamon

¼ teaspoon kosher salt

6 tablespoons (85 grams) cold unsalted butter, cut into ½-inch cubes

Note

If blackberries aren't your thing, feel free to use raspberries or blueberries in this recipe instead. Just avoid using berries that are very juicy, such as strawberries, which have a tendency to bleed quite a bit, causing the blondies to be soggy.

Storage

The blondies will keep in an airtight container for up to 1 week.

01 Make the Blackberry Blondies batter: Arrange a rack in the middle of the oven and preheat to 350°F. Grease a 9 × 13-inch baking pan with nonstick pan spray. Line with parchment paper, leaving some overhang on all sides so it's easy to lift the bars out of the pan after baking. Lightly coat the paper with pan spray.

02 In a medium bowl, combine the blackberries and cornstarch and toss to coat them. Set aside.

03 In a large bowl, whisk together the melted butter and brown sugar. Add the eggs, vanilla extract, and lemon zest, and whisk until smooth. Add the flour, baking powder, salt, and cinnamon, and stir with a rubber spatula until a smooth, soft dough forms.

04 Transfer the dough to the prepared baking pan and spread into an even layer using an offset spatula. Scatter the blackberries evenly over the top (including any of the cornstarch left in the bottom of the bowl) and gently press them into the dough surface.

05 Make the Cinnamon Streusel Topping: In a medium bowl, combine the flour, brown sugar, cinnamon, and salt. Add the butter cubes and press them into the dry ingredients with your fingertips until small, pea-sized pebbles form. At first the mixture will appear too dry, but keep working in the butter until clumps start forming. Scatter the streusel evenly over the top of the dough, pressing it in slightly with your hands.

06 Bake until the top is browned and the edges are set but the center still feels slightly soft, 38 to 43 minutes. Transfer the pan to a wire rack and let cool for at least 1 hour, then use the parchment to pull the bars out of the pan. Set on a cutting board and cut into 24 pieces (6 short rows and 4 long rows).

Caramelized Pineapple Skillet Cookie

Makes one 10-inch skillet cookie

Crunchy macadamia nuts, caramelized pineapple, and melted white chocolate turn this classic skillet cookie into a completely new dessert. The trick here is to cook the pineapple in melted butter until the fruit is golden brown and practically falling apart. This helps concentrate the pineapple flavor and bring out its natural sweetness. (If you've ever had pineapple upside-down cake, you know what I'm talking about.) I like to top the freshly baked cookie with toasted coconut flakes and several scoops of vanilla ice cream while still warm so the ice cream melts into the cookie, but you can also wait until the cookie is cool for a firmer texture.

1½ **sticks (12 tablespoons/170 grams)** unsalted butter, cut into ½-inch cubes

2 **cups (400 grams)** diced fresh or canned pineapple (drained, if canned)

2 **cups** spooned and leveled all-purpose flour (256 grams)

½ **teaspoon** baking soda

1 **teaspoon** kosher salt

1 **cup (200 grams)** packed light brown sugar

¼ **cup (50 grams)** granulated sugar

1 **large egg**, room temperature

1 **tablespoon** vanilla extract

½ **cup (85 grams)** white chocolate chips or chopped white chocolate

½ **cup (70 grams)** toasted, salted macadamia nuts, roughly chopped (see page 18)

Toasted coconut flakes and vanilla ice cream, for serving (optional; see page 18)

Make Ahead

The cookie dough can be made several days in advance and stored in the fridge, tightly covered in plastic wrap. When ready to bake, press it into the bottom of a skillet coated with nonstick pan spray and bake as instructed.

Storage

Remove any leftover cookie from the skillet and transfer to an airtight container. Store at room temperature for up to 1 week. I like to microwave leftovers for about 30 seconds to warm them up before eating.

01   Arrange a rack in the middle of the oven and preheat to 350°F.

02   In a 10-inch cast-iron skillet over medium-high heat, melt the butter. Add the pineapple and cook, stirring occasionally, until it is soft, dark golden brown, and fragrant, 7 to 10 minutes. (Don't worry if the butter begins to brown.) Immediately pour the butter and pineapple into a large heatproof bowl and let cool at room temperature for 20 minutes. Do not wash the skillet.

03   As the pineapple is cooling, whisk together the flour, baking soda, and salt in a medium bowl and set aside.

04   Add both sugars to the bowl with the melted butter and stir vigorously with a rubber spatula until smooth. Add the egg and vanilla extract and vigorously stir until glossy. Add the flour mixture and stir until a soft dough forms. Stir in the white chocolate chips and macadamia nuts.

05   Transfer the dough to the cooled skillet and spread into an even layer using an offset spatula. Bake until browned around the edges but the center is still slightly soft when touched, 22 to 25 minutes. (The cookie will continue cooking in the skillet after it comes out of the oven. Do not overbake.) Transfer the skillet to a wire rack and cool for 10 minutes before serving. The cookie will be soft and gooey when hot, but firm and sliceable once cooled. If you prefer your skillet cookies on the softer side, eat within 1 hour of baking.

Peach Crisp Skillet Cookie

Makes one 10-inch skillet cookie

At first glance this oatmeal skillet cookie might look like any other, but its unassuming appearance masks a ripe peach flavor within. Made with a generous amount of peach preserves, the cookie is soft and chewy with a bold fruity flavor. It's finished with an oat streusel punctuated with spicy cinnamon for a crunchy contrast. You can slice it into wedges and eat as is or top it with slices of fresh peaches and vanilla ice cream for a crowd-pleasing treat eaten right out of the skillet.

Oatmeal Cookie Base

1 stick (8 tablespoons/113 grams) unsalted butter, room temperature

1 cup spooned and leveled all-purpose flour (128 grams)

1 teaspoon ground cinnamon

¼ teaspoon ground allspice

¼ teaspoon baking soda

1 teaspoon kosher salt

⅓ cup (100 grams) peach preserves

¾ cup (150 grams) packed light brown sugar

1 large egg, room temperature

1 tablespoon vanilla extract

1½ cups (130 grams) old-fashioned rolled oats

Crunchy Oat Topping

¼ cup spooned and leveled all-purpose flour (32 grams)

2 tablespoons (23 grams) packed light brown sugar

¼ cup (22 grams) old-fashioned rolled oats

½ teaspoon ground cinnamon

Pinch of kosher salt

2 tablespoons (28 grams) cold unsalted butter, cut into ½-inch cubes

Make Ahead

The cookie dough can be made several days in advance and stored in the fridge, tightly covered with plastic wrap. When ready to bake, press the dough into the bottom of a skillet coated with nonstick pan spray and bake as instructed.

Storage

Remove any leftover cookie from the skillet and transfer to an airtight container. Store at room temperature for up to 1 week. I like to microwave leftovers for about 30 seconds to warm them up before eating.

01 Make the Oatmeal Cookie Base: In a 10-inch cast-iron skillet over medium heat, melt the butter. Continue cooking, stirring often to prevent the milk solids from burning and swirling so it coats the sides, until the butter foams and then darkens in color slightly and is very fragrant, 3 to 4 minutes. Transfer the butter to a large heatproof bowl, scraping any browned bits stuck to the bottom with a spatula. Let cool at room temperature for 30 minutes. Do not wash the skillet; set it aside.

02 As the butter is cooling, combine the flour, cinnamon, allspice, baking soda, and salt in a medium bowl.

03 Position a rack in the middle of the oven and preheat to 325°F.

04 Add the peach preserves and brown sugar to the bowl with the melted butter and whisk until smooth. Add the egg and vanilla extract and whisk until fully combined. Add the flour mixture and stir with a rubber spatula until a smooth, wet dough forms. Add the oats and stir to combine.

05 Transfer the dough to the skillet and spread into an even layer using a rubber spatula.

06 Make the Crunchy Oat Topping: In a medium bowl, combine the flour, brown sugar, oats, cinnamon, and salt. Add the butter cubes and press them into the dry ingredients with your fingertips until small, pea-sized pebbles form. Scatter the topping evenly over the dough in the skillet, pressing it into the dough slightly so they stick.

07 Bake until the cookie is browned but still slightly soft in the center, 26 to 28 minutes. (The cookie will continue cooking in the skillet after it comes out of the oven.) Transfer the skillet to a wire rack and cool for 10 minutes before serving. The cookie will be soft and gooey when hot, but firm and sliceable once cooled. If you prefer your skillet cookies on the softer side, eat within 1 hour of baking.

Vanilla Bean, Rosewater & Raspberry Meringues

Makes 12 large meringues

This recipe uses an Italian meringue to create perfectly glossy cookies that are crisp throughout. All you have to do is make a sugar syrup with sugar and water, and then add the hot syrup to whipping egg whites, which transforms them into the most luxurious, glossy, and cloudlike meringue imaginable. A splash of rosewater gives the meringue a subtle floral flavor, the freeze-dried raspberries add a pop of tartness, and the salty pistachios balance the sweetness.

01 Preheat the oven to 200°F and set 2 racks at the upper-middle and lower-middle positions. Line 2 baking sheets with parchment paper or nonstick baking mats.

02 Rub the inside of the bowl of a stand mixer with the cut lemon and fit the mixer with the whisk attachment. If any lemon juice accumulates in the bottom of the bowl, wipe it away with a paper towel. Add the egg whites, cornstarch, cream of tartar, and salt and whip on medium speed until almost tripled in volume and stiff peaks form, 3 to 4 minutes.

03 In a small pot fitted with a candy thermometer, combine the sugar, vanilla extract, and ⅓ cup (79 ml) water. Without stirring, bring to a simmer over medium heat and cook until the temperature reaches 235°F. If any sugar crystals form, use a wet pastry brush to dab the sides of the pot to dissolve them (don't stir the syrup).

04 Turn the mixer on to low speed and slowly pour the hot sugar syrup on the side of the whipping egg whites. (Avoid pouring it onto the whisk attachment.) Increase the mixer speed to high and whip until the egg whites are glossy, doubled in volume, and stiff, about 3 minutes. You should be able to lift up the whisk and see peaks that hold their shape.

05 Turn the mixer off and add the rosewater and vanilla seeds. Mix on low speed just until incorporated.

06 Use 2 spoons to dollop large ⅓-cup mounds of meringue onto the prepared baking sheets, spacing them 2 inches apart. Sprinkle the tops with the pistachios. Bake both sheets at the same time, until the meringues are completely dry on the outside, 2 to 2½ hours. Depending on your oven, the outsides of the meringues might brown slightly, but that's okay. Immediately smash the freeze-dried raspberries using your fingertips and sprinkle them on top of the meringues while they are still warm. Let cool for at least 20 minutes on the baking sheets before moving to a serving plate.

1 **medium** lemon, halved

5 **large** egg whites, room temperature

1 **teaspoon** cornstarch

¼ **teaspoon** cream of tartar

¼ **teaspoon** kosher salt

1 **cup (200 grams)** granulated sugar

1 **teaspoon** vanilla extract

1 **teaspoon** rosewater

1 vanilla bean, split in half and seeds scraped out (reserve bean for another use)

¼ **cup (25 grams)** roasted salted pistachios, finely chopped (see page 18)

¼ **cup (8 grams)** freeze-dried raspberries

Note
Rubbing your bowl with lemon helps make sure it's completely clean and supplies additional acid to help stabilize the meringue.

Storage
The meringues will keep in an airtight container for several days. The centers might become slightly chewy, but they will be delicious, nonetheless.

Strawberry Shortbread Cookies with Crème Fraîche Glaze

Makes 12 shortbread wedges

Buttery shortbread is transformed into a sweet-tart and tangy summertime treat with the addition of strawberry jam added straight to the dough, a glossy crème fraîche glaze, and a finishing sprinkle of crushed freeze-dried strawberries. The easy-to-make dough gets pressed into a tart pan and baked, then finished with the glaze and bright pink strawberry bits. The glaze's slightly sour flavor tames the shortbread's sweetness, making it just-sweet-enough; if your grocery store doesn't carry crème fraîche, you can easily swap it out for sour cream.

Shortbread Cookies

Nonstick pan spray

2 sticks (16 tablespoons/226 grams) unsalted butter, softened

2 tablespoons (40 grams) strawberry jam or preserves

⅔ cup (66 grams) confectioners' sugar

1 teaspoon vanilla extract

2 cups spooned and leveled all-purpose flour (256 grams)

1 tablespoon cornstarch

1 teaspoon kosher salt

1 teaspoon granulated sugar

Crème Fraîche Glaze

⅓ cup (66 grams) crème fraîche (see Note)

1¼ cups (125 grams) confectioners' sugar

1 teaspoon vanilla extract

Pinch of salt

2 tablespoons (6 grams) freeze-dried strawberries, lightly crushed with your fingertips (optional)

Note

Crème fraîche is a thick soured cream typically sold in the cheese or yogurt sections of well-stocked grocery stores. If unavailable, use full-fat sour cream or plain full-fat Greek yogurt in its place. Just note that you may need to adjust the consistency of the glaze by adding more confectioners' sugar. The glaze should be thick yet easily spreadable.

Make Ahead

The shortbread base can be baked and sliced into wedges the day before you glaze it and stored at room temperature, placed back into the tart pan and tightly wrapped with plastic.

Storage

The cookies will keep in an airtight container in a single layer for up to 1 week.

01 Make the Shortbread Cookies: Position a rack in the middle of the oven and preheat to 325°F. Spray a 9-inch springform pan or tart pan with a removable bottom with the nonstick pan spray.

02 In the bowl of a stand mixer fitted with the paddle attachment, combine the butter, strawberry jam, confectioners' sugar, and vanilla extract. (Alternatively, use an electric hand mixer and large bowl.) Beat on medium speed, scraping down the sides of the bowl as needed, until smooth and fluffy, 2 minutes. Turn the mixer off and add the flour, cornstarch, and salt. Mix on low speed until a soft dough forms, 1 to 2 minutes.

03 Transfer the dough to the prepared pan and press into an even layer from edge to edge using an offset spatula. (If the dough is too sticky to spread easily, feel free to lightly wet your hands and press the dough with them.) Sprinkle the granulated sugar over the top and prick several times with a fork.

04 Bake until the top is deeply and evenly browned, 40 to 45 minutes. Let the shortbread cool for 10 minutes, then remove from the pan, leaving the bottom circle underneath, and cut into 12 wedges. (Careful, the pan will still be hot.) After slicing, don't separate the wedges; instead, let the shortbread cool for at least 1 hour with the wedges still touching and in a circle.

05 While the shortbread is cooling, make the Crème Fraîche Glaze: In a medium bowl, whisk together the crème fraîche, confectioners' sugar, vanilla extract, and salt until completely smooth. Pour the glaze into the center of the cookie round and use the back of a spoon to smear the icing all over the top. Sprinkle the top with the freeze-dried strawberries (if using) and then disconnect the wedges slightly so they are not touching. Let set for 1 hour before serving.

Chewy Toasted Sesame Cookies

Nutty

PB&J Crème Pies

These sandwich cookies reinterpret the flavors of a classic PB&J sandwich with the chewy texture of a Little Debbie oatmeal crème pie—and they just happen to be gluten-free.

Peanut Butter Cookies

2 large eggs

1 tablespoon vanilla extract

1⅓ cups (267 grams) packed light brown sugar

1 cup (200 grams) granulated sugar, divided

2 cups (480 grams) smooth peanut butter, such as Jif or Skippy (see Note)

2 teaspoons baking soda

1 teaspoon kosher salt

Filling

1 stick (8 tablespoons/113 grams) unsalted butter, softened

½ cup (120 grams) smooth peanut butter, such as Jif or Skippy

1 teaspoon vanilla extract

Pinch of kosher salt

2 cups (200 grams) confectioners' sugar

¾ cup (218 grams) strawberry jam

Note

Avoid using natural peanut butter varieties in this recipe, as they have a tendency to separate. I find that using them results in inconsistent cookies that come out either too dry or too oily.

Make Ahead

This cookie dough might dry out if left unbaked, which is why it's best to bake the dough as soon as it's made. You can make the filling several days in advance and refrigerate in an airtight container. When ready to assemble, let the filling come to room temperature for at least 1 hour before dolloping.

Storage

The cookies will keep in an airtight container in a single layer for up to 1 week.

01 Make the cookies: Preheat the oven to 350°F and set 2 racks at the upper-middle and lower-middle positions. Line 3 baking sheets (or as many as you have) with parchment paper or nonstick baking mats.

02 In a large bowl, combine the eggs, vanilla, brown sugar, and ½ cup (100 grams) of the granulated sugar. Whisk until smooth, pale yellow, and slightly ribbony. Add the peanut butter, baking soda, and salt and stir with a rubber spatula until a thick, smooth dough forms. At first the mixture will look very thin, but after about 30 seconds of mixing it will thicken up into a Play-Doh–like consistency.

03 Place the remaining ½ cup (100 grams) granulated sugar in a shallow, wide bowl. Using a medium 1¾-inch (#40) cookie scoop or 2 tablespoons, portion out the dough and roll into balls. Roll the balls in the granulated sugar and place at least 3 inches apart on the prepared baking sheets (10 per sheet). Press the dough balls down with the palm of your hand. The dough discs should be about ½ inch thick, so take care not to flatten them too much.

04 Bake 2 sheets at the same time, swapping them midway, until the tops begin to crack, 9 to 11 minutes. Then bake the last baking sheet on either rack. (If reusing one of the baking sheets, allow it to cool for 15 minutes before baking another batch on it.) Remove from the oven and let the cookies cool completely on the baking sheets.

05 Make the filling: In the bowl of a stand mixer fitted with the paddle attachment, combine the butter, peanut butter, vanilla, and salt. (Alternatively, use a hand mixer and large bowl.) With the mixer running on low speed, slowly add the confectioners' sugar until incorporated, 3 to 4 minutes. Increase the mixer speed to medium-high and whip until fluffy, 1 to 2 minutes.

06 Dollop or pipe about 2 tablespoons of the filling onto the undersides of half the cookies. Dollop about 2 teaspoons of jam on the underside of the remaining cookies. Sandwich the buttercream cookies with the jelly cookies, and let sit uncovered at room temperature for 2 hours to let the filling firm up.

Matcha Amaretti Cookies

Makes 18 cookies

These vibrant amaretti cookies get their bright green color and earthy green tea flavor from matcha powder. The rich, slightly bitter taste of the matcha pairs wonderfully with the nutty almond flavor and helps tame the cookies' sweetness. Rolling them in granulated sugar first, followed by confectioners' sugar, helps create beautiful cracks and a crunchy exterior—preventing the confectioners' sugar from melting in the oven.

01 Preheat the oven to 325°F and set 2 racks at the upper-middle and lower-middle positions. Line 2 baking sheets with parchment paper or nonstick baking mats.

02 In a large bowl, combine the almond flour, matcha powder, salt, and 1 cup (200 grams) of the granulated sugar. Whisk until the matcha powder is evenly distributed throughout.

03 In the bowl of a stand mixer fitted with the whisk attachment, combine the egg whites and almond and vanilla extracts. (Alternatively, use a hand mixer and large bowl.) Mix on medium speed until slightly frothy, 2 to 3 minutes, then increase the speed to high and whip until doubled in volume and stiff peaks form, 1 to 2 minutes more.

04 Transfer the whipped egg whites to the bowl of dry ingredients and mix with a rubber spatula or with clean hands until a thick dough forms.

05 Place the remaining ½ cup (100 grams) granulated sugar in a shallow, wide bowl or a plate and the confectioners' sugar in a second shallow bowl or plate.

06 Using a medium 1¾-inch (#40) cookie scoop or 2 tablespoons, portion out the dough and roll into balls. Roll a dough ball in the granulated sugar, then in the confectioners' sugar, then roll in the palms of your hands above the bowl, shaking off any excess confectioners' sugar. Place the dough balls at least 3 inches apart on the prepared baking sheets (9 per sheet.) Using the bottom of a measuring cup or drinking glass, gently press down the tops of the cookies to flatten them so they are ½ inch thick.

07 Bake both sheets at the same time, swapping the top sheet to the bottom rack and bottom sheet to the top midway through baking, until the cookies are cracked and just starting to brown on the bottoms, 23 to 26 minutes. Remove from the oven and let cool slightly on the baking sheets, then transfer to a wire rack to cool completely.

2⅓ cups (235 grams) almond flour (see Note)

1 tablespoon (6 grams) matcha powder

¼ teaspoon kosher salt

1½ cups (300 grams) granulated sugar, divided

3 large egg whites, room temperature

1 teaspoon almond extract

2 teaspoons vanilla extract

1 cup (100 grams) confectioners' sugar

Note

Make sure to use almond flour, not almond meal. Almond flour has a finer texture and is made with blanched almonds, allowing the bright green color of the matcha to shine. If you can't find it, you can easily make your own by grinding blanched almonds in a food processor until they are the texture of fine sand. If there are any large pieces of almond still remaining, sift the flour through a fine-mesh sieve to remove them.

Storage

The cookies will keep in an airtight container in a single layer for up to 1 week.

Black-and-White
Tahini Cookies

Tahini Cookies

2 cups spooned and leveled all-purpose flour (256 grams)

½ teaspoon baking powder

¼ teaspoon baking soda

½ teaspoon kosher salt

1 stick (8 tablespoons/113 grams) unsalted butter, softened

⅔ cup (156 grams) tahini

1 cup (200 grams) granulated sugar

1 large egg, room temperature

1 tablespoon vanilla extract

½ teaspoon grated lemon zest (optional; see Note)

½ cup (120 grams) sour cream

Icing

2 cups (200 grams) confectioners' sugar, plus more as needed

3 tablespoons (44 ml) light corn syrup

1 teaspoon vanilla extract

Pinch of kosher salt

¼ cup (23 grams) unsweetened cocoa powder

Toasted black and white sesame seeds, for sprinkling (see page 18)

Note
Some people add lemon juice or zest to their black-and-white cookies to give them a subtle citrus flavor. I like to add just a small amount of zest to brighten up the flavor of the cookies, but if you're opposed to it, leave it out.

Make Ahead
The cookies can be baked several days before icing and stored in an airtight container at room temperature, but the icing should be made the day you plan to use it.

Storage
The cookies will keep in an airtight container in a single layer for up to 1 week. I like to wrap them individually in plastic wrap so they are easy to eat on the go.

Makes 12 large cookies

This version of a classic, cakey New York black-and-white cookie adds the nuttiness of tahini, giving them a rich, slightly earthy flavor that rounds out the sweetness. After the cookies get baked, they get flipped over so their rounded tops flatten slightly as they cool. A contrasting sesame pattern on top makes them flashy and provides a clue to the flavor within. Their texture is supple, moist, and perfect for wrapping in plastic wrap and eating on the go.

01 Make the Tahini Cookies: Preheat the oven to 350°F and set 2 racks at the upper-middle and lower-middle positions. Line 2 baking sheets with parchment paper or nonstick baking mats.

02 In a medium bowl, whisk together the flour, baking powder, baking soda, and salt.

03 In the bowl of a stand mixer fitted with the paddle attachment, combine the butter, tahini, and sugar. Beat on medium speed until light and fluffy, 2 to 3 minutes. (Alternatively, use a hand mixer and large bowl.) Turn the mixer off and add the egg, vanilla extract, lemon zest (if using), and sour cream. Mix on medium speed until pale and ribbony, 2 to 3 minutes. With the mixer running on low speed, gradually add the dry ingredients, beating just until a soft, sugar cookie-like dough forms, about 1 minute.

04 Using heaping portions from a large 2⅓-inch (#16) cookie scoop or a scant scoop from a ⅓-cup measure, portion out the dough into mounds on the prepared baking sheets, spacing them at least 3 inches apart (6 per sheet). Bake both sheets at the same time, swapping the top sheet to the bottom rack and bottom sheet to the top midway through baking, until just starting to brown, 15 to 17 minutes total. Remove the cookies from the oven and let them rest just until cool enough to handle but still hot, then flip them upside down and gently push them down if they are lopsided. Let them cool completely on the baking sheets. (This helps them flatten slightly.)

05 While the cookies are cooling, make the icing: Place the confectioners' sugar, corn syrup, vanilla extract, salt, and 2 tablespoons water in a large bowl and whisk until smooth. Transfer half the icing (about ½ cup/125 grams) to a medium bowl and add the cocoa powder and an additional 1 tablespoon water. Whisk until completely smooth. Both icings should be the same consistency. If one is thicker than the other, thin it with water ½ teaspoon at a time; if

thinner, add 1 teaspoon confectioners' sugar at a time. (Make sure the white icing is not so thin that it's opaque.) Tightly cover the chocolate icing with plastic wrap.

06   Using either an offset spatula or a small spoon, ice half of the flat side (the side that is now facing up) of each cookie with the white icing and sprinkle the tops with black sesame seeds. Let the icing set at room temperature for 15 minutes, then ice the other half with the chocolate frosting and sprinkle the top with the white sesame seeds. (To get a clean line in the middle, I like to use a piping bag or zip-top bag with the corner cut off to create a thin line of the chocolate frosting on top of the center edge where the white icing ends, then fill in the rest by using a small offset spatula to spread the frosting to the cookie's edge.)

07   Let the cookies set at room temperature for 1 hour before serving.

Pistachio Thumbprint Cookies with Raspberry Rosewater Jam

Tender thumbprint cookies get coated with salted pistachios and filled with a quick home-made raspberry jam scented with rosewater. These cookies express a combination of textures and flavors that are sweet, salty, and floral. A smidge of ground cardamom adds an alluring aroma that rounds out the sweetness and adds a subtle spice. If rosewater isn't your thing, you can omit it or replace it with orange blossom water—the jam will work just fine and still taste wonderful with the cookies. Or, to save yourself time, you can use your favorite store-bought jam instead; strawberry, blackberry, or apricot would all pair wonderfully with the pistachios.

Pistachio Cookies

2 sticks (16 tablespoons/226 grams) unsalted butter, room temperature

1 cup (200 grams) granulated sugar

2 large eggs, separated

1 tablespoon vanilla extract

½ teaspoon kosher salt

½ teaspoon ground cardamom

2¾ cups spooned and leveled all-purpose flour (352 grams)

1⅓ cups (165 grams) toasted salted pistachios (see page 18)

Raspberry Rosewater Jam

2 cups (290 grams) fresh raspberries

½ cup (100 grams) granulated sugar

1 tablespoon rosewater

1 teaspoon vanilla extract

Pinch of kosher salt

½ teaspoon cornstarch

Make Ahead

The jam can be made up to 1 week in advance and stored in the fridge in an airtight container. If wrapped tightly in plastic, the dough can be stored in the refrigerator for several days before baking. If it's too firm to portion, let sit at room temperature for 15 minutes and try again.

Storage

The cookies will keep in an airtight container in a single layer for up to 1 week.

01 Make the Pistachio Cookies: In the bowl of a stand mixer fitted with the paddle attachment, combine the butter and sugar. (Alternatively, use a hand mixer and large bowl.) Mix on medium speed, scraping down the sides and bottom of the bowl halfway through, until light and fluffy, 2 to 3 minutes. Turn the mixer off, add the egg yolks (saving the whites for later), the vanilla extract, salt, and cardamom, and mix on medium speed until completely incorporated, 1 to 2 minutes. With the mixer running on low speed, slowly add the flour until fully incorporated and a stiff, crumbly dough forms. Cover the bowl tightly with plastic wrap and chill for 2 hours or up to 2 days.

02 While the dough is chilling, make the Raspberry Rosewater Jam: Combine the raspberries, sugar, rosewater, vanilla extract, and salt in a medium saucepan. Cook over medium heat, stirring often to prevent the bottom from burning, until the raspberries are completely broken down and the jam is deep red in color, 9 to 11 minutes. Dissolve the cornstarch in 1 tablespoon of cold water and pour into the jam while stirring. Continue cooking until the mixture has thickened slightly and is the texture of a loose jam, about 2 minutes more. Remove from the heat and let cool at least 30 minutes before using. (The jam will be slightly looser than a typical jam, but don't fret. Once baked, it will thicken. I like to keep the seeds in the jam, but if you prefer the jam to be completely smooth, use a rubber spatula to press it through a fine-mesh sieve while still warm.)

03 Place the pistachios for the cookies in the bowl of a food processor fitted with the blade attachment and process for 10 to 15 seconds, until they are the size of small pebbles. (Alternatively, use a knife and chop as fine as possible.) Place them in a shallow, wide bowl.

04 Preheat the oven to 350°F and set 2 racks at the upper-middle and lower-middle positions. Line 2 baking sheets with parchment paper or nonstick baking mats. Place the reserved egg whites in a medium bowl and whisk until foamy.

05 Using a medium 1¾-inch (#40) cookie scoop or 2 tablespoons, portion out the dough and roll into balls. Dip the dough balls in the egg whites, then in the ground pistachios, pressing them into the sides of the dough to help them stick. Place the dough balls at least 3 inches apart on the prepared baking sheets (12 per sheet). Using your thumb, press down on the center of each dough ball to create an indentation where the jam will go. If the sides of the balls crack while pressing them, just pinch them back together so the jam doesn't seep out.

06 Bake both sheets at the same time, swapping the top sheet to the bottom rack and bottom sheet to the top midway through baking, until the cookies are just starting puff slightly, 8 to 10 minutes. Remove from the oven and immediately press down with a small spoon on any indentations that might have puffed up. Fill each indentation with about 1 heaping teaspoon of the raspberry jam, then bake once more until the cookies are deep golden brown, 10 to 12 minutes more. Let cool for at least 1 hour on the baking sheets before serving to allow time for the jam to set.

Cashew Caramel Cookies

These cashew cookies are salty, sweet, and filled with a chewy caramel center. The trick to getting that perfectly pullable caramel interior is to use two soft caramel candies that have been smashed together and rolled into a ball. I find that using store-bought caramels rather than making your own results in chewier cookies—a shortcut I fully support. I recommend eating the cookies while they're warm so the caramel center is still molten.

01 Preheat the oven to 350°F and set 2 racks at the upper-middle and lower-middle positions. Line 3 baking sheets (or as many as you have) with parchment paper or nonstick baking mats.

02 Add the melted butter, brown sugar, and granulated sugar to a large bowl and whisk to combine. Add the eggs and vanilla extract and whisk until ribbony and smooth. Add the flour, baking powder, baking soda, salt, cinnamon, and chopped cashews. Stir with a rubber spatula until a soft dough forms.

03 Using your hands, take 2 caramel candies, press them together, and roll them into a smooth ball. (Depending on the brand and freshness of your caramel candies, they might be too firm to press together. If so, scatter the caramels in a single layer on a large microwave-safe plate and microwave for 30 seconds until the caramels are warm but not melting. If you accidently microwave them too long and they start to melt, just let them cool for a few minutes.)

04 Using a large 2⅓-inch (#16) cookie scoop or ¼-cup measure, portion out the dough and roll into large balls. Flatten the balls slightly, press a caramel ball into the center, and tightly form the dough around it, then reroll into a ball again. Make sure there are no cracks so the caramel does not ooze out during baking. Place the dough balls 3 inches apart on the prepared baking sheets (6 to 8 per sheet).

05 Bake 2 sheets at the same time, swapping the top sheet to the bottom rack and bottom sheet to the top midway through baking, until the tops of the cookies are lightly browned, 14 to 17 minutes. Remove from the oven and bake the last baking sheet on either rack. Let the cookies cool on the baking sheets for at least 30 minutes before moving. (If you try to pick up the cookies while still hot, the caramel will fall out—and potentially burn you—so be patient.) If reusing sheet pans to bake multiple batches, I recommend leaving the cookie dough at room temperature as you allow the cookies to cool.

1 cup (16 tablespoons/226 grams) unsalted butter, melted and cooled slightly

1⅓ cups (267 grams) packed light brown sugar

⅓ cup (67 grams) granulated sugar

2 large eggs

1 tablespoon vanilla extract

3 cups spooned and leveled all-purpose flour (384 grams)

1 teaspoon baking powder

1 teaspoon baking soda

1 teaspoon kosher salt

1 teaspoon ground cinnamon

2 cups (260 grams) toasted cashews (salted or unsalted), roughly chopped (see page 18)

36 soft caramel candies (about 1½ cups/293 grams total) such as Kraft brand, unwrapped

Make Ahead

If wrapped tightly in plastic, the dough can be stored in the refrigerator for several days before baking. Let sit at room temperature for about 30 minutes, until it's warm enough to easily form into balls.

Storage

The cookies will keep in an airtight container for up to 1 week.

Milk Chocolate–Peanut Butter Cookie Bars

Nonstick pan spray

2¾ **cups** spooned and leveled all-purpose flour (352 grams)

¾ **teaspoon** baking soda

1 **teaspoon** kosher salt

1½ **sticks (12 tablespoons/226 grams)** unsalted butter, softened

1½ **cups (300 grams)** packed light brown sugar

½ **cup (100 grams)** granulated sugar

¾ **cup (180 grams)** creamy peanut butter, such as Jif or Skippy

3 **large** eggs, room temperature

1 **tablespoon** vanilla extract

2 **cups (12 ounces/340 grams)** milk chocolate chips, divided (see Note)

Note

Milk chocolate chips are typically sold in 11.5- or 12-ounce bags. The small difference is nothing to be concerned about and either can be used in this recipe.

Storage

The bars will keep in an airtight container for up to 1 week.

Makes 24 bars

These chewy peanut butter cookie bars have a rich, blondie-like texture with pockets of molten milk chocolate throughout. They're like the gooey, soft center of a freshly baked peanut butter cookie—only better. Using milk chocolate chips instead of dark mimics the beloved flavor of peanut butter cups and brings a creamy richness to the bars. I like to eat them while still a little warm with a scoop of melting ice cream on top, although they are plenty decadent all on their own.

01 Arrange a rack in the middle of the oven and heat to 325°F. Grease a 9 × 13-inch metal baking pan with nonstick pan spray. Line with parchment paper, leaving some overhang on all sides so it's easy to lift the bars out of the pan after baking. Lightly coat the paper with pan spray.

02 In a medium bowl, combine the flour, baking soda, and salt.

03 In the bowl of a stand mixer fitted with the paddle attachment, combine the butter, brown sugar, and granulated sugar. (Alternatively, use a hand mixer and large bowl.) Beat on medium speed until light and fluffy, scraping down the sides and bottom of the bowl halfway through, 2 to 3 minutes. Turn the mixer off and add the peanut butter, eggs, and vanilla extract. Mix on medium speed until the mixture is the texture of light cake batter and very fluffy, 2 to 3 minutes. With the mixer running on low speed, gradually add the dry ingredients, beating until just combined. Stir in 1½ cups (255 grams) of the chocolate chips with a rubber spatula.

04 Transfer the dough to the prepared baking pan and spread into an even layer using an offset spatula coated with pan spray. Sprinkle the remaining ½ cup (85 grams) chocolate chips over the top and press them into the dough slightly so they stick. Bake for 35 to 40 minutes or until the top is lightly browned and starting to crack and a toothpick inserted into the center comes out with only a few moist crumbs attached. (Just be careful not to insert your toothpick into a pocket of melted chocolate.) Remove the bars from the oven and immediately bang the baking pan on the countertop several times to deflate them slightly. (If you only have a glass baking pan, you can skip this step.)

05 Let the bars cool in the baking pan for at least 1 hour, then slice into 24 pieces (6 long rows by 4 short rows). The bars will be very soft when warm but will firm up once cooled.

Salted Brown Butter–Pecan Tassies

Pastry Dough

1 stick (8 tablespoons/113 grams) salted butter, room temperature

4 ounces (½ block/113 grams) cream cheese, room temperature

1 teaspoon vanilla extract

1¼ cups spooned and leveled all-purpose flour (160 grams)

Nonstick pan spray

Filling

½ stick (4 tablespoons/57 grams) salted butter

1 cup (200 grams) packed light brown sugar

1 large egg

1 tablespoon vanilla extract

½ teaspoon ground cinnamon

1 cup (125 grams) toasted unsalted pecans, coarsely chopped, divided (see page 18)

Make Ahead

The pastry dough can be made several days in advance, formed into a disc, then wrapped in plastic and stored in the fridge. When ready to bake, let the dough sit out at room temperature for 30 minutes to soften slightly.

Storage

The tassies will keep in an airtight container in a single layer for up to 1 week.

Makes 24 pecan tassies

A pecan tassie is essentially a pecan pie in cookie form. A buttery crust houses a gooey pecan filling that bakes into a bite-sized treat. This version amps up the flavor with salted butter in both the crust and the filling. And for an added pop, the butter in the filling gets browned too, offering a toasty flavor that highlights the pecans.

01 Make the pastry dough: In the bowl of a stand mixer fitted with the paddle attachment, combine the butter, cream cheese, and vanilla extract. (Alternatively, use a hand mixer and large bowl.) Beat on medium speed until light and fluffy, 1 to 2 minutes. Turn the mixer off, add the flour, and mix on low speed just until a dry dough forms, 1 to 2 minutes.

02 Press the dough together into a ball in the bowl and tightly cover the bowl with plastic wrap. Refrigerate for 1 hour.

03 Make the filling: In a small saucepan over medium heat, melt the butter. Continue cooking, stirring often to prevent burning, until the butter foams and then darkens in color slightly and is very fragrant, 3 to 4 minutes. Immediately pour the butter into a medium heatproof bowl and let cool at room temperature for 20 minutes.

04 Add the brown sugar to the bowl with the butter and whisk until combined. Add the egg, vanilla extract, and cinnamon and whisk until no streaks of egg remain. Stir in ¾ cup (94 grams) of the chopped pecans with a rubber spatula.

05 Arrange a rack in the middle of the oven and preheat to 350°F. Spray a 24-cup mini muffin tin with the nonstick pan spray.

06 Portion out the pastry dough into tablespoon-sized portions (or weigh out into 15 gram portions) and roll into balls. Place one ball of dough in each of the muffin cups and use your fingers to evenly press the dough into the bottom and up the sides of the cups until it's flush with the tops of the cups.

07 Add enough filling to the center of each crust to reach about three-fourths full (about 2 teaspoons per tin). Top each with the remaining ¼ cup (31 grams) pecans, pressing them into the filling slightly. (If you have filling left over, don't fret. It's better to underfill the crusts than to have the filling ooze out.)

08 Bake until the tops are golden brown and the filling has puffed slightly, 18 to 22 minutes. Remove from the oven and let the tassies cool in the muffin tin for at least 30 minutes before removing.

Chewy Flourless Pistachio Cookies

These chewy pistachio cookies come together within a matter of minutes, are gluten-free, and call for only a handful of ingredients. They have the chewy texture of an amaretti cookie with crispy, meringue-like edges. The trick is to bake the cookies just until the tops are cracked. Fresh from the oven, they will be soft and practically impossible to pick up, but once cooled, they will be perfectly chewy. They are salty, sweet, and fragrant, thanks to the ground cardamom—the perfect cookie for pistachio lovers.

01 Preheat the oven to 350°F and set 2 racks at the upper-middle and lower-middle positions. Line 2 baking sheets with parchment paper or nonstick baking mats.

02 In the bowl of a food processor fitted with the blade attachment, combine the pistachios, granulated sugar, confectioners' sugar, salt, and cardamom. Process until the pistachios are the texture of fine sand and there are no visible pieces of pistachio left, 60 to 90 seconds. Transfer the mixture to a large bowl and add the egg whites and vanilla extract. Mix with a rubber spatula until a thick, paste-like dough forms.

03 Using a medium 1¾-inch (#40) cookie scoop or 2 tablespoons, portion out the dough and roll into balls. (The dough will be sticky, so don't fret if they are not perfect balls.) Place the dough balls at least 3 inches apart on the prepared baking sheets (8 per sheet).

04 Bake both sheets at the same time, swapping the top sheet to the bottom rack and bottom sheet to the top midway through baking, until the tops of the cookies crack and the bottoms are just starting to brown, 12 to 14 minutes. (Don't overbake the cookies. They aren't the kind of cookie that browns that much on the top. It's best to err on the side of underbaking for this recipe.) Let the cookies cool completely on the baking sheets before removing with an offset spatula.

2 cups (280 grams) raw or toasted unsalted pistachios (see Note)

1 cup (200 grams) granulated sugar

¾ cup (75 grams) confectioners' sugar

½ teaspoon kosher salt

¼ teaspoon ground cardamom

2 large egg whites

1 tablespoon vanilla extract

Note

The cookie pictured in the photo is made with raw pistachios. Using raw pistachios will result in bright green cookies, but they'll be a tad milder in flavor. Cookies made with toasted pistachios will be slightly brown with a robust nutty flavor. See page 18 for instructions on toasting the pistachios.

Make Ahead

If wrapped tightly in plastic, the dough can be stored in the refrigerator for several days before baking. If too firm to scoop, let sit at room temperature for 15 minutes and try again.

Storage

The cookies will keep in an airtight container for up to 1 week.

Coconut-Crusted Peanut Butter Cookies

These chewy peanut butter cookies are everything you love about a classic peanut butter cookie, amped up with a bold coconutty flavor. They get rolled in shredded and chopped coconut before baking to give them a delicate exterior that practically shatters when you bite into one. If you love both coconut and peanut butter, this is the recipe for you.

01 In the bowl of a stand mixer fitted with the paddle attachment, combine the butter and brown sugar. Beat on medium speed until light and fluffy, 2 to 3 minutes. (Alternatively, use a hand mixer and large bowl.) Turn the mixer off and add the peanut butter, egg, and vanilla extract. Mix on medium speed until pale yellow and ribbony, 2 to 3 minutes. Turn the mixer off and add the flour, salt, and baking soda. Mix on low speed just until a soft dough forms, 1 to 2 minutes. Cover the bowl tightly with plastic wrap and refrigerate for 2 hours. (Don't skip this step or else your cookies will spread too much.)

02 Preheat the oven to 350°F and set 2 racks at the upper-middle and lower-middle positions. Line 2 baking sheets with parchment paper or nonstick baking mats.

03 Place the coconut in a shallow, wide bowl or on a plate. Using a large 2⅓-inch (#16) cookie scoop or ¼-cup measure, portion out the dough and roll into balls. Roll the dough balls in the coconut, pressing the coconut into the dough slightly to help it stick, and place the dough balls at least 3 inches apart on the prepared baking sheets (8 per sheet).

04 Bake both sheets at the same time, swapping the top sheet to the bottom rack and bottom sheet to the top midway through baking, until the coconut is lightly toasted and the tops of the cookies begin to crack, 15 to 17 minutes. Let cool completely on the baking sheets.

---

1 stick (8 tablespoons/113 grams) unsalted butter, softened

1 cup (200 grams) packed light brown sugar

½ cup (120 grams) creamy peanut butter, such as Jif or Skippy

1 large egg, room temperature

1 tablespoon vanilla extract

1¼ cups spooned and leveled all-purpose flour (160 grams)

½ teaspoon kosher salt

⅛ teaspoon baking soda

1 cup (80 grams) sweetened shredded coconut, finely chopped with a knife (see Note)

Note

Make sure to use sweetened coconut shreds for this recipe, such as Baker's, instead of the drier, unsweetened varieties. Chopping the shredded coconut slightly with a knife will help the coconut stick and prevent any long pieces from burning.

Make Ahead

If wrapped tightly in plastic, the dough can be stored in the refrigerator for several days before baking. If the coconut is not sticking to the cold dough, let sit at room temperature for 15 minutes and try again.

Storage

The cookies will keep in an airtight container for up to 1 week.

Chewy Toasted Sesame Cookies

Makes 24 cookies

Toasted sesame oil is one of those powerhouse ingredients that can completely transform a dish. It's rich and nutty, with a distinct, alluring aroma. Many cooks save toasted sesame oil for finishing a dish, owing to its strong flavor, but I like to add it to my baked goods for depth. Here, the sesame oil combines with butter and canola oil to create a cookie that is pleasantly chewy with a distinct sesame finish and a somewhat savory quality. The addition of cream cheese in the dough gives the cookies a soft, moist texture—it's a clever technique borrowed from *Cook's Illustrated*'s chewy sugar cookies, from which this recipe is adapted. The cookies are easy yet impressive, and the black and white sesame seeds on top give them a striking look to match their bold taste.

2½ **cups** spooned and leveled all-purpose flour (320 grams)

1 **teaspoon** baking powder

½ **teaspoon** baking soda

¼ **teaspoon** kosher salt

6 **tablespoons (85 grams)** unsalted butter, softened

2 **ounces (57 grams)** cream cheese, room temperature

1 **tablespoon** toasted sesame oil (see Note)

¼ **cup (60 ml)** canola or vegetable oil

1¼ **cups (250 grams)** granulated sugar, divided

½ **cup (100 grams)** packed light brown sugar

1 **large** egg, room temperature

2 **tablespoons (30 ml)** whole milk

1 **tablespoon** vanilla extract

⅓ **cup (36 grams)** toasted white sesame seeds (see page 18)

⅓ **cup (36 grams)** toasted black sesame seeds (see page 18)

Note
Toasted sesame oil can be found in most well-stocked grocery stores. If unavailable, regular sesame oil can be used, but will not provide the same bold sesame flavor.

Make Ahead
If wrapped tightly in plastic, the dough can be stored in the refrigerator for several days before baking. If the dough is too hard to scoop, let sit at room temperature for 15 minutes and try again.

Storage
Cookies will keep in an airtight container at room temperature for up to 1 week.

01 Preheat the oven to 350°F and set 2 racks at the upper-middle and lower-middle positions. Line 2 baking sheets with parchment paper or nonstick baking mats.

02 In a medium bowl, combine the flour, baking powder, baking soda, and salt.

03 In the bowl of a stand mixer fitted with the paddle attachment, combine the butter, cream cheese, toasted sesame oil, canola oil, 1 cup (200 grams) of the granulated sugar, and the brown sugar. Beat on medium speed until smooth and fully combined, 2 minutes. (Alternatively, use a hand mixer and large bowl.) Turn the mixer off and add the egg, milk, and vanilla extract. Mix on medium speed until light and ribbony, 2 to 3 minutes. With the mixer running on low speed, gradually add the flour mixture, beating until just combined. Let the dough rest for 10 minutes. (The dough will be very soft at first but will firm up after a few minutes.)

04 Combine the white and black sesame seeds in a shallow, wide bowl. Using a medium 1¾-inch (#40) cookie scoop or 2 tablespoons, portion out the dough and roll into balls. Roll the dough balls in the sesame seeds, then place the dough balls at least 3 inches apart on the prepared baking sheets (12 per sheet) and sprinkle the tops with the remaining ¼ cup (50 grams) granulated sugar.

05 Bake both sheets at the same time, swapping the top sheet to the bottom rack and bottom sheet to the top midway through baking, until the tops of the cookies are lightly browned, 10 to 12 minutes. Let cool slightly on the baking sheets, then transfer to a wire rack to cool completely.

Peanut Butter Caramel Millionaire's Shortbread

Makes 36 bars

This nutty take on millionaire's shortbread swaps out the caramel center for one made with peanut butter and chopped salted peanuts. It starts with a shortbread base made in one bowl and without a mixer and bakes up into a tender, buttery foundation for the peanut caramel added right on top, which is followed by a rich, fudgy ganache. The resulting bars are a salty-sweet treat that cram everything good into one bite.

Shortbread Base

Nonstick pan spray

1⅔ cups spooned and leveled all-purpose flour (214 grams)

⅓ cup (67 grams) granulated sugar

½ teaspoon kosher salt

1½ sticks (12 tablespoons/170 grams) unsalted butter, melted and cooled slightly

2 large egg yolks

1 teaspoon vanilla extract

Peanut Butter Caramel

¾ cup (175 grams) packed light brown sugar

½ stick (4 tablespoons/57 grams) unsalted butter

¼ cup (59 ml) light corn syrup

1 14-ounce can (414 ml) sweetened condensed milk

¼ cup (66 grams) creamy peanut butter, such as Jif or Skippy

1 tablespoon vanilla extract

½ teaspoon kosher salt

¼ cup (66 grams) toasted salted peanuts, coarsely chopped (see page 18)

Chocolate Ganache

1 cup (about 6 ounces/170 grams) semisweet or bittersweet chocolate chips or chopped chocolate

3 tablespoons (35 ml) heavy cream

1 teaspoon vanilla extract

Pinch of kosher salt

Make Ahead

The shortbread base can be baked several days in advance and stored at room temperature, tightly wrapped in plastic. The caramel and ganache layers should be made the day of assembly.

Storage

The cookies will keep in an airtight container in a single layer at room temperature for up to 1 week.

01 Make the Shortbread Base: Arrange a rack in the middle of the oven and preheat to 350°F. Grease an 8 × 8-inch square baking pan with nonstick pan spray. Line with parchment paper, leaving some overhang on all sides. Lightly coat the paper with pan spray.

02 In a large bowl, combine the flour, granulated sugar, and salt. Add the melted butter, egg yolks, and vanilla extract and stir using a rubber spatula until a crumbly, moist dough forms that holds together when you squeeze it.

03 Transfer the dough to the prepared baking pan and press into an even layer using the bottom of a measuring cup or clean hands. Prick the top several times with a fork. Bake until the shortbread is slightly puffed and golden brown at the edges, 23 to 28 minutes. Remove from the oven and set aside to cool slightly.

04 While the shortbread is cooling, make the Peanut Butter Caramel: In a medium pot fitted with a candy thermometer, combine the brown sugar, butter, corn syrup, sweetened condensed milk, peanut butter, vanilla extract, and salt. Cook over medium-low heat, stirring constantly to prevent the bottom and sides from burning, until the mixture reaches 235°F, 10 to 12 minutes. The caramel should be thick and slightly darkened in color. Remove from the heat and stir in the chopped peanuts. Pour over the still-warm shortbread base and transfer to the fridge for 20 minutes.

05 As the caramel is cooling, make the Chocolate Ganache: Combine the chocolate, heavy cream, vanilla extract, and salt in a medium, microwave-safe bowl. Microwave on high power in 10-second increments, stirring between each, until fully melted, 30 to 50 seconds total.

06 Pour the chocolate over the caramel and smooth it out with an offset spatula or spoon. Let the shortbread set in the fridge for 2 hours, then cut into a 6 x 6 grid to make 36 squares.

Tart

Salt-and-Vinegar Potato Chip Cookies

Key Lime Pie Meringues

Makes 20 meringue cookies

These crisp meringue cookies are filled with zesty homemade lime curd that tastes just like Key lime pie. It's the sweet and tart flavor combination you know and love from the iconic dessert, transformed into cookies.

01 Make the meringues: Preheat the oven to 200°F and set the racks at the upper-middle and lower-middle positions. Line 2 baking sheets with parchment paper or nonstick baking mats.

02 In the bowl of a stand mixer fitted with the whisk attachment, combine the egg whites, cream of tartar, salt, and vanilla extract. Mix on medium speed until the cream of tartar is completely dissolved and the eggs are very foamy, 2 to 3 minutes.

03 With the mixer running on medium speed, gradually add the sugar 1 tablespoon at a time, waiting until the sugar is completely dissolved and smooth before adding the next, 7 to 9 minutes total. Increase the mixer speed to medium-high and whip until the meringue is glossy, very fluffy, and almost tripled in volume, 3 to 4 minutes more.

Meringues

3 large egg whites, room temperature

¾ teaspoon cream of tartar

Pinch of kosher salt

1 teaspoon vanilla extract

¾ cup (150 grams) granulated sugar

¼ cup (25 grams) graham cracker crumbs (from about 2 full crackers)

Key Lime Curd

⅓ cup (79 ml) Key lime juice (see Note)

3 large egg yolks (about 46 grams)

1 whole egg

⅓ cup (67 grams) granulated sugar

1 teaspoon vanilla extract

3 tablespoons (43 grams) unsalted butter

04 Use a medium 1¾-inch (#40) cookie scoop or 2 spoons to dollop small 2-tablespoon-sized mounds of the meringue onto the prepared baking sheets, spacing them 1 inch apart (10 per sheet). Use a spoon to create small wells in the center of the meringues where the curd will go. (I find it easiest to insert a spoon vertically into the center of the meringues and twist it to channel out holes.) Sprinkle the tops with the crushed graham crackers.

05 Bake for 2 hours, until matte and dry on the outsides. (Do not open the oven during baking.) Turn the oven off and let the meringues cool in the oven for an additional 1 hour with the door shut. (Don't be tempted to check on them. You need the residual heat from the oven to continue cooking them.)

06 Make the curd: Combine the Key lime juice, egg yolks, whole egg, sugar, and vanilla extract in a medium saucepan and whisk to combine. Add the butter and cook over medium heat, stirring frequently with a rubber spatula to prevent lumps from forming, until the curd is starting to bubble and is thick enough to coat the back of a spoon, 3 to 4 minutes. Remove from the heat and strain through a fine-mesh sieve into a medium heatproof bowl. Press plastic wrap onto the top of the curd and transfer to the fridge. Let cool for at least 30 minutes.

07 Fill the center of each meringue with about 1 tablespoon of the lime curd and serve immediately.

Note

Key lime juice can be found in plastic or glass bottles in the baking section of most well-stocked grocery stores. My favorite brand is Nellie & Joe's Famous Key West Lime Juice. If you can't find it, regular lime juice can be used instead.

Make Ahead

Feel free to bake the meringues for 2 hours and leave them in a cold oven overnight in place of the final 1 hour of cooling. Just make sure the oven door is completely closed and try your best not to open it. The lime curd can be prepared several days in advance and stored in an airtight container in the fridge. If you're not planning to serve all the cookies at once, feel free to fill only the amount you do want to serve. Unfilled meringue shells can be stored at room temperature in an airtight container for up to 1 week.

Lemon Poppy Seed Tea Cookies

1½ sticks (12 tablespoons/170 grams) unsalted butter, softened

1 tablespoon vanilla extract

¼ teaspoon kosher salt

2 tablespoons (10 grams) grated lemon zest (from about 2 large lemons)

1⅓ cups (266 grams) granulated sugar, divided

1⅔ cups spooned and leveled all-purpose flour (213 grams), plus more for dusting

1 tablespoon cornstarch

3 tablespoons (26 grams) poppy seeds (see Note)

Note
Poppy seeds go bad rather quickly, so I recommend storing any leftovers in the fridge or freezer to prolong their life.

Make Ahead
The cut-out cookies can be stored in the freezer, tightly wrapped in plastic, for several months. When ready to make, bake directly from frozen.

Storage
The cookies will keep in an airtight container at room temperature for up to 1 week.

Makes 24 cookies

These simple shortbread cookies rely on the classic combination of lemon and poppy seeds to create an understated cookie that's flavorful yet delicate enough to be paired with tea. Tossing the baked cookies in sugar while still warm gives them a sparkling, crunchy coating and hides any imperfections, so there's no need to be too precious when rolling out the dough.

01 Line 2 baking sheets with parchment paper or nonstick baking mats.

02 In the bowl of a stand mixer fitted with the paddle attachment, combine the butter, vanilla extract, salt, lemon zest, and ⅔ cup (133 grams) of the granulated sugar. (Alternatively, use an electric hand mixer and large bowl.) Beat on medium speed until smooth and fluffy, 2 to 3 minutes. Turn the mixer off and add the flour, cornstarch, and poppy seeds. Mix on low speed until a soft dough forms, 2 to 3 minutes. Stop the mixer and squeeze a small amount of dough—it should hold together. If it doesn't, add 1 tablespoon of water and keep mixing for about 15 seconds.

03 Transfer the dough to a lightly floured work surface and press together into a ball. Dust the top of the dough with flour and roll it out to a ½-inch-thick sheet. Using a 1½-inch round cookie cutter, cut out the cookies and use an offset metal spatula to transfer them to the prepared baking sheets, spacing about 1 inch apart (12 per sheet). Press the dough scraps together into a ball and repeat the rolling and cutting process. Freeze the cookies for 15 minutes. (If you can't fit both sheets in your freezer at once, consolidate them all onto 1 sheet, then divide them back onto 2 sheets for baking.)

04 While the cookies are freezing, place the remaining ⅔ cup (133 grams) granulated sugar in a medium bowl. Preheat the oven to 350°F and set the racks at the upper-middle and lower-middle positions.

05 Bake both sheets at the same time, swapping the top sheet to the bottom rack and bottom sheet to the top midway through baking, until the tops of the cookies are light golden brown, 13 to 15 minutes. Let the cookies sit for 5 minutes, until cool enough to handle, then gently toss them one by one in the sugar to coat them on all sides. (The cookies need to be warm for the sugar to stick, so don't wait too long.) Place the cookies back onto the baking sheets and let them cool completely.

Preserved Lemon Crinkle Cookies

Preserved lemons are a popular ingredient in Middle Eastern and North African cuisines, used in a variety of recipes, from tagines to stews. They're made by soaking whole lemons in a salty brine, transforming them into an earthier, tangier version of their former selves. Here, the preserved lemon peel is used to give classic crinkle cookies a robust, intensely lemony flavor and subtle salty bite. You can usually find preserved lemons in glass jars in well-stocked grocery stores, or you can easily order them online. But if unavailable, you can make this recipe with 2 tablespoons of grated fresh lemon zest with an added ½ teaspoon of kosher salt in the dough—but the flavor will not be the same.

1 stick (8 tablespoons/113 grams) unsalted butter, softened

1⅓ cups (267 grams) granulated sugar, divided

2 tablespoons (20 grams) chopped preserved lemon peel (see Note; recipe follows)

2 large eggs, room temperature

1 tablespoon vanilla extract

2½ cups spooned and leveled all-purpose flour (320 grams)

1½ teaspoons baking powder

¾ cup (75 grams) confectioners' sugar

Note

Two medium preserved lemons will yield about 2 tablespoons of chopped peel. To prepare them, run the preserved lemons under cold water to wash off some of the salt, then cut the peels into quarters. Using your fingers, pull the peel away from the flesh, and finely chop the peel. You will only use the peel in this recipe.

Make Ahead

The dough can be stored in the bowl in the refrigerator, tightly covered with plastic wrap, for several days before baking. If the dough is too hard to portion, let it sit at room temperature for 10 minutes and try again.

Storage

The cookies will keep in an airtight container at room temperature for up to 1 week.

DIY Preserved Lemons

Trim about ¼ inch from the stem tip of 6 lemons, then cut them lengthwise in half to within ½ inch of the bottom. Make another cut at a right angle almost all the way down again, as if to quarter the lemons. Sprinkle about 1 tablespoon kosher salt into the center of each lemon and massage it in so it dissolves slightly. Stack the lemons in a sterilized 2-quart glass jar, pressing them in so they snugly fit. If they didn't purge enough of their juices to cover themselves, add the juice of 1 or 2 large lemons until they are covered. Tightly cover with a lid and refrigerate for at least 1 week and up to several months.

01 In the bowl of a stand mixer fitted with the paddle attachment, combine the butter, 1 cup (200 grams) of the granulated sugar, and the chopped preserved lemon peel. Beat on medium speed until light and fluffy, scraping down the sides and bottom of the bowl halfway through, 2 to 3 minutes. Turn the mixer off, add the eggs and vanilla extract, and mix until pale yellow and very light, 2 to 3 minutes. Turn the mixer off, add the flour and baking powder, and mix on low speed just until a soft dough forms, 1 to 2 minutes. Tightly cover the bowl with plastic and chill in the refrigerator for 2 hours.

02 As the dough chills, place the remaining ⅓ cup (67 grams) granulated sugar in a shallow, wide bowl or on a plate and put the confectioners' sugar in a second shallow bowl or on a plate.

03 Preheat the oven to 350°F and set the racks at the upper-middle and lower-middle positions. Line 2 baking sheets with parchment paper or nonstick baking mats.

04 Using a medium 1¾-inch (#40) cookie scoop or 2 tablespoons, portion out the dough and roll into balls. Working with one dough ball at a time, roll in the granulated sugar, then in the confectioners' sugar, then roll in the palms of your hands above the bowl of confectioners' sugar to reshape them. Place the dough balls 3 inches apart on the prepared baking sheets (11 per sheet).

05 Bake both sheets at the same time, swapping the top sheet to the bottom rack and bottom sheet to the top midway through baking, until the cookies are puffed and the cracks no longer look wet, 13 to 15 minutes. Let cool completely on the baking sheets.

Chewy Coconut-Lime Cookies

Makes 20 large cookies

These chewy, coconut-laden cookies get a bright, citrusy burst of flavor from fresh lime zest. They're crispy on the outside and soft in the center, with specks of green throughout. Toasting the coconut before adding it to the dough lends a stronger toasted-coconut flavor and a beautiful golden hue, so don't skip it. Although time-consuming, this pays off by giving the cookies a bold, tropical aroma reminiscent of coconut candies.

01 Preheat the oven to 300°F and set 2 racks at the upper-middle and lower-middle portions. Line 2 baking sheets with parchment paper or nonstick baking mats. Scatter the coconut in a single layer divided between the baking sheets. Bake, rotating the sheets halfway through and stirring so the coconut toasts evenly, just until the edges start to turn golden brown but the center shreds remain fairly white, 10 to 12 minutes. Remove from the oven and cool for 10 minutes. Turn the oven off.

02 While the coconut cools, add the melted butter, brown sugar, granulated sugar, and lime zest to a large bowl and whisk to combine. Add the eggs and vanilla extract and whisk until ribbony and smooth, about 1 minute. Add the flour, baking powder, baking soda, and salt, and stir with a rubber spatula just until a soft dough forms. Mix in the cooled coconut. Cover the bowl tightly with plastic wrap and refrigerate for 2 hours. (Don't skip this step or your cookies will spread too much.)

03 Preheat the oven to 350°F. Line 3 baking sheets (or as many as you have) with parchment paper or nonstick baking mats. Using a large 2½-inch (#10) cookie scoop or ¼-cup measure, portion out the dough and roll into large balls. Place at least 3 inches apart on the prepared baking sheets (6 to 8 per sheet).

04 Bake 2 sheets at the same time, swapping the top sheet to the bottom rack and bottom sheet to the top midway through baking, until the tops of the cookies are lightly browned, 14 to 16 minutes, then bake the last baking sheet on either rack. (If reusing one of the baking sheets, allow it to cool for 15 minutes before placing another batch on it.) Immediately bang the baking sheets on the countertop to deflate the cookies a bit as they come out of the oven. Let them cool slightly on the baking sheets, then transfer to a wire rack to cool completely.

1 14-ounce bag (about 4 lightly packed cups/397 grams) sweetened shredded coconut

2 sticks (16 tablespoons/226 grams) unsalted butter, melted and cooled slightly

1⅓ cups (267 gram) packed light brown sugar

⅓ cup (67 grams) granulated sugar

1 tablespoon grated fresh lime zest (from about 2 medium limes)

2 large eggs

1 tablespoon vanilla extract

2¼ cups spooned and leveled all-purpose flour (288 grams)

1 teaspoon baking powder

1 teaspoon baking soda

¼ teaspoon kosher salt

Make Ahead

The coconut can be toasted and stored in an airtight container at room temperature for up to 1 week. The dough can be stored in the refrigerator, wrapped tightly in plastic, for several days before baking. If it's too cold to scoop, let sit at room temperature for 15 minutes and try again.

Storage

The cookies will keep in an airtight container at room temperature for up to 1 week.

Pink Grapefruit
Soft Sugar Cookies

Cookies

2¾ cups spooned and leveled all-purpose flour (352 grams)

¼ cup (33 grams) cornstarch

¾ teaspoon baking powder

¾ teaspoon baking soda

½ teaspoon kosher salt

1 stick (8 tablespoons/113 grams) unsalted butter, softened

1 cup (200 grams) granulated sugar

2 teaspoons grated fresh grapefruit zest (from about 1 medium grapefruit)

1 large egg, room temperature

⅓ cup (75 grams) sour cream, room temperature

1 tablespoon vanilla extract

Frosting

1 stick (8 tablespoons/113 grams) unsalted butter, softened

4 cups (400 grams) confectioners' sugar

½ cup (118 ml) heavy cream

1 teaspoon vanilla extract

1 teaspoon grated fresh grapefruit zest (from about ½ medium grapefruit)

Pinch of kosher salt

Red food coloring (optional)

Rainbow sprinkles, for sprinkling (optional)

Note
Any variety of fresh grapefruit will work well in this recipe, but if grapefruit isn't your favorite, any citrus (including limes, oranges, and lemons) can work in its place.

Make Ahead
The cookies can be baked the day before frosting and stored at room temperature in an airtight container.

Storage
Leftover frosted cookies can be kept in an airtight container in a single layer in the fridge for up to 1 week. The buttercream frosting will dry slightly but will be delicious nonetheless.

Makes 24 cookies

These sugar cookies are everything you love about the nostalgic lunchbox treat, here reimagined with the unexpected addition of pink grapefruit zest. The bright, citrusy flavor helps balance the sweetness of the cookies and lends a fresh, perfume-like aroma. They are soft, buttery, and pleasantly cakey with a tender texture.

01 Make the cookies: Preheat the oven to 350°F and set the oven racks at the upper-middle and lower-middle positions. Line 2 baking sheets with parchment paper or nonstick baking mats.

02 In a medium bowl, whisk together the flour, cornstarch, baking powder, baking soda, and salt.

03 In the bowl of a stand mixer fitted with the paddle attachment, combine the butter, sugar, and grapefruit zest. Beat on medium speed until smooth and fluffy, 2 to 3 minutes. (Alternatively, use a hand mixer and large bowl.) Turn the mixer off and add the egg, sour cream, and vanilla extract. Mix on medium speed until light and ribbony, 2 to 3 minutes. With the mixer running on low speed, gradually add the flour mixture, beating until just combined.

04 Using a medium 1¾-inch (#40) cookie scoop or 2 tablespoons, portion out the dough and roll into balls. Place the dough balls at least 3 inches apart on the prepared baking sheets (12 per sheet). Use the palm of your hand to gently flatten the dough balls to ½ inch thickness.

05 Bake until the tops of the cookies no longer look wet, rotating the sheets from top to bottom halfway through, 11 to 13 minutes. (You don't want much browning on these cookies. They should be pale.) Let cool slightly on the baking sheets, then transfer to a wire rack to cool completely.

06 As the cookies are cooling, make the frosting: In the bowl of the stand mixer fitted with the whisk attachment, combine the butter, confectioners' sugar, heavy cream, vanilla extract, grapefruit zest, and salt. (Alternatively, use a hand mixer and large bowl.) Mix on low speed to incorporate the confectioners' sugar, then increase the speed to medium-high and whip until light and fluffy, 2 to 3 minutes. Reduce the speed to low and add the red food coloring (if using) 1 drop at a time until your desired color is achieved.

07 Frost the tops of the cookies with 1 heaping tablespoon of frosting per cookie and use the rounded side of a spoon to artfully swoosh it. Sprinkle the tops with rainbow sprinkles, if using.

Lemon-Thyme Shortbread Cookies

These simple shortbread cookies have a bright lemon flavor and alluring herbal aroma from the addition of fresh thyme. It gives the cookies a pop of freshness and subtle savory flavor that transforms the simple shortbread into something new and exciting. The recipe uses the zest of three lemons, giving them a bold edge despite their unassuming appearance. One bite and a citrusy rush of lemon hits your nose. If thyme isn't your thing, feel free to use rosemary instead. Its woody flavor goes well with the lemon and provides a similar flavor profile.

01 Line a baking sheet with parchment paper or a nonstick baking mat.

02 In the bowl of a stand mixer fitted with the paddle attachment, combine the butter, confectioners' sugar, vanilla extract, salt, and lemon zest. (Alternatively, use an electric hand mixer and large bowl.) Beat on medium speed until smooth and fluffy, scraping down the sides and bottom halfway through, 2 to 3 minutes. Turn the mixer off and add the flour and chopped thyme. Mix on low speed just until a crumbly dough forms, 1 to 2 minutes.

03 Transfer the dough to a lightly floured work surface and press together into a ball. Dust the top of the dough with flour and roll out into an 8 × 8-inch square that's ½ inch thick. Sprinkle the granulated sugar over the top of the dough and gently press it in with your hands. Use a knife or pizza cutter to make a 4 × 4 grid of 4 rows in either direction, yielding 16 squares. (Feel free to trim the edges of the side pieces so they are perfectly square or leave them rounded—your choice.) Transfer the squares to the prepared baking sheet, spacing them about 1 inch apart. Freeze for 30 minutes.

04 Arrange a rack in the middle of the oven and preheat to 350°F.

05 Bake the cookies until just starting to brown on the tops, 18 to 23 minutes. Let cool completely on the baking sheet. The cookies will feel very soft when warm but will firm up once cooled.

2 sticks (16 tablespoons/226 grams) unsalted butter, softened

1¼ cups (125 grams) confectioners' sugar

1 tablespoon vanilla extract

1 teaspoon kosher salt

2 tablespoons (16 grams) grated fresh lemon zest (from 3 or 4 medium lemons)

2½ cups spooned and leveled all-purpose flour (320 grams), plus more for dusting

2 teaspoons chopped fresh thyme leaves

1 tablespoon granulated sugar

Make Ahead

The dough can be stored in the fridge, tightly wrapped in plastic, for several days in advance. When ready to roll out, let sit at room temperature for 20 minutes to warm up slightly.

Storage

The cookies will keep in an airtight container at room temperature for up to 1 week.

Cilantro-Lime Sugar Cookies

Makes 30 cookies

Cilantro lovers, this is the cookie for you. Chewy sugar cookies get flavored with fresh lime zest and just enough chopped cilantro to give the cookies a subtle, herbal freshness. Their flavor doesn't scream cilantro—rather, it whispers it. If you've ever had a cilantro-lime margarita, think of that flavor profile: fresh, perfumy, and bright. But if cilantro isn't your thing, you can make these cookies without adding it or substitute fresh basil instead and still end up with a delicious lime sugar cookie. Or you can use just two tablespoons of chopped cilantro instead of a quarter cup for a more nuanced flavor.

01 Preheat the oven to 375°F and set 2 racks at the upper-middle and lower-middle positions. Line 3 baking sheets (or as many as you have) with parchment paper or nonstick baking mats.

02 In a medium bowl, combine the flour, baking powder, baking soda, and salt.

03 In a large bowl, whisk together the melted butter and 1¾ cups (350 grams) of the granulated sugar until combined. Add the lime zest, vanilla extract, egg, and egg yolk, and whisk until smooth and glossy. Add the flour mixture and stir with a rubber spatula until a soft dough forms, then mix in the chopped cilantro.

04 Place the remaining ½ cup (100 grams) granulated sugar in a shallow, wide bowl. Using a medium 1¾-inch (#40) cookie scoop or 2 tablespoons, portion out the dough and roll into balls. Roll the balls in the sugar and place at least 3 inches apart on the prepared baking sheets (10 per sheet). The dough will be very soft, so don't fret if the balls are not perfectly round.

05 Bake 2 sheets at the same time, swapping the top sheet to the bottom rack and bottom sheet to the top midway through baking, until the tops of the cookies are very lightly browned, 12 to 14 minutes, then bake the last sheet on either rack. (If reusing one of the baking sheets, allow it to cool for 15 minutes before baking another batch on it.) Let the cookies cool completely on the baking sheets.

2¾ **cups** spooned and leveled all-purpose flour (352 grams)

½ **teaspoon** baking powder

½ **teaspoon** baking soda

½ **teaspoon** kosher salt

2 **sticks (16 tablespoons/226 grams)** unsalted butter, melted and cooled slightly

2¼ **cups (450 grams)** granulated sugar, divided

1 **tablespoon** grated fresh lime zest (from 2 or 3 medium limes)

1 **tablespoon** vanilla extract

1 **large** egg

1 **large** egg yolk

¼ **cup (22 grams)** packed finely chopped fresh cilantro leaves (about ½ bunch), or less depending on preference

Make Ahead

If wrapped tightly in plastic, the dough can be stored in the refrigerator for several days before baking. If too firm to scoop, let sit at room temperature for 15 minutes and try again.

Storage

The cookies will keep in an airtight container at room temperature for up to 1 week.

Brownie Sandwich Cookies with Blood Orange Marshmallow Crème

These soft and chewy brownie cookies get sandwiched together with a homemade marshmallow crème made with fresh blood orange juice. This gives the marshmallow filling a pretty pastel pink color and a subtle tartness that cuts through the richness of the brownies. If you've ever had a Terry's Chocolate Orange, this is similar: bold, citrusy, and aromatic. Because blood oranges are seasonal, feel free to make the marshmallow with bottled blood orange juice instead of fresh, or simply swap in regular orange juice. Although the filling won't be pink, it will taste just as good.

Chocolate Brownie Cookies

2 cups spooned and leveled all-purpose flour (256 grams)

3 tablespoons (21 grams) natural, unsweetened cocoa powder

½ teaspoon kosher salt

¼ teaspoon baking soda

¾ stick (6 tablespoons/84 grams) unsalted butter, cut into ½-inch cubes

1 cup (6 ounces/170 grams) semisweet or bittersweet chocolate chips

2 teaspoons vanilla extract

3 large eggs, room temperature

1 cup (200 grams) granulated sugar

½ cup (100 grams) packed light brown sugar

Blood Orange Marshmallow Crème

1 cup (237 ml) blood orange juice (from 5 medium blood oranges), strained and divided (see Note)

2 teaspoons unflavored powdered gelatin

¾ cup (150 grams) granulated sugar

⅓ cup (79 ml) light corn syrup

1 teaspoon vanilla extract

Pinch of kosher salt

Nonstick pan spray

Note
Bottled blood orange juice can be found year-round in specialty grocery stores and can be used in place of freshly squeezed. Make sure to strain out any pulp before using.

Make Ahead
The chocolate cookies can be baked several days in advance and stored in an airtight container at room temperature before filling with the marshmallow crème.

Storage
The filled cookies will keep in an airtight container at room temperature for up to 1 week.

(recipe continues)

01   Make the Chocolate Brownie Cookies: Preheat the oven to 350°F and set 2 racks at the upper-middle and lower-middle positions. Line 2 baking sheets with parchment paper or nonstick baking mats.

02   Combine the flour, cocoa powder, salt, and baking soda in a medium bowl and whisk to combine. Set aside.

03   In a medium heatproof bowl, combine the butter and chocolate chips. Microwave on high power in 10-second increments, stirring between each, until fully melted, about 1 minute. Add the vanilla extract and mix until smooth.

04   Add the eggs, granulated sugar, and brown sugar to the bowl of a stand mixer fitted with the whisk attachment. (Alternatively, use a hand mixer and large bowl.) Whip on high speed until the eggs are pale yellow, ribbony, and almost tripled in volume, about 4 minutes.

05   Reduce the mixer speed to low and slowly pour in the melted chocolate mixture. Mix until just combined, about 1 minute. Turn the mixer off and add the flour mixture. Stir with a rubber spatula just until a loose dough forms similar to brownie batter.

06   Working quickly, use a medium 1¾-inch (#40) cookie scoop or 2 table-spoons to immediately portion the dough onto the prepared baking sheets, spacing at least 2 inches apart (14 per sheet). The dough will be more like cake batter than cookie dough.

07   Bake both sheets at the same time, swapping the top sheet to the bottom rack and bottom sheet to the top midway through baking, until the tops of the cookies begin to crack, 11 to 13 minutes. Immediately bang the baking sheets several times on the countertop to deflate the cookies slightly. Let the cookies cool completely on the baking sheets. (The cookies will be very soft when warm but firm up once cooled. Do not be tempted to overbake them.)

08   While the cookies are cooling, make the Blood Orange Marshmallow Crème: In the bowl of a stand mixer fitted with the whisk attachment, combine ⅓ cup (79 ml) of the blood orange juice and the gelatin and stir with a spoon until the gelatin dissolves. Set aside to bloom.

09   In a large pot fitted with a candy thermometer, whisk together the remaining ⅔ cup (158 ml) blood orange juice, the granulated sugar, corn syrup, vanilla extract, and salt. (The syrup will bubble quite a bit, so make sure to use a large enough pot so it does not overflow.) Without stirring, bring to a simmer over medium heat and cook until the temperature reaches 245°F, 13 to 15 minutes. If any sugar crystals form on the sides of the pot during cooking, use a wet pastry brush to dissolve them.

10   Immediately pour the hot syrup on top of the bloomed gelatin in the mixer bowl. Gradually increase the mixer speed from low to high to prevent splashing, then whip on high speed until the marshmallow is very sticky, glossy, and doubled in volume, 9 to 11 minutes.

11   Spray a medium 1¾-inch (#40) cookie scoop or metal spoon with nonstick pan spray and dollop about 2 tablespoons of the marshmallow crème onto the undersides of half the cookies. Sandwich with the remaining cookies and let set for 2 hours at room temperature.

Rhubarb & White Chocolate Cookie Bars

½ **pound (227 grams/about 4 medium stalks)** fresh rhubarb, cut into ½-inch slices (about 2 cups; see Note)

1 **cup (200 grams)** granulated sugar, divided, plus more for prepping the pan

Nonstick pan spray

2¾ **cups** spooned and leveled all-purpose flour (352 grams)

¾ **teaspoon** baking soda

½ **teaspoon** kosher salt

2 **sticks (16 tablespoons/226 grams)** unsalted butter, softened

1½ **cups (300 grams)** packed light brown sugar

3 **large eggs,** room temperature

1 **tablespoon** vanilla extract

1½ **cups (9 ounces/255 grams)** white chocolate chips

Note

If fresh rhubarb isn't available, feel free to use frozen sliced rhubarb instead. To do so, let the rhubarb defrost in the fridge overnight in its bag and then drain off the liquid before tossing it with the sugar and macerating for 1 hour. Because frozen rhubarb tends to bleed more of its juices compared to fresh, make sure to thoroughly squeeze it free of excess moisture before spreading it on the dough.

Storage

Leftover bars will keep in an airtight container at room temperature for up to 1 week or frozen in a zip-top bag for several months. To defrost, let sit at room temperature for 2 hours or microwave individual bars for 20 to 30 seconds on high power until warm.

Makes 24 bars

If you've ever spotted fresh rhubarb at the market and haven't known what to do with it, these cookie bars are the perfect place to start. They're studded with bright pink slices of rhubarb that provide a tart contrast to the sweet pockets of molten white chocolate. The trick here is to macerate the sliced rhubarb in sugar for an hour before making the cookies. This helps rid the rhubarb of its excess moisture and tames its sour bite, resulting in cookie bars that are delightfully chewy and just tart enough.

01   Combine the rhubarb and ½ cup (100 grams) of the granulated sugar in a medium bowl and massage the sugar into the rhubarb, lightly squeezing it to release some of its juices, until the rhubarb turns bright pink and most of the sugar has been dissolved into a syrup consistency. Transfer the rhubarb to a colander placed over a bowl (for catching the rhubarb juice, which is great added to a cocktail or spooned over ice cream) and let sit at room temperature for 1 hour, stirring every now and then.

02   Arrange a rack in the middle of the oven and preheat to 325°F. Grease a 9 × 13-inch metal baking pan with the nonstick pan spray. Line with parchment paper, leaving some overhang on the long sides so it's easy to lift out the bars after baking, and coat once more with the pan spray. Sprinkle the sides and bottom of the pan with a thin layer of granulated sugar. (I find it easiest to add about 1 tablespoon of sugar to the pan, shake the pan to coat, then turn it upside down and tap out any excess.)

03   In a medium bowl, whisk together the flour, baking soda, and salt.

04   In the bowl of a stand mixer fitted with the paddle attachment, combine the butter, brown sugar, and remaining ½ cup (100 grams) granulated sugar. (Alternatively, use a hand mixer and large bowl.) Beat on medium speed until light and fluffy, scraping down the sides and bottom of the bowl halfway through, 2 to 3 minutes. Turn the mixer off and add the eggs and vanilla extract. Mix on medium speed until the mixture is the texture of light cake batter and very fluffy, 2 to 3 minutes. With the mixer running on low speed, gradually add the dry ingredients, beating until just combined and no pockets of dry flour remain. Stir in the white chocolate chips with a rubber spatula.

05 Add the cookie dough to the prepared pan and spread into an even layer using an offset spatula coated with pan spray. Give the rhubarb a few good squeezes to get rid of as much juice as you can. Scatter the rhubarb evenly on top of the cookie dough and press the pieces into the dough so they stick. Bake for 55 to 65 minutes, until the top is lightly browned and a toothpick inserted into the center comes out with only a few moist crumbs attached. (Just be careful not to insert your toothpick into a pocket of melted chocolate or a piece of rhubarb.) Immediately bang the pan on the countertop several times to deflate the bars slightly.

06 Let the bars cool in the baking pan for at least 2 hours (the bars will firm up as they cool) before slicing into 24 pieces (6 short rows and 4 long rows).

Salt-and-Vinegar Potato Chip Cookies

Salt-and-vinegar potato chips might sound like a strange mix-in to add to cookie dough, but it *works*. The acidic flavor of the potato chips brightens the cookies, balancing out their richness and making them taste lighter and more balanced—trust me! If you've ever added lemon juice to a bland meal only to discover that all it needed was a touch of acid, this recipe embraces the same philosophy. Milk chocolate perfectly balances the sharpness of the potato chips and gives the cookies a wonderful snacky vibe. Any milk chocolate bar found in the candy aisle will work perfectly.

01 Preheat the oven to 375°F and set 2 racks at the upper-middle and lower-middle positions. Line 3 baking sheets (or as many as you have) with parchment paper or nonstick baking mats.

02 In a medium bowl, combine the flour, baking powder, baking soda, and 1 cup (70 grams) of the crushed potato chips. Stir with a rubber spatula until the potato chips are completely coated with flour.

03 In a large bowl, whisk together the melted butter, brown sugar, and granulated sugar until combined. Add the eggs and vanilla extract and whisk until smooth and glossy. Add the flour mixture and stir with a rubber spatula just until a soft dough forms. Mix in the chopped chocolate.

04 Place the remaining 1 cup (70 grams) crushed potato chips in a large, shallow bowl. Using a large 2⅓-inch (#16) cookie scoop or ¼-cup measure, portion out the dough and roll into large balls. Roll the dough balls in the crushed potato chips, pressing the chips into the dough so they stick, and place at least 3 inches apart on the prepared baking sheets (7 to 8 per sheet).

05 Bake 2 sheets at the same time, swapping the top sheet to the bottom rack and bottom sheet to the top midway through baking, until the tops of the cookies are lightly browned, 12 to 14 minutes, then bake the last sheet on either rack. (If reusing one of the baking sheets, allow it to cool for 15 minutes before baking another batch on it.) Immediately bang the baking sheets on the countertop several times as they come out of the oven to deflate the cookies slightly and let them cool completely on the baking sheets.

3½ cups spooned and leveled all-purpose flour (448 grams)

1 teaspoon baking powder

¾ teaspoon baking soda

2 cups (140 grams) crushed salt-and-vinegar potato chips (from a 5-ounce bag), divided (preferably kettle-style chips, but any will work)

2 sticks (16 tablespoons/226 grams) unsalted butter, melted and cooled slightly

1⅓ cups (267 grams) packed light brown sugar

⅓ cup (67 grams) granulated sugar

2 large eggs, room temperature

1 tablespoon vanilla extract

8 ounces (227 grams) milk chocolate, roughly chopped (about 1⅓ cups)

Make Ahead

If wrapped tightly in plastic, the dough can be stored in the refrigerator for several days before baking. If it's too firm to portion, let sit at room temperature for 20 minutes and try again.

Storage

The cookies will keep in an airtight container at room temperature for up to 1 week.

Macadamia Nut Shortbread Cookies with Hibiscus-Lime Glaze

Makes 18 shortbread cookies

These tender macadamia nut shortbread cookies get coated with a tart, neon-pink glaze made with fresh lime juice and dried hibiscus flowers. The two ingredients work together to create a bold, citrusy glaze with a refreshingly sour flavor.

Macadamia Nut Shortbread Cookies

½ **cup (63 grams)** toasted salted macadamia nuts (see page 18)

2¾ **cups** spooned and leveled all-purpose flour (352 grams), plus more for dusting

½ **teaspoon** kosher salt

2 **sticks (16 tablespoons/226 grams)** unsalted butter, softened

½ **cup (100 grams)** confectioners' sugar

¼ **cup (50 grams)** granulated sugar

1 **large** egg yolk

1 **teaspoon** vanilla extract

Hibiscus-Lime Glaze

¼ **cup (59 ml)** fresh lime juice (from about 2 medium limes)

¼ **cup (8 grams)** dried hibiscus flowers, lightly crushed with your fingers (see Note)

1 **teaspoon** vanilla extract

2½ **cups (250 grams)** confectioners' sugar, plus more as needed

Fresh lime zest, for garnish (optional)

Note

Dried hibiscus flowers can be found in either the tea or the produce section of most well-stocked grocery stores, sometimes near the dried mushrooms. If unavailable, look for a tea blend that includes dried hibiscus as a main ingredient, such as Celestial Seasonings' Red Zinger tea. Although not ideal, it will provide a similar flavor.

Make Ahead

Unbaked, cut-out shortbread cookies can be stored in the freezer, tightly wrapped in plastic, for several months.

Storage

The cookies will keep in an airtight container at room temperature for up to 1 week.

01 Make the cookies: Line a baking sheet with parchment paper or a nonstick baking mat.

02 In the bowl of a food processor fitted with the blade attachment, combine the nuts, flour, and salt. Process until the nuts are the texture of fine sand and there are no visible pieces left, 30 to 45 seconds.

03 In the bowl of a stand mixer fitted with the paddle attachment, combine the butter, confectioners' sugar, and granulated sugar. (Alternatively, use a hand mixer and large bowl.) Beat on medium speed until light and fluffy, 2 to 3 minutes. Add the egg yolk and vanilla extract and continue mixing on medium speed until fully incorporated, 1 to 2 minutes. With the mixer running on low speed, slowly add the ground nut mixture until a crumbly dough forms, about 1 minute.

04 Transfer the dough to a lightly floured work surface and press together into a ball. Roll out until about ⅓ inch thick. Using a 3-inch rectangular cookie cutter, cut out cookies and place on the prepared baking sheet, spacing 1 inch apart. Press the dough scraps together into a ball and repeat the rolling and cutting process. Freeze for 30 minutes.

05 Arrange a rack in the middle of the oven and preheat to 350°F. Bake the cookies until the tops are just starting to turn light golden brown, 21 to 25 minutes. Let cool on the baking sheet for at least 30 minutes.

06 Make the glaze: Combine the lime juice and hibiscus flowers in a microwave-safe bowl and microwave on high for 30 seconds, just until hot. Let steep at room temperature for 10 minutes.

07 Strain the mixture through a fine-mesh sieve into a medium bowl. Add the vanilla extract and confectioners' sugar and whisk until completely smooth. The glaze should be thick yet pourable. If it's too thin, add 1 tablespoon confectioners' sugar to thicken it up; if too thin, add 1 to 2 teaspoons water.

08 Dip the tops of the shortbread cookies in the glaze, holding them above the bowl for several seconds to let the excess drip off. Place back on the baking sheet and let set for 30 minutes. Garnish with fresh lime zest, if using.

Chewy Triple-Citrus Poppy Seed Cookies

2¾ **cups** spooned and leveled all-purpose flour
(352 grams)

½ **teaspoon** baking soda

½ **teaspoon** kosher salt

¼ **cup plus 2 tablespoons (57 grams)** poppy seeds,
divided (see page 18 for storing info)

2 **teaspoons** grated fresh lemon zest (from about
2 medium lemons)

2 **teaspoons** grated fresh lime zest (from about
0 medium limes)

2 **teaspoons** grated fresh orange zest (from about
1 medium orange)

¾ **cup (150 grams)** packed light brown sugar

1½ **cups (300 grams)** granulated sugar, divided

2 **sticks (16 tablespoons/226 grams)** unsalted butter,
softened

1 **large** egg, room temperature

2 **large** egg yolks, room temperature

1 **tablespoon** vanilla extract

Make Ahead

If wrapped tightly in plastic, the dough can be stored in
the refrigerator for several days before baking.

Storage

The cookies will keep in an airtight container at room
temperature for up to 1 week.

Makes 24 cookies

This spin on lemon poppy seed cookies adds both
orange and lime zest to the mix for a bold, citrusy
cookie that tastes almost like tropical punch. The
trick to getting the most flavor out of the zest is to
massage it into the sugar. This helps release some
of the oils from the zest, perfuming the sugar with
a bright flavor that infuses the cookies. If one of
the citruses isn't your favorite, feel free to omit it
or swap it out with any other citrus of your liking.
Grapefruit, pomelos, and clementines would all
work well as substitutes.

01 In a medium bowl, combine the flour, baking soda,
salt, and ¼ cup (38 grams) of the poppy seeds.

02 In the bowl of a stand mixer fitted with the paddle
attachment, combine the lemon zest, lime zest,
orange zest, brown sugar, and 1 cup (200 grams)
of the granulated sugar. Massage the zest into the
sugar with your fingertips until the sugar is tinted a
light yellow and is very fragrant.

03 Add the butter and beat on medium speed, scraping
down the sides and bottom of the bowl halfway
through, until smooth and fluffy, 2 to 3 minutes.
(Alternatively, use a hand mixer and large bowl.) Turn
the mixer off and add the egg, egg yolks, and vanilla
extract. Mix on medium speed until very fluffy, 2 to
3 minutes. With the mixer running on low speed,
gradually add the flour mixture, beating until just
combined. Tightly cover the bowl with plastic wrap
and refrigerate for 2 hours.

04 Preheat the oven to 350°F and set 2 racks at the
upper-middle and lower-middle positions. Line
2 baking sheets with parchment paper or nonstick
baking mats.

05 Place the remaining ½ cup (100 grams) granulated
sugar and remaining 2 tablespoons (19 grams)
poppy seeds in a shallow, wide bowl and mix with a
spoon to combine. Using a medium 1¾-inch (#40)
cookie scoop or 2 tablespoons, portion out the
dough and roll into balls. Roll the balls in the sugar
mixture to coat them and place at least 2 inches
apart on the prepared baking sheets (12 per sheet).

06 Bake both sheets at the same time, swapping the
top sheet to the bottom rack and bottom sheet to
the top midway through baking, until the cookies are
puffed and very lightly browned, 14 to 17 minutes.
Immediately bang the baking sheets on the
countertop as they come out of the oven to deflate
the cookies slightly. Let cool slightly on the baking
sheets, then transfer to a wire rack to cool completely.

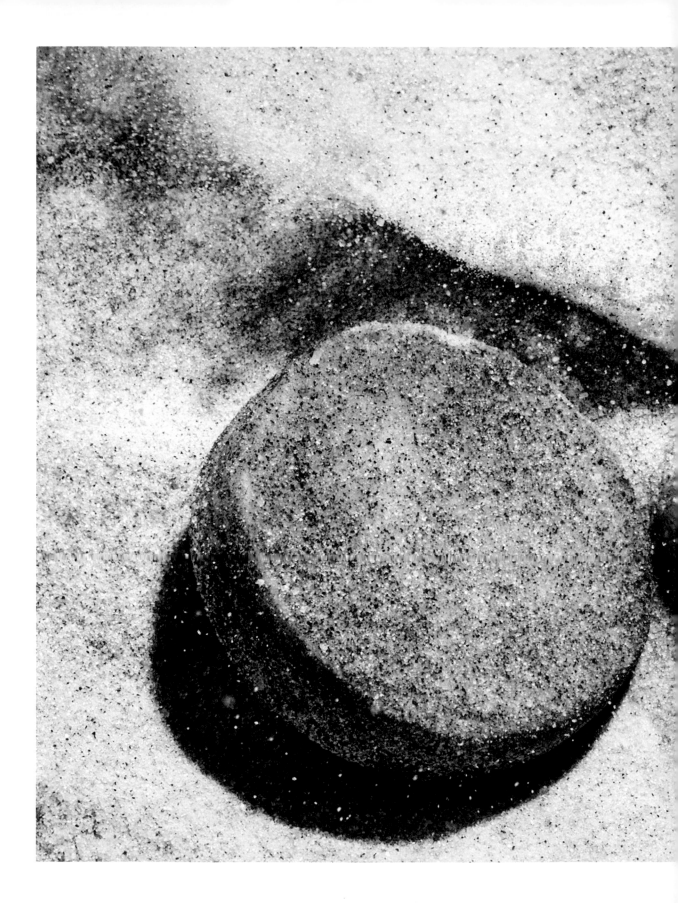

Snickerdoodle Shortbread

Spiced

Cardamom Palmiers

Makes 24 palmiers

Palmiers are impressive cookies that seem like a lot of work but actually come together in no time at all, thanks to frozen puff pastry. If you've never had one before, imagine the crunchy, flaky, sugar-crusted edge of a pie crust, and that's what you're in for. Ground cardamom gives these a citrusy and bright aromatic flavor that hits your nose the moment you bite into them with a crisp, caramel-like texture that shatters in your mouth. I like to eat them with black tea or coffee, or as a late-night snack.

01 Set a rack in the middle of the oven and preheat to 450°F. Line 3 baking sheets (or as many as you have) with parchment paper or nonstick baking mats.

02 In a medium bowl, combine the sugar, cardamom, and salt and stir with a spoon.

03 Unfold 1 sheet of the puff pastry onto a clean work surface. Sprinkle ¼ cup (50 grams) of the sugar mixture evenly over the top and press it in slightly with your hands. Flip the sheet of pastry over and sprinkle the other side with another ¼ cup (50 grams) of the sugar mixture. (This process is a bit messy, so feel free to put a piece of parchment paper on the countertop to make cleanup easier. A lot of the sugar will end up on the countertop.)

04 Fold two opposite sides of the square toward the middle so they go halfway into the center, then fold them once more toward the center so the folds meet exactly in the middle. Brush the top of the puff pastry with water, then fold one half over the other like a book so you end up with one long rectangle that has 6 layers. Press the puff pastry together slightly so all the layers stick. Cut the rectangle crosswise into ½-inch-thick slices (about 12), sprinkle both sides of the slices with the excess sugar left on the countertop and arrange the slices on the prepared baking sheets spacing them at least 3 inches apart (8 per sheet). Repeat the process with the remaining sheet of puff pastry.

05 Bake 1 baking sheet at a time, turning the palmiers over after 8 minutes and continuing to cook for an additional 5 to 7 minutes on the other side until dark golden brown (13 to 15 minutes total). Remove the baking sheet from the oven and set aside—the palmiers should cool completely on the sheet. Repeat with the remaining baking sheets. (If reusing one of the baking sheets, allow it to cool for 15 minutes before baking another batch on it.)

1 cup (200 grams) granulated sugar

2 teaspoons ground cardamom

½ teaspoon kosher salt

1 package (2 sheets/490 grams) frozen puff pastry, thawed (preferably an all-butter brand such as Dufour)

Make Ahead
Sliced, unbaked palmiers can be stored in a zip-top bag in the freezer for several months and baked from frozen.

Storage
The palmiers will keep in an airtight container for up to 1 week.

Chewy Crystalized Ginger Cookies

Makes 24 cookies

Crisp on the edges and chewy in the center, these spicy molasses cookies are a ginger lover's dream. Packed with both ground and crystallized ginger, the cookies don't shy away from heat. The ground ginger provides a peppery kick, while the crystallized variety adds a chewy texture and sweeter, more complex ginger flavor. Don't let the addition of black pepper scare you—it's there to give the cookies a subtle, tingly background note that highlights the ginger.

3 cups spooned and leveled all-purpose flour (384 grams)

1 cup (185 grams) crystallized ginger, very finely chopped (see Note)

2 teaspoons baking soda

1 tablespoon ground cinnamon

1 tablespoon ground ginger

½ teaspoon kosher salt

¼ teaspoon finely ground black pepper

1½ sticks (12 tablespoons/170 grams) unsalted butter, softened

1¼ cups (250 grams) packed light brown sugar

1 large egg

⅓ cup (79 ml) unsulphured molasses

1 tablespoon vanilla extract

⅓ cup (67 grams) granulated sugar

Note

Crystallized ginger can be found in most well-stocked grocery stores in either the candy or the natural food sections, sometimes labeled as candied ginger or ginger cubes. Just make sure not to use ginger-flavored candies, as they are not the same thing. To make chopping it easier, I like to spray the blade of my knife with nonstick pan spray so it doesn't stick.

Make Ahead

If wrapped tightly in plastic, the dough can be stored in the refrigerator for several days before baking. If too firm to scoop, let sit at room temperature for 15 minutes and try again.

Storage

The cookies will keep in an airtight container for up to 1 week.

01 Preheat the oven to 350°F and set 2 racks at the upper-middle and lower-middle positions. Line 2 baking sheets with parchment paper or nonstick baking mats.

02 In a medium bowl, whisk together the flour, crystallized ginger, baking soda, cinnamon, ground ginger, salt, and black pepper.

03 In the bowl of a stand mixer fitted with the paddle attachment, combine the butter and brown sugar. Beat on medium speed, scraping down the sides and bottom of the bowl halfway through, until smooth and fluffy, 2 to 3 minutes. (Alternatively, use a hand mixer and large bowl.) Turn the mixer off and add the egg, molasses, and vanilla extract. Mix on medium speed until very fluffy and lightened in color slightly, 2 to 3 minutes. With the mixer running on low speed, gradually add the flour mixture, beating until just combined.

04 Place the granulated sugar in a shallow, wide bowl. Using a large 2⅓-inch (#16) cookie scoop or ¼-cup measure, portion out the dough and roll into balls. Roll the dough balls in the sugar, then place at least 3 inches apart on the prepared baking sheets (12 per sheet).

05 Bake both sheets at the same time, swapping the top sheet to the bottom rack and bottom sheet to the top midway through baking, until the tops of the cookies crack and puff slightly, 13 to 15 minutes. Let cool completely on the baking sheets.

Sweet Potato Snickerdoodles

Nonstick pan spray

1 large sweet potato (about 10 ounces/283 grams)

1 stick (8 tablespoons/113 grams) unsalted butter

⅓ cup (67 grams) packed light or dark brown sugar

1 cup (200 grams) granulated sugar, divided

1 tablespoon vanilla extract

1¾ cups spooned and leveled all-purpose flour (224 grams)

1 teaspoon kosher salt

1 teaspoon cream of tartar

1 teaspoon baking soda

2 tablespoons (15 grams) ground cinnamon

Make Ahead

The sweet potato can be roasted several days before making the dough and stored in an airtight container in the fridge. If wrapped tightly in plastic, the finished dough can be stored in the refrigerator for several days before baking. If too firm to scoop, let sit at room temperature for 15 minutes and try again.

Storage

The cookies will keep in an airtight container for up to 1 week.

Makes 10 large cookies

Sweet potatoes and cinnamon are a match made in heaven, and this snickerdoodle is proof positive. The sweet potato gives the dough a buttery, earthy richness and a bright orange color, creating the perfect base to highlight the cinnamon.

01　Preheat the oven to 375°F and set 2 racks at the upper-middle and lower-middle positions. Line a baking sheet with parchment paper or a nonstick baking mat and lightly coat with nonstick pan spray.

02　Cut the sweet potato in half vertically and place the halves cut side down on the prepared baking sheet. Roast on the top rack until a knife can be inserted into it without any resistance, 50 to 55 minutes. Let cool on the baking sheet.

03　As the potato is cooling, melt the butter in a small saucepan over medium heat. Continue cooking, stirring often to prevent the milk solids from burning, until the butter foams and then darkens in color slightly and is very fragrant, 3 to 4 minutes. Immediately pour the butter into a large heatproof bowl and let cool for 10 minutes.

04　As the butter is cooling, spoon out the flesh of the sweet potato (discard the skin) and place in a medium bowl. Smash the flesh with a fork until completely smooth and measure out ½ cup (130 grams). Reserve any extra for another use.

05　Add the brown sugar, ½ cup (100 grams) of the granulated sugar, the vanilla extract, and the measured sweet potato to the bowl with the melted butter. Whisk until smooth. Add the flour, salt, cream of tartar, and baking soda and stir with a rubber spatula just until a soft dough forms.

06　Line 2 baking sheets with fresh parchment paper or nonstick baking mats. Mix the remaining ½ cup (100 grams) granulated sugar and the cinnamon in a shallow, wide bowl. Using a large 2⅓-inch (#16) cookie scoop or ¼-cup measure, portion out the dough and roll into balls. Roll in the cinnamon sugar and then place the dough balls at least 2 inches apart on the prepared baking sheets (5 per sheet).

07　Bake both sheets at the same time, swapping them midway, until the cookies are puffy and cracked, 14 to 17 minutes. Immediately bang the baking sheets on the countertop as they come out of the oven to deflate the cookies slightly and then let cool completely on the baking sheets.

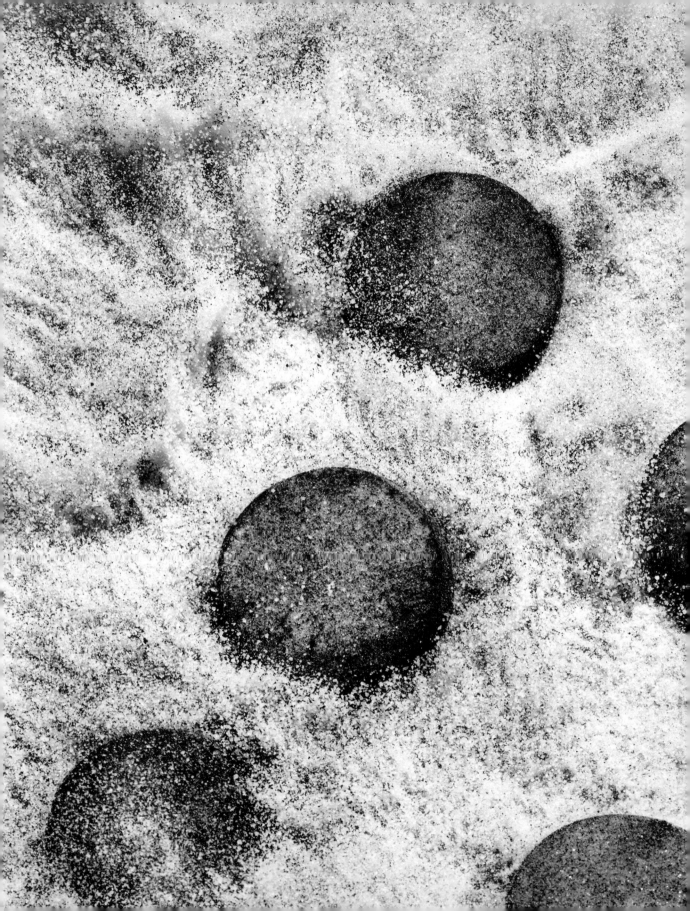

Snickerdoodle Shortbread

These cookies borrow all the flavors of classic snickerdoodles and reimagine them as buttery shortbread rounds. A simple shortbread base made with cream of tartar mimics the slightly tangy flavor of snickerdoodle dough. As soon as the cookies are done baking, they get tossed in cinnamon sugar, transforming the pale shortbreads into sparkling, browned beauties with a bold cinnamon-y flavor.

2¾ **cups** spooned and leveled all-purpose flour (352 grams), plus more for dusting

1 **teaspoon** kosher salt

½ **teaspoon** cream of tartar (see Note)

2 **sticks (16 tablespoons/226 grams)** unsalted butter, softened

½ **cup (50 grams)** confectioners' sugar

½ **cup (100 grams)** granulated sugar, divided

1 **large** egg yolk

2 **teaspoons** vanilla extract

2 **teaspoons** ground cinnamon

Note
Cream of tartar can be found in the spice or baking sections of most well-stocked grocery stores. If you want to put it to use, the Brown Butter–Bourbon Snickerdoodles (page 67), Sweet Potato Snickerdoodles (page 180), and the Crunchy Muscovado Meringues (page 222) all use it.

Make Ahead
Unbaked, cut-out shortbread cookies can be stored in the freezer for several months. To freeze them, place the cut-out cookies on a baking sheet, freeze uncovered for 30 minutes, then transfer to a zip-top bag.

Storage
The cookies will keep in an airtight container for up to 1 week.

01 Line 2 baking sheets with parchment paper or nonstick baking mats.

02 In a medium bowl, whisk together the flour, salt, and cream of tartar.

03 In the bowl of a stand mixer fitted with the paddle attachment, combine the butter, confectioners' sugar, and ¼ cup (50 grams) of the granulated sugar. (Alternatively, use a hand mixer and large bowl.) Beat on medium speed until light and fluffy, 2 to 3 minutes. Add the egg yolk and vanilla extract and continue mixing on medium speed until fully incorporated, 1 to 2 minutes. Turn the mixer off and add the flour mixture. Mix on low speed just until a crumbly dough forms, about 1 minute.

04 Transfer the dough to a lightly floured work surface and press together into a ball. Roll out until about ⅓ inch thick. Using a 2-inch round cookie cutter, cut out cookies and place on the prepared baking sheets, spacing about 1 inch apart (12 per sheet). Press the dough scraps together into a ball and repeat the rolling and cutting process. Freeze for 30 minutes. (If you can't fit both sheets in your freezer at once, feel free to consolidate the cookies onto 1 sheet, then divide again onto 2 sheets for baking.)

05 Preheat the oven to 350°F and set 2 racks at the upper-middle and lower-middle positions. Combine the remaining ¼ cup (50 grams) granulated sugar and the cinnamon in a small bowl.

06 Bake both sheets from frozen at the same time, swapping the top sheet to the bottom rack and bottom sheet to the top midway through baking, until the sides of the cookies are just starting to turn light golden brown and the cookies are fragrant, 19 to 22 minutes. Let the cookies cool for 5 minutes on the baking sheets until they are cool enough to handle, then toss them one at a time in the cinnamon sugar, taking your time to generously coat them on all sides. Place the cookies back on the baking sheets and let cool completely.

Vanilla Bean
& Sumac Cookies

Makes 24 cookies

Bright pink flecks of sumac bleed their rosy color into these soft sugar cookies that are crisp on the edges and chewy in the center. As they bake, the citrusy scent of sumac blends with the vanilla, creating an alluring aroma that's bright and inviting. The cookies' flavor is buttery, sweet, and a tad tart—the perfect platform to show off the sumac's unique flavor.

01 Preheat the oven to 375°F and set 2 racks at the upper-middle and lower-middle positions. Line 3 baking sheets (or as many as you have) with parchment paper or nonstick baking mats.

02 In a medium bowl, whisk together the flour, baking powder, baking soda, salt, and 2 teaspoons of the sumac.

03 In a large bowl, whisk together the melted butter and 1¾ cups (350 grams) of the granulated sugar until combined. Add the vanilla seeds, egg, and egg yolk, and whisk until smooth and glossy. Add the flour mixture and stir with a rubber spatula until a soft dough forms.

04 Place the remaining ½ cup (100 grams) granulated sugar and remaining ½ teaspoon sumac in a shallow, wide bowl and stir with a spoon. Using a medium 1¾-inch (#40) cookie scoop or 2 tablespoons, portion out the dough and roll into balls. Roll the balls in the sumac sugar and place at least 3 inches apart on the prepared baking sheets (8 per sheet).

05 Bake 2 sheets at the same time, swapping the top sheet to the bottom rack and bottom sheet to the top midway through baking, until the tops of the cookies are very lightly browned, 13 to 15 minutes, then bake the last sheet on either rack. (If reusing one of the baking sheets, allow it to cool for 15 minutes before baking another batch on it.) Let cool completely on the baking sheets.

2¾ **cups** spooned and leveled all-purpose flour (352 grams)

½ **teaspoon** baking powder

½ **teaspoon** baking soda

½ **teaspoon** kosher salt

2½ **teaspoons** ground sumac, divided (see Note)

2 **sticks (16 tablespoons/226 grams)** unsalted butter, melted and cooled slightly

2¼ **cups (450 grams)** granulated sugar, divided

2 vanilla beans, seeds scraped out (reserve beans for another use; see Note)

1 **large** egg

1 **large** egg yolk

Note
Sumac can be found in the spice section of most well-stocked grocery stores, such as Whole Foods. If you don't have vanilla beans, feel free to use 1 tablespoon vanilla extract or vanilla bean paste in its place.

Make Ahead
If wrapped tightly in plastic, the dough can be stored in the refrigerator for several days before baking. If too firm to scoop, let sit at room temperature for 15 minutes and try again.

Storage
The cookies will keep in an airtight container for up to 1 week.

Giant Five-Spice Molasses Cookies

Makes 12 large cookies

This recipe uses one of my favorite spice blends—five-spice powder—to give the cookies a warm, aromatic flavor that's an unexpected departure from the typical molasses cookie. The spice blend is often used in Chinese and Vietnamese cooking and is typically made with star anise, fennel, cinnamon, cloves, and peppercorns. Here it's used to infuse the cookies with a sweet and savory flavor profile that works beautifully with the molasses to create large, chewy cookies with a bold, spicy flavor.

01 In a medium bowl, whisk together the flour, baking soda, five-spice powder, and salt.

02 In the bowl of a stand mixer fitted with the paddle attachment, combine the butter and brown sugar. Beat on medium speed, scraping down the sides and bottom of the bowl halfway through, until smooth and fluffy, 2 to 3 minutes. (Alternatively, use a hand mixer and large bowl.) Turn the mixer off and add the egg, molasses, and vanilla extract. Mix on medium speed until very fluffy and lightened in color slightly, 2 to 3 minutes. With the mixer running on low speed, gradually add the flour mixture, beating just until a soft dough forms with no pockets of dry flour. Tightly cover the bowl with plastic wrap and refrigerate for 1 hour.

03 Preheat the oven to 350°F and set 2 racks at the upper-middle and lower-middle positions. Line 2 baking sheets with parchment paper or nonstick baking mats. Place the turbinado sugar in a shallow, wide bowl.

04 Using a large 2⅓-inch (#16) cookie scoop or ¼-cup measure, portion out the dough and roll into large balls. Roll the dough balls in the turbinado sugar and then place at least 3 inches apart on the prepared baking sheets (6 per sheet).

05 Bake both sheets at the same time, swapping the top sheet to the bottom rack and bottom sheet to the top midway through baking, until the tops of the cookies crack and puff slightly, 15 to 18 minutes. Let cool completely on the baking sheets.

3 cups spooned and leveled all-purpose flour (384 grams)

2 teaspoons baking soda

1 tablespoon five-spice powder (see Note)

½ teaspoon kosher salt

1½ sticks (12 tablespoons/170 grams) unsalted butter, softened

1¼ cups (250 grams) packed light brown sugar

1 large egg

⅓ cup (79 ml) ulsulphured molasses

1 tablespoon vanilla extract

½ cup (100 grams) turbinado sugar

Note
Five-spice powder can be found in the spice section of most well-stocked grocery stores.

Make Ahead
If wrapped tightly in plastic, the dough can be stored in the refrigerator for several days before baking. If too firm to scoop, let sit at room temperature for 15 minutes and try again.

Storage
Store the cookies in an airtight container at room temperature for up to 1 week.

Chewy Triple-Spice Sugar Cookies

Makes 24 cookies

Soft and chewy sugar cookies get a fiery upgrade with the addition of three bold spices: cinnamon, ginger, and allspice. The trio gives the cookies a bold bite similar to a gingersnap, while brown sugar lends a caramel-y flavor and soft texture. Enjoy them with a hot cider for the ultimate cool-weather treat.

01 Preheat the oven to 375°F and set 2 racks at the upper-middle and lower-middle positions. Line 2 baking sheets with parchment paper or nonstick baking mats.

02 In a medium bowl, whisk together the flour, cinnamon, ginger, allspice, baking powder, baking soda, and salt.

03 In a large bowl, whisk together the melted butter, brown sugar, and ¾ cup (150 grams) of the granulated sugar until combined. Add the vanilla extract, egg, and egg yolk, and whisk until smooth. Add the flour mixture and stir with a rubber spatula just until a soft dough forms and no pockets of dry flour remain.

04 Place the remaining ½ cup (100 grams) granulated sugar in a shallow, wide bowl. Using a medium 1¾-inch (#40) cookie scoop or 2 tablespoons, portion out the dough and roll into balls. Roll the balls in the sugar and place at least 3 inches apart on the prepared baking sheets (12 per sheet).

05 Bake both sheets at the same time, swapping the top sheet to the bottom rack and bottom sheet to the top midway through baking, until the bottom edges of the cookies are starting to brown and the tops are cracked, 12 to 14 minutes. Let cool completely on the baking sheets.

2¾ cups spooned and leveled all-purpose flour (352 grams)

2 tablespoons (15 grams) ground cinnamon

1 tablespoon ground ginger

1 teaspoon ground allspice

½ teaspoon baking powder

½ teaspoon baking soda

½ teaspoon kosher salt

2 sticks (16 tablespoons/226 grams) unsalted butter, melted and cooled slightly

1 cup (200 grams) packed light brown sugar

1¼ cups (250 grams) granulated sugar, divided

1 tablespoon vanilla extract

1 large egg

1 large egg yolk

Storage
If wrapped tightly in plastic, the dough can be stored in the refrigerator for several days before baking. If too firm to scoop, let sit at room temperature for 15 minutes and try again.

Storage
The cookies will keep in an airtight container for up to 1 week.

Chocolate Chunk Gingersnaps

Makes 18 large cookies

Chocolate chip cookies meet gingersnaps in this decadent hybrid recipe. A rich, spiced cookie dough made with molasses gets studded with chopped bittersweet chocolate pieces, creating large pools of molten chocolate as the cookies bake. The result is everything you love about the world's most famous cookie, upgraded with warm winter spices.

01 Preheat the oven to 350°F and set 2 racks at the upper-middle and lower-middle positions. Line 3 baking sheets (or as many as you have) with parchment paper or nonstick baking mats.

02 In a medium bowl, whisk together the flour, cinnamon, ginger, cloves, allspice, baking soda, and salt.

03 In the bowl of a stand mixer fitted with the paddle attachment, combine the butter and brown sugar. (Alternatively, use a hand mixer and large bowl.) Beat on medium speed, scraping down the sides and bottom of the bowl halfway through, until smooth and fluffy, 2 to 3 minutes. Turn the mixer off and add the egg, molasses, and vanilla extract. Mix on medium speed until very fluffy and lightened in color slightly, 2 to 3 minutes. With the mixer running on low speed, gradually add the flour mixture, beating just until a soft dough forms. Add the chopped chocolate and mix on low speed just until distributed. (It's okay if the mixer crushes the chocolate slightly.)

04 Place the granulated sugar in a shallow, wide bowl. Using a large 2⅓-inch (#16) cookie scoop or ¼-cup measure, portion out the dough and roll into balls. Roll the balls in the granulated sugar and place at least 3 inches apart on the prepared baking sheets (6 per sheet).

05 Bake 2 sheets at the same time, swapping the top sheet to the bottom rack and bottom sheet to the top midway through baking, until the tops of the cookies crack and puff slightly, 14 to 17 minutes, then bake the remaining sheet on either rack. (If reusing one of the baking sheets, allow it to cool for 15 minutes before baking another batch on it.) Immediately bang the baking sheets on the countertop as they come out of the oven to deflate the cookies slightly and let cool completely on the baking sheets.

3¼ cups spooned and leveled all-purpose flour (416 grams)

1 tablespoon ground cinnamon

1 tablespoon ground ginger

¼ teaspoon ground cloves

¼ teaspoon ground allspice

2 teaspoons baking soda

½ teaspoon kosher salt

1½ sticks (12 tablespoons/170 grams) unsalted butter, softened

1½ cups (300 grams) packed light brown sugar

1 large egg

⅓ cup (79 ml) unsulphured molasses

1 tablespoon vanilla extract

6 ounces (170 grams) semisweet or bittersweet chocolate, finely chopped (about 1 cup)

½ cup (100 grams) granulated sugar

Make Ahead
If wrapped tightly in plastic, the dough can be stored in the refrigerator for several days before baking. If too firm to scoop, let sit at room temperature for 15 minutes and try again.

Storage
The cookies will keep in an airtight container for up to 1 week.

Spiced Apple Butter Cookies

Apple butter's ultra-concentrated flavor gives these sugar cookies a bold, autumnal vibe. It also makes them the perfect fall cookie: crisp on the outside and soft in the center, with warm baking spices throughout. Browning the butter lends the cookies an extra layer of nutty flavor, while tossing them in sugar gives them added crunch and sparkle. As a bonus, the apple butter helps keep the cookies soft for several days. If your market has other fruit butters—such as pear or pumpkin—you can feel free to use those in place of the apple butter.

01   Melt the butter in a small saucepan over medium heat. Continue cooking, stirring often to prevent the milk solids from burning, until the butter foams and then darkens in color slightly and is very fragrant, 3 to 4 minutes. Immediately pour the butter into a large heatproof bowl and let cool for 20 minutes.

02   As the butter is cooling, preheat the oven to 375°F and set 2 racks at the upper-middle and lower-middle positions. Line 3 baking sheets (or as many as you have) with parchment paper or nonstick baking mats.

03   In a medium bowl, whisk together the flour, cinnamon, ginger, allspice, baking powder, baking soda, and salt.

04   Add 1¾ cups (350 grams) of the granulated sugar to the bowl with the melted butter and whisk to combine. Add the apple butter, egg, and vanilla extract and whisk until smooth. Add the flour mixture and stir with a rubber spatula just until a soft dough forms with no pockets of dry flour.

05   Place the remaining ½ cup (100 grams) granulated sugar in a shallow, wide bowl. Using a medium 1¾-inch (#40) cookie scoop or 2 tablespoons, portion out the dough and roll into balls. Roll the balls in the sugar and then place at least 3 inches apart on the prepared baking sheets (10 per sheet).

06   Bake 2 sheets at the same time, swapping the top sheet to the bottom rack and bottom sheet to the top midway through baking, until the cookies are puffy and cracked, 11 to 14 minutes, then bake the remaining sheet on either rack. (If reusing one of the baking sheets, allow it to cool for 15 minutes before baking another batch on it.) Immediately bang the baking sheets on the countertop several times to deflate the cookies slightly as they come out of the oven and let cool completely on the baking sheets.

2 sticks (16 tablespoons/226 grams) unsalted butter

3¼ cups spooned and leveled all-purpose flour (416 grams)

1 tablespoon ground cinnamon

1 teaspoon ground ginger

¼ teaspoon ground allspice

½ teaspoon baking powder

½ teaspoon baking soda

½ teaspoon kosher salt

2¼ cups (450 grams) granulated sugar, divided

½ cup (130 grams) apple butter (see Note)

1 large egg

1 tablespoon vanilla extract

Note
Apple butter is a concentrated, cooked-down version of applesauce that has an intense apple flavor with notes of caramel. It can be found near the jams or applesauce in well-stocked grocery stores or is easily ordered online.

Make Ahead
If wrapped tightly in plastic, the dough can be stored in the refrigerator for several days before baking. If too firm to scoop, let sit at room temperature for 15 minutes and try again.

Storage
The cookies will keep in an airtight container for up to 1 week.

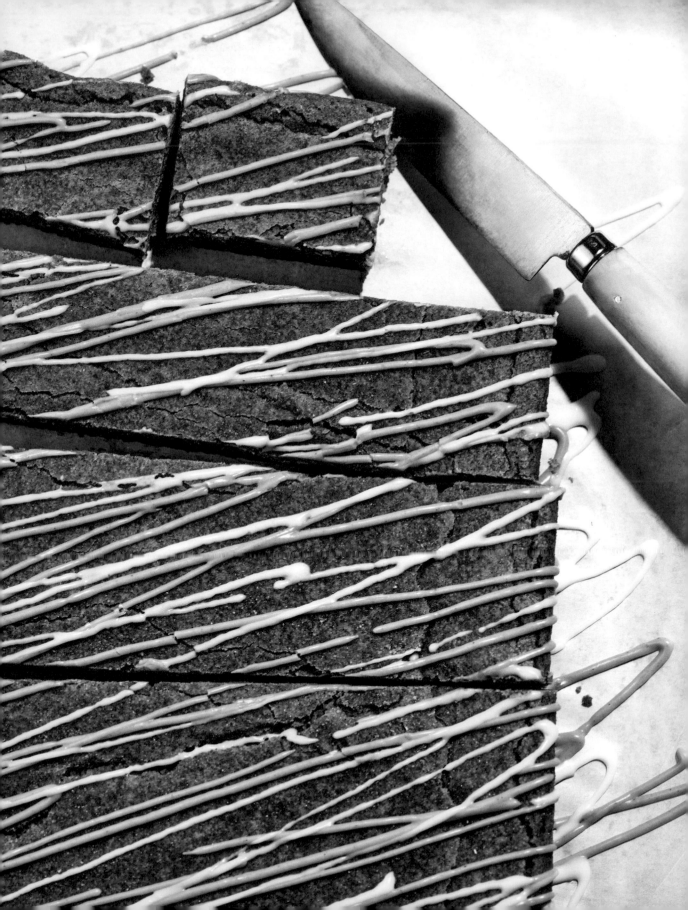

Cinnamon Sugar
Speculoos Squares

Speculoos are gingerbread-like spice cookies popular throughout Europe. They're especially good with coffee, but *even better* when ground into a thick, spreadable paste called "cookie butter." The texture is similar to peanut butter, yet the flavor is sweet with a pleasant warm spice, perfect for spreading on toast or English muffins. This recipe uses it to create chewy, blondie-like bars that get topped with crunchy cinnamon sugar and a warm spiced glaze.

01 Make the Speculoos Squares: Position a rack in the middle of the oven and preheat to 325°F. Grease a 9 × 13-inch metal baking pan with the nonstick pan spray. Line with parchment paper, leaving some overhang on the long sides so it's easy to lift out after baking. Lightly coat the paper with pan spray.

02 Place the cookie butter and butter in a large, microwave-safe bowl and microwave in 30-second increments, stirring between each, until completely melted, 60 to 90 seconds total. Add the brown sugar and whisk until smooth. Add the eggs and vanilla extract and whisk until smooth and ribbony. Add the flour, baking powder, baking soda, salt, and ¼ teaspoon of the cinnamon. Stir with a rubber spatula just until a soft dough forms with no pockets of dry flour.

03 Transfer the dough to the prepared baking pan and press into an even layer using clean hands coated with pan spray. Combine the granulated sugar and remaining ¼ teaspoon cinnamon in a small bowl and sprinkle over the top. Lightly press the sugar into the dough with your hands.

04 Bake until the top is lightly browned and the edges are set and a toothpick inserted into the center comes out clean, 30 to 35 minutes. Let cool at room temperature for at least 2 hours.

05 As the bars cool, make the glaze: In a medium bowl, whisk together the confectioners' sugar and milk until smooth. Transfer half the glaze (about 1½ tablespoons) to a second medium bowl and add the cookie butter and cinnamon. Whisk until completely smooth, adding additional milk to thin it as needed. Both glazes should be thick yet pourable. If either of them is too thick, add additional milk; if too thin, add additional confectioners' sugar.

06 Drizzle the top of the bars with the glazes and let set for 20 minutes, then slice into 24 pieces (6 long rows by 4 short rows).

Speculoos Squares

Nonstick pan spray

½ cup (150 grams) speculoos cookie butter (see Note)

2 sticks (16 tablespoons/226 grams) unsalted butter, cut into ½-inch cubes

2 cups (400 grams) packed light brown sugar

2 large eggs, room temperature

1 tablespoon vanilla extract

2½ cups spooned and leveled all-purpose flour (320 grams)

½ teaspoon baking powder

¼ teaspoon baking soda

¾ teaspoon kosher salt

½ teaspoon ground cinnamon, divided

1 tablespoon granulated sugar

Glaze

¾ cup (75 grams) confectioners' sugar, plus more as needed

1 tablespoon plus 1 teaspoon (20 ml) milk, plus more as needed

1 tablespoon speculoos cookie butter

¼ teaspoon ground cinnamon

Note
The cookie butter can be found next to the nut butters in well-stocked grocery stores, including Trader Joe's.

Storage
The bars will keep in an airtight container at room temperature for up to 1 week.

Pumpkin Spice Sandwich Cookies with Brown Butter–Cream Cheese Frosting

Pumpkin Spice Cookies

1 stick (8 tablespoons/113 grams) unsalted butter

1⅔ cups spooned and leveled all-purpose flour (213 grams)

2 tablespoons (15 grams) pumpkin pie spice (see Note)

½ teaspoon kosher salt

¾ teaspoon baking powder

¾ teaspoon baking soda

¾ cup (150 grams) packed light brown sugar

1 cup (200 grams) granulated sugar, divided

½ cup (120 grams) canned pumpkin puree (not pumpkin pie filling)

1 tablespoon vanilla extract

Brown Butter–Cream Cheese Frosting

4 ounces (½ block/113 grams) cold cream cheese, cut into large cubes

½ stick (4 tablespoons/57 grams) unsalted butter

1 teaspoon vanilla extract

Pinch of kosher salt

2 cups (200 grams) confectioners' sugar

Note

Pumpkin pie spice can be found in the spice section of most well-stocked grocery stores. If unavailable, you can make your own by combining 4 teaspoons ground cinnamon, 2½ teaspoons ground ginger, ½ teaspoon ground allspice, ½ teaspoon ground cloves, and ½ teaspoon ground nutmeg. This will give you just enough spice mixture to make this recipe.

Make Ahead

The pumpkin cookies can be baked several days before filling with the cream cheese frosting and kept in an airtight container at room temperature.

Storage

The assembled cookies will keep in an airtight container in a single layer in the fridge for up to 1 week.

Makes 9 sandwich cookies

Pumpkin and cream cheese are a classic flavor combination, and this recipe takes full advantage of it. Chewy pumpkin cookies are sandwiched with a brown butter–cream cheese frosting, creating a cookie that tastes like pumpkin cheesecake.

01   Make the Pumpkin Spice Cookies: Preheat the oven to 375°F and set 2 racks at the upper-middle and lower-middle positions. Line 2 baking sheets with parchment paper or nonstick baking mats.

02   Melt the butter in a small saucepan over medium heat, stirring often until the butter foams and then darkens in color slightly and is very fragrant, 3 to 4 minutes. Immediately pour the butter into a large heatproof bowl and let cool for 10 minutes.

03   Whisk together the flour, pumpkin pie spice, salt, baking powder, and baking soda in a medium bowl.

04   Add the brown sugar, ½ cup (100 grams) of the granulated sugar, the pumpkin puree, and vanilla extract to the bowl with the melted butter and whisk until smooth. Add the flour mixture and stir just until a soft dough forms with no pockets of dry flour.

05   Place the remaining ½ cup (100 grams) granulated sugar in a shallow, wide bowl. Using a medium 1¾-inch (#40) cookie scoop or 2 tablespoons, portion out the dough and roll into balls. Roll the balls in the sugar and place at least 3 inches apart on the prepared baking sheets (9 per sheet).

06   Bake both sheets at the same time, swapping them midway, until the cookies are puffy and cracked, 13 to 15 minutes. Immediately bang the baking sheets on the countertop several times to deflate the cookies and let cool completely on the baking sheets.

07   Make the frosting: Place the cream cheese cubes in a large heatproof bowl. Melt the butter in a small saucepan over medium heat. Continue cooking, stirring often, until the butter foams and then darkens in color slightly and is very fragrant, 3 to 4 minutes. Immediately pour the butter over the cream cheese cubes and let sit for 10 minutes.

08   Add the vanilla extract and salt to the butter mixture and stir with a rubber spatula until the cream cheese is softened. Add the confectioners' sugar ½ cup (50 grams) at a time, stirring between each addition, until the mixture is completely smooth.

09   Dollop or pipe about 3 tablespoons of the filling onto the undersides of half the cookies. Sandwich with the remaining cookies and chill in the refrigerator for 30 minutes to set the filling.

Spiced Maple Cookies

Makes 24 cookies

Maple sugar gives these cookies a warm, caramel-like flavor and perfumes your home with the sweet scent of Sunday breakfast as they are baking. The addition of cinnamon and ginger highlight the maple's complex flavor and makes these cookies the perfect thing to bake on a cold fall day. The cookies come out of the oven feeling very soft, then firm up after a few minutes of cooling, so don't be tempted to overbake them. As soon as you see cracks forming on the tops, they are done.

01 Preheat the oven to 375°F and set 2 racks at the upper-middle and lower-middle positions. Line 2 baking sheets with parchment paper or nonstick baking mats.

02 In a medium bowl, whisk together the flour, cinnamon, ginger, baking powder, baking soda, and salt.

03 In a large bowl, whisk together the melted butter, brown sugar, and maple sugar until smooth and glossy. Add the vanilla extract, egg, and egg yolk, and whisk until smooth. Add the flour mixture and stir with a rubber spatula just until a soft dough forms with no pockets of dry flour.

04 Using a medium 1¾-inch (#40) cookie scoop or 2 tablespoons, portion out the dough and roll into balls. Place at least 3 inches apart on the prepared baking sheets (12 per sheet).

05 Bake both sheets at the same time, swapping the top sheet to the bottom rack and bottom sheet to the top midway through baking, until the cookies are slightly puffy and starting to crack, 9 to 12 minutes. (It's best to err on the side of underbaking these cookies.) Let cool completely on the baking sheets.

2¾ cups spooned and leveled all-purpose flour (352 grams)

2 teaspoons ground cinnamon

1 teaspoon ground ginger

½ teaspoon baking powder

½ teaspoon baking soda

1 teaspoon kosher salt

2 sticks (16 tablespoons/226 grams) unsalted butter, melted and cooled slightly

1 cup (200 grams) packed light brown sugar

¾ cup (150 grams) maple sugar (see Note)

1 tablespoon vanilla extract

1 large egg

1 large egg yolk

Note
Maple sugar can be found in the baking or organic sections of specialty grocery stores or easily ordered online. My favorite brand to bake with is from Coombs Family Farms; one 6-ounce bag is just enough to make this recipe.

Make Ahead
If wrapped tightly in plastic, the dough can be stored in the refrigerator for several days before baking. If too firm to scoop, let sit at room temperature for 15 minutes and try again.

Storage
The cookies will keep in an airtight container for up to 1 week.

Chewy Apple Cider Sugar Cookies

Ⓧ

Makes 30 cookies

Few treats can match a warm apple cider doughnut—but these cookies come close. They're made with cider that is slowly simmered until it reduces and its flavors concentrate, giving them an incredibly bold apple flavor.

01 In a small saucepan over medium heat, melt the butter. Continue cooking, stirring often to prevent the milk solids from burning, until the butter foams and then darkens in color slightly and is very fragrant, 4 to 6 minutes. Immediately pour the butter and any browned bits into a large heatproof bowl. Do not wash the saucepan.

02 Add the apple cider to the saucepan and bring to a simmer over high heat. (Be careful; the cider will sizzle when you pour it in the pan.) Reduce the heat to medium to maintain a simmer and cook, stirring occasionally, until reduced to ⅓ cup (79 ml), 18 to 22 minutes. (The easiest way to test if the reduction is ready is to pour it into a heatproof measuring glass.) Pour the reduced cider into the bowl with the butter and let the mixture cool for 5 minutes.

03 While the cider is cooling, whisk together the flour, baking powder, baking soda, ginger, allspice, and salt in a medium bowl. Preheat the oven to 350°F and set 2 racks at the upper-middle and lower-middle positions. Line 3 baking sheets (or as many as you have) with parchment paper or nonstick baking mats.

2 sticks (16 tablespoons/226 grams) unsalted butter

2 cups (473 ml) apple cider or apple juice (see Note)

3½ cups spooned and leveled all-purpose flour (448 grams)

1 teaspoon baking powder

1 teaspoon baking soda

1 teaspoon ground ginger

½ teaspoon ground allspice

½ teaspoon kosher salt

1 cup (200 grams) packed light brown sugar

1½ cups (300 grams) granulated sugar, divided

2 large eggs, room temperature

1 tablespoon vanilla extract

2 tablespoons (15 grams) ground cinnamon

04 Add the brown sugar and 1 cup (200 grams) of the granulated sugar to the butter mixture and whisk until smooth and glossy. Add the eggs and vanilla extract and whisk until smooth. Add the flour mixture and mix with a rubber spatula just until a soft dough forms with no pockets of dry flour.

Note

Both apple cider and apple juice can be used in this recipe. I prefer using apple cider and find that it gives the cookies a stronger apple flavor, but juice works just fine if cider is unavailable.

05 In a shallow medium bowl, combine the remaining ½ cup (100 grams) granulated sugar with the cinnamon. Using a medium 1¾-inch (#40) cookie scoop or 2 tablespoons, portion out the dough and roll into balls. Roll the balls in the cinnamon sugar and place at least 3 inches apart on the prepared baking sheets (10 per sheet).

Make Ahead

If wrapped tightly in plastic, the dough can be stored in the refrigerator for several days before baking. If too firm to scoop, let sit at room temperature for 15 minutes and try again.

06 Bake 2 sheets at the same time, swapping the top sheet to the bottom rack and bottom sheet to the top midway through baking, until the cookies crack and are very fragrant, 12 to 15 minutes, then bake the last sheet on either rack. (If reusing one of the baking sheets, allow it to cool for 15 minutes before baking another batch on it.) Let the cookies cool completely on the baking sheets.

Storage

The cookies will keep in an airtight container for up to 1 week.

Spiced Peanut Butter–Coconut Squares

Makes 16 bars

No-bake peanut butter squares are a classic homemade dessert. This version kicks it up a notch with hints of coconut and warm spices. Ginger, cayenne, cinnamon, and a touch of toasted sesame oil come together to create an alluring combination of flavors that pairs perfectly with creamy peanut butter and rich dark chocolate. They're spicy, cold, and creamy. Make these in advance and stash them in the fridge or freezer—and make sure to serve them chilled so the filling stays nice and firm.

01 Make the base: Grease an 8 × 8-inch square baking pan with the nonstick pan spray. Line with parchment paper, leaving some overhang on all sides so it's easy to lift the bars out of the pan after they set. Lightly coat the paper with pan spray.

02 Whisk together the melted butter, peanut butter, toasted sesame oil, vanilla extract, cinnamon, ginger, cayenne, and salt in a large bowl until smooth. Add the confectioners' sugar and graham cracker crumbs and stir with a rubber spatula until the sugar is completely dissolved and the mixture is very thick. (It should be the texture of Play-Doh.) Transfer the mixture to the prepared baking pan and press into an even layer using clean hands.

03 Make the Coconut Ganache: Add the chocolate, heavy cream, coconut oil, and vanilla extract to a medium microwave-safe bowl. Microwave in 10-second increments, stirring between each, until the chocolate is completely melted, 60 to 90 seconds total. Stir the mixture until completely smooth and pour over the peanut butter base. Spread into an even layer using an offset spatula if needed and refrigerate for at least 6 hours.

04 When ready to serve, take the bars out of the fridge and sprinkle with the flaky sea salt (if using). Lift the bars out of the pan using the parchment paper and transfer to a cutting board. Run a large chef's knife under hot water, dry with a paper towel, and slice into a 4 × 4 grid to make 16 pieces. Serve chilled.

Base

Nonstick pan spray

1 stick (8 tablespoons/113 grams) unsalted butter, melted and cooled slightly

1 cup (240 grams) creamy peanut butter, such as Jif or Skippy

1 tablespoon toasted sesame oil

2 teaspoons vanilla extract

1½ teaspoons ground cinnamon

1½ teaspoons ground ginger

¼ teaspoon cayenne

½ teaspoon kosher salt

2 cups (200 grams) confectioners' sugar

1 cup (112 grams) graham cracker crumbs (from 1 sleeve/9 full crackers)

Coconut Ganache

8 ounces (227 grams) semisweet or bittersweet chocolate, roughly chopped (about 1⅓ cups)

½ cup (120 ml) heavy cream

½ cup (110 grams) virgin coconut oil (see Note)

2 teaspoons vanilla extract

Flaky sea salt (optional)

Note

Virgin coconut oil (also called unrefined coconut oil) is made from fresh coconuts and has a strong coconutty flavor and aroma. If all you have on hand is refined coconut oil, you can use that, although the coconut flavor will be more mild.

Storage

The bars will keep in an airtight container in the fridge in a single layer for up to 1 week.

Smoky

Smoked Butter & Chocolate Chunk Cookies

The sweet, fruity flavor of charred wood has a distinct quality that's alluring and complex. It's the secret ingredient that makes barbecued meats so delicious and what gives Scotch whiskey its signature bite. I'm a firm believer that just about anything tastes better when smoked—chocolate chunk cookies being no exception.

¾ cup (40 grams) fine applewood smoking chips (see Note)

2 sticks (16 tablespoons/226 grams) unsalted butter, cut into ½-inch cubes

3¼ cups spooned and leveled all-purpose flour (416 grams)

1 teaspoon baking powder

1 teaspoon baking soda

1 teaspoon kosher salt

1⅓ cups (267 grams) packed light brown sugar

⅔ cup (134 grams) granulated sugar, divided

2 large eggs

1 tablespoon vanilla extract

8 ounces (227 grams) semisweet or bittersweet chocolate, finely chopped (about 1⅓ cups)

Note
Fine smoking chips can be found in the grilling section of specialty grocery and hardware stores or can be easily ordered online.

Make Ahead
The butter can be smoked and stored in an airtight container in the fridge for up to 1 week. When ready to use, heat in the microwave in 10-second bursts until fully melted. If wrapped tightly in plastic, the dough can be stored in the refrigerator for several days before baking. If too firm to scoop, let sit at room temperature for 15 minutes and try again.

Storage
The cookies will keep in an airtight container for up to 1 week.

01 Line the bottom and sides of a large, lidded, heavy-bottomed pot with foil and place the applewood chips in the bottom. Place the butter in a medium heatproof metal bowl that can easily fit into the pot without touching the sides. Scrunch up a sheet of foil to create a ring that's large enough to prop up the bowl so it's not touching the bottom of the pot and place the foil ring on the wood chips. Nestle the bowl in the center of the ring, transfer the pot to the stovetop, and heat over high heat. As soon as you see smoke starting to rise, place the lid on. Continue cooking for 5 minutes, turn the heat off, and let sit for 20 minutes. Do not remove the lid.

02 Carefully remove the lid to let the smoke out; leave the pot uncovered until the bowl of butter is cool enough to touch, 20 to 25 minutes.

03 Meanwhile, preheat the oven to 350°F and set 2 racks at the upper-middle and lower-middle positions. Line 3 baking sheets (or as many as you have) with parchment paper or nonstick baking mats. In a medium bowl, whisk together the flour, baking powder, baking soda, and salt.

04 Skim any foam off the top of the butter, discard it, and transfer the melted smoked butter to a large bowl. Add the brown sugar and ⅓ cup (67 grams) of the granulated sugar and whisk to combine. Add the eggs and vanilla extract and whisk until ribbony and smooth, 1 minute. Add the flour mixture and stir just until a soft dough forms with no pockets of dry flour. Mix in the chopped chocolate.

05 Place the remaining ⅓ cup (67 grams) granulated sugar in a shallow, wide bowl. Using a medium 1¾-inch (#40) cookie scoop or 2 tablespoons, portion out the dough and roll into balls. Roll each ball in the sugar and place at least 3 inches apart on the prepared baking sheets (8 to 10 per sheet).

06 Bake 2 sheets at the same time, swapping them midway, until the tops of the cookies are lightly browned, 14 to 16 minutes, then bake the last sheet on either rack. (If reusing one of the baking sheets, allow it to cool for 15 minutes before baking another batch on it.) Let the cookies cool slightly on the baking sheets, then transfer to a wire rack to cool completely.

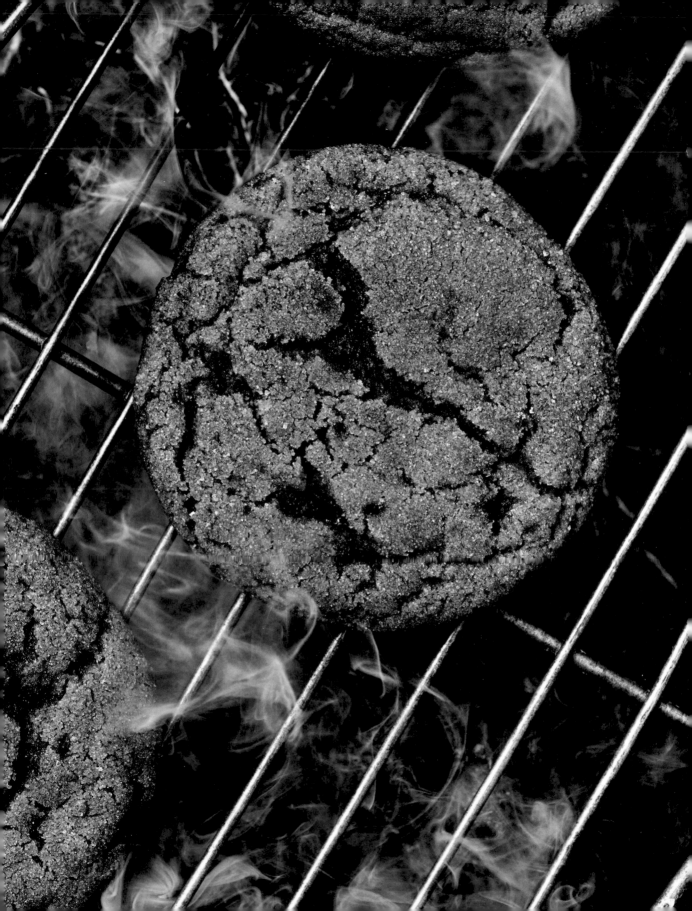

Smoky Muscovado
Sugar Cookies

2¾ **cups** spooned and leveled all-purpose flour
(352 grams)

½ **teaspoon** baking powder

½ **teaspoon** baking soda

1 **teaspoon** kosher salt

2 **sticks (16 tablespoons/226 grams)** unsalted butter,
melted and cooled slightly

1¼ **cups (250 grams)** packed dark muscovado sugar
(see Note)

1 **cup (200 grams)** granulated sugar, divided

1 **tablespoon** vanilla extract

¼ **teaspoon** liquid smoke (optional; **see Note**)

1 **large egg**

2 **tablespoons (30 ml)** unsulphured molasses

Note
Muscovado sugar is an unrefined cane sugar that can
be found in specialty grocery stores or easily ordered
online. Liquid smoke can be found in the spice or hot
sauce section of most well-stocked grocery stores. If
unavailable, the muscovado sugar alone will still provide
a subtle smokiness.

Make Ahead
If wrapped tightly in plastic, the dough can be stored
in the refrigerator for several days before baking. If too
firm to scoop, let sit at room temperature for 15 minutes
and try again.

Storage
The cookies will keep in an airtight container for up
to 1 week.

Makes 24 cookies

These dark sugar cookies are made with one
of my favorite ingredients: muscovado sugar. It
gives the cookies a bold, caramel-like flavor that
verges on smoky. To highlight the intensity of
the muscovado sugar, a touch of liquid smoke is
added to amplify its uniqueness. The resulting
cookies are compelling, rich, and a tad less
sweet compared to most sugar cookies. Don't be
alarmed if the muscovado sugar is not completely
incorporated into the batter. These clumps are to
be expected, and they transform into tiny bursts of
caramel while baking.

01 Preheat the oven to 375°F and set 2 racks at the
upper-middle and lower-middle positions. Line
2 baking sheets with parchment paper or nonstick
baking mats.

02 In a medium bowl, combine the flour, baking powder,
baking soda, and salt.

03 In a large bowl, whisk together the melted butter,
muscovado sugar, and ½ cup (100 grams) of the
granulated sugar. Add the vanilla extract, liquid
smoke (if using), egg, and molasses, and whisk until
smooth. Add the flour mixture and stir with a rubber
spatula until a soft dough forms and no pockets of
dry flour remain. Let the dough sit for 10 minutes to
firm up. (The dough will be very soft when first mixed
but will thicken up after a few minutes.)

04 Place the remaining ½ cup (100 grams) granulated
sugar in a shallow, wide bowl. Using a medium
1¾-inch (#40) cookie scoop or 2 tablespoons,
portion out the dough and roll into balls. Roll the
balls in the sugar and then place at least 3 inches
apart on the prepared baking sheets (12 per sheet).

05 Bake both sheets at the same time, swapping the
top sheet to the bottom rack and bottom sheet to
the top midway through baking, until the tops of
the cookies are starting to crack, 11 to 13 minutes.
Immediately bang the baking sheets on the
countertop to deflate the cookies a bit. Let them cool
slightly on the baking sheets, then transfer to a wire
rack to cool completely.

Burnt S'mores Skillet Cookie

Nonstick pan spray

2¼ cups (250 grams) mini marshmallows, divided

1½ sticks (12 tablespoons/170 grams) unsalted butter

2 cups spooned and leveled all-purpose flour (256 grams)

½ teaspoon baking soda

1 teaspoon kosher salt

1 cup (200 grams) packed light brown sugar

¼ cup (50 grams) granulated sugar

1 large egg

1 tablespoon vanilla extract

8 ounces (227 grams) semisweet or bittersweet chocolate, roughly chopped (about 1⅓ cups), divided

4 full graham cracker sheets (about 60 grams), broken into large, irregular pieces (about 1 ¼ cups), divided

Make Ahead
The cookie dough can be made several days in advance and stored in the fridge, tightly covered with plastic wrap. When ready to bake, press the dough into the bottom of a skillet coated with pan spray, then top with the marshmallows and bake as instructed.

Storage
Remove any leftover cookie from the skillet and transfer to an airtight container. Store at room temperature for up to 1 week.

Makes one 10-inch skillet cookie

While I typically discourage adding burnt ingredients to your cookie dough, that's precisely what makes this recipe so good. Crushed graham crackers, chopped chocolate, and a generous amount of charred marshmallows lend it that signature combination of flavors that makes it taste like it came straight from the campfire. The trick is to actually burn the marshmallows under a broiler, then add them to the dough so they melt into it.

01 Arrange a rack in the middle of the oven and preheat the broiler to high.

02 Line a baking sheet with aluminum foil and coat with nonstick pan spray. Scatter 2 cups (200 grams) of marshmallows in the center of the pan. Place the pan under the broiler until the marshmallows are charred on the top, rotating the pan halfway through so they char evenly, 2 to 2½ minutes total. Remove from the oven and turn off the broiler. Set the oven to bake and preheat to 350°F.

03 In a 10-inch cast-iron skillet over medium-high heat, melt the butter, swirling it so it coats the sides of the pan. Pour the butter into a large heatproof bowl and let cool for 10 minutes. Do not wash the skillet.

04 As the butter is cooling, whisk together the flour, baking soda, and salt in a medium bowl.

05 Add both sugars to the bowl with the melted butter and whisk until smooth. Add the egg and vanilla extract and whisk until smooth. Add the flour mixture and stir with a rubber spatula until no pockets of dry flour remain and a soft dough forms.

06 Scrape the marshmallows off the sheet pan using a rubber spatula and transfer them to the bowl of cookie dough. Stir them into the dough until they practically melt into it and form streaks of gooey marshmallow. (It's okay if there are some large clumps that stick together.) Stir in about 1 cup (170 grams) of the chopped chocolate and 1 cup (about 48 grams) of the graham crackers pieces.

07 Transfer the dough to the cooled skillet and spread into an even layer using an offset spatula. Top with the remaining ¼ cup (about 12 grams) graham crackers, ⅓ cup (56 grams) chocolate, and ¼ cup (50 grams) marshmallows, pressing them into the dough slightly so they stick. Bake until browned around the edges but still slightly gooey in the center, 25 to 28 minutes. (Do not overbake.) Transfer the skillet to a wire rack and cool for 10 minutes before serving. If you prefer your skillet cookies on the softer side, eat within 1 hour of baking.

Ancho & Chocolate Slice-and-Bakes

1½ **cups** spooned and leveled all-purpose flour (192 grams)

2 **tablespoons (14 grams)** natural, unsweetened cocoa powder

1 **teaspoon** ancho chile powder, or less depending on preference (see Note)

½ **teaspoon** ground cinnamon

¼ **teaspoon** kosher salt

10 **tablespoons (142 grams)** unsalted butter, softened

½ **cup (50 grams)** confectioners' sugar

1 **large** egg yolk

1 **tablespoon** vanilla extract

3 **ounces (85 grams)** semisweet chocolate, finely chopped (about ½ cup)

¼ **cup (50 grams)** turbinado sugar

1 **large** egg

Note

Pure ancho chile powder (not to be confused with chili powder, which is a combination of several different spices) is made solely from ground ancho chiles and can be found in the spice section of well-stocked grocery stores or easily ordered online.

Make Ahead

The dough log can be stored in the fridge, tightly wrapped in plastic, for several days before baking. If it's too cold to slice easily, let sit out at room temperature for 15 minutes and try again.

Storage

The cookies will keep in an airtight container for up to 1 week.

Makes 16 cookies

These tender, shortbread-like cookies are spiced with cinnamon and ground ancho chile, giving them a warm, smoky flavor that lingers long after you bite into them. Rolling them in turbinado sugar gives them an added layer of crunch, while sweet pockets of molten dark chocolate help tame their heat. If you're sensitive to spice, try eating them with a cold glass of milk or crumble them on top of a scoop of vanilla ice cream—or use just half the amount of spice called for. Just note that the dough requires two hours of chilling before baking, so plan accordingly.

01 In a large bowl, whisk together the flour, cocoa powder, chile powder, cinnamon, and salt.

02 In the bowl of a stand mixer fitted with the paddle attachment, combine the butter, confectioners' sugar, egg yolk, and vanilla extract. Beat on medium speed, scraping down the sides and bottom of the bowl halfway through, until smooth, 2 to 3 minutes. (Alternatively, use a hand mixer and large bowl.) Turn the mixer off and add the flour mixture. Mix on low speed just until a crumbly dough forms, about 1 minute. Stir in the chopped chocolate with a rubber spatula.

03 Transfer the dough to a large sheet of plastic wrap. Form into a 1½-inch-diameter log and gently wrap in the plastic, twisting the ends tightly to help form a cylinder shape. Chill in the fridge for 2 hours, rotating it every so often to help keep its round shape.

04 Place the turbinado sugar in a large, shallow bowl or plate. Crack the egg into a small bowl and stir with a fork until no streaks of yolk remain.

05 Position a rack in the middle of the oven and preheat to 350°F. Line a baking sheet with parchment paper or a nonstick baking mat.

06 Unwrap the chilled dough and use a pastry brush to lightly coat the outside with the beaten egg. Roll the log in the turbinado sugar, firmly pressing the sugar into the sides of the log to help it stick. Use a sharp, thin knife to slice the log into ½-inch-thick slices (about 16 slices). Arrange the slices on the prepared baking sheet, spacing about 2 inches apart.

07 Bake until the tops of the cookies look matte and are very fragrant, 16 to 18 minutes. Let cool completely on the baking sheet. The cookies will feel very soft when hot but will firm up once cooled.

Blackstrap Molasses & Buckwheat Chocolate Chunk Cookies

Makes 16 large cookies

Buckwheat flour has a bold earthiness that is unlike anything else. It's slightly bitter, with a nutty flavor that pairs perfectly with chocolate. Here, the flavor is amped up with the intensity of blackstrap molasses—a rich, dark, almost salty variety of molasses that has a subtle smoky taste. The resulting cookies are anything but bland, with a caramel-like quality that is big and unreserved.

2½ **cups** spooned and leveled all-purpose flour (320 grams)

½ **cup** spooned and leveled buckwheat flour (73 grams; see Note)

2 **teaspoons** baking soda

1 **teaspoon** kosher salt

1½ **sticks (12 tablespoons/170 grams)** unsalted butter, softened

1¼ **cups (250 grams)** packed light brown sugar

1 **large** egg

⅓ **cup (79 ml)** blackstrap molasses (see Note)

1 **tablespoon** vanilla extract

6 **ounces (170 grams)** semisweet or bittersweet chocolate, finely chopped (about 1 cup)

Flaky sea salt, for sprinkling (optional)

Note
Buckwheat flour can be found in the baking section of most well-stocked grocery stores. My favorite brand is Bob's Red Mill. Blackstrap molasses can be found next to conventional molasses in almost all grocery stores. If unavailable, look for molasses that is labeled "robust" and feel free to use that instead.

Make Ahead
If wrapped tightly in plastic, the dough can be stored in the refrigerator for several days before baking. If too firm to scoop, let sit at room temperature for 15 minutes and try again.

Storage
The cookies will keep in an airtight container for up to 1 week.

01 Preheat the oven to 350°F and set 2 racks at the upper-middle and lower-middle positions. Line 2 baking sheets with parchment paper or nonstick baking mats.

02 In a medium bowl, whisk together both flours, the baking soda, and salt.

03 In the bowl of a stand mixer fitted with the paddle attachment, combine the butter and brown sugar. Beat on medium speed, scraping down the sides and bottom of the bowl halfway through, until smooth and fluffy, 2 to 3 minutes. (Alternatively, use a hand mixer and large bowl.) Turn the mixer off and add the egg, molasses, and vanilla extract. Mix on medium speed until very fluffy and lightened in color slightly, 2 to 3 minutes. With the mixer running on low speed, gradually add the flour mixture, beating until just combined. Stir in the chopped chocolate with a rubber spatula.

04 Using a large 2⅓-inch (#16) cookie scoop or ¼-cup measure, portion out the dough and roll into large balls. Place at least 3 inches apart on the prepared baking sheets (8 per sheet) and sprinkle with flaky sea salt (if using).

05 Bake both sheets at the same time, swapping the top sheet to the bottom rack and bottom sheet to the top midway through baking, until the tops of the cookies crack and puff slightly, 13 to 15 minutes. Immediately bang the baking sheets on the countertop as they come out of the oven to deflate the cookies. Let cool slightly on the baking sheets, then transfer to a wire rack to cool completely.

Fudgy Smoked Paprika Cookies

Makes 18 large cookies

Smoked paprika gives these cookies a bold smokiness that hits your nose the moment you bite into them. They aren't spicy, only flavorful, with an alluring smoky aroma that highlights the chocolate. They have a rich, brownie-like texture with pockets of molten dark chocolate throughout. Try these on their own or sandwich two together with a scoop of vanilla or cinnamon-swirl ice cream for a decadent, sweet-and-smoky treat.

01   Preheat the oven to 375°F and set 2 racks at the upper-middle and lower-middle positions. Line 3 baking sheets (or as many as you have) with parchment paper or nonstick baking mats.

02   In a medium bowl, whisk together the flour, cocoa powder, baking powder, baking soda, smoked paprika, and salt.

03   In a large bowl, whisk together the melted butter, brown sugar, and granulated sugar until combined. Add the eggs and vanilla extract and whisk until smooth and glossy. Add the flour mixture and stir with a rubber spatula until a soft dough forms. Stir in the chopped chocolate with a rubber spatula. (If the dough is too thick to easily mix in the chocolate, feel free to mix using clean hands.)

04   Using a large 2⅓-inch (#16) cookie scoop or ¼-cup measure, portion out the dough and roll into large balls. (The dough will be sticky, so don't fret if the balls are not perfectly shaped.) Place the balls at least 3 inches apart on the prepared baking sheets (6 per sheet).

05   Bake 2 sheets at the same time, swapping the top sheet to the bottom rack and bottom sheet to the top midway through baking, until the tops of the cookies are cracked and matte, 12 to 14 minutes, then bake the last sheet on either rack. (If reusing one of the baking sheets, allow it to cool for 15 minutes before baking another batch on it.) Immediately smack the baking sheets on the countertop as they come out of the oven to deflate the cookies slightly. Let the cookies cool completely on the baking sheets.

3 cups spooned and leveled all-purpose flour (384 grams)

½ cup (45 grams) natural, unsweetened cocoa powder

1 teaspoon baking powder

1 teaspoon baking soda

1 tablespoon smoked paprika (see Note)

½ teaspoon kosher salt

2 sticks (16 tablespoons/226 grams) unsalted butter, melted and cooled slightly

1⅔ cups (334 grams) packed light brown sugar

⅓ cup (67 grams) granulated sugar

2 large eggs

1 tablespoon vanilla extract

8 ounces (227 grams) semisweet or bittersweet chocolate, roughly chopped (about 1⅓ cups)

Note
Smoked paprika can be found in the spice section of most well-stocked grocery stores. Regular paprika will not give the same smoky flavor and should not be used in this recipe.

Make Ahead
If wrapped tightly in plastic, the dough can be stored in the refrigerator for several days before baking. If too firm to scoop, let sit at room temperature for 15 minutes and try again.

Storage
The cookies will keep in an airtight container for up to 1 week.

Maple & Peppered-Bacon Cookies

These cookies are crisp on the outside, chewy in the center, and strike the perfect balance of salty and sweet. The trick to getting their rich bacon flavor is to use not only the cooked bacon but the rendered fat as well. This gives the entire cookie a savory, smoky bacon flavor that works beautifully with the maple syrup and brown sugar.

01 Line a large plate with a paper towel. Add the chopped bacon to a large nonstick skillet and cook over medium heat, stirring often to prevent burning, until the bacon is crispy and dark brown, 11 to 13 minutes. Use a slotted spoon to transfer the bacon to the paper towel to drain. Pour the rendered bacon fat (and any burnt bits stick to the bottom of the pot) into a large heatproof bowl. Carefully wipe out the skillet with a paper towel.

02 Add the butter to the skillet and cook over medium-high heat, stirring often to prevent the milk solids from burning, until the butter foams and then darkens in color slightly and is very fragrant, 2 to 4 minutes. Immediately pour the butter into the bowl with the reserved bacon fat and let cool for 15 minutes.

03 As the butter is cooling, preheat the oven to 375°F and set 2 racks at the upper-middle and lower-middle positions. Line 2 baking sheets with parchment paper or nonstick baking mats. Whisk together the flour, baking powder, baking soda, salt, and pepper in a medium bowl.

04 Add the brown sugar and granulated sugar to the melted butter mixture and whisk until combined. Add the maple syrup, vanilla extract, and egg and whisk until smooth. Add the flour mixture and stir with a rubber spatula just until a soft dough forms with no pockets of flour.

05 Chop the cooked bacon into small, pea-sized pieces and stir into the dough.

06 Using a medium 1¾-inch (#40) cookie scoop or 2 tablespoons, portion out the dough and roll into balls. Place at least 3 inches apart on the prepared baking sheets (12 per sheet).

07 Bake both sheets at the same time, swapping the top sheet to the bottom rack and bottom sheet to the top midway through baking, until the cookies are slightly puffy and starting to crack, 11 to 13 minutes. (It's best to err on the side of underbaking these cookies.) Let cool slightly on the baking sheets, then transfer to a wire rack to cool completely.

7 slices (about 8 ounces/227 grams) thick-cut bacon, cut into 1-inch-wide pieces

1½ sticks (12 tablespoons/170 grams) unsalted butter

2¾ cups spooned and leveled all-purpose flour (352 grams)

½ teaspoon baking powder

½ teaspoon baking soda

½ teaspoon kosher salt

½ teaspoon freshly ground black pepper

1 cup (200 grams) packed light brown sugar

¾ cup (150 grams) granulated sugar

¼ cup (59 ml) maple syrup

1 tablespoon vanilla extract

1 large egg

Make Ahead
If wrapped tightly in plastic, the finished dough can be stored in the refrigerator for several days before baking. If too firm to scoop, let sit at room temperature for 15 minutes and try again.

Storage
The cookies will keep in an airtight container for up to 1 week.

Chipotle Fudge Squares with Crunchy Raw Sugar

Makes 36 fudge squares

These simple fudge squares might look unassuming, but their flavor is anything but. They're a quick, no-bake treat perfect for making in summer, when the last thing you want to do is turn on your oven, thus providing a pop of spice without heating up your kitchen. A combination of cinnamon and chipotle chile powder gives them a fragrant, subtle heat that builds as you eat. They're not necessarily spicy; rather, they are warming and slightly tingly. The chipotle's smoky flavor perfumes the fudge, giving it an added layer that highlights the richness of the chocolate. A showering of crunchy raw sugar on top gives them an added layer of texture that contrasts with the smooth fudge and makes them sparkle.

01 Grease an 8 × 8-inch square baking pan with the nonstick pan spray. Line with parchment paper, leaving some overhang on all sides so it's easy to lift out the fudge after it sets, and coat the paper once more with the pan spray.

02 Fill a medium saucepan halfway with water and bring to a simmer over medium heat, then reduce the heat to low to maintain a very gentle simmer.

03 In a large heatproof bowl slightly larger than the saucepan, combine the chocolate chips, sweetened condensed milk, whole milk, vanilla extract, chile powder, cinnamon, and salt. Stir to evenly coat the chocolate and then place the bowl on top of the saucepan (the bottom of the bowl shouldn't touch the simmering water). Melt the chocolate, stirring often, until the mixture is completely smooth, 5 to 7 minutes (it will be very thick).

04 Pour the fudge into the prepared baking pan and spread into an even layer using an offset spatula or spoon. Immediately sprinkle the top with the raw sugar and dust with additional cinnamon and chipotle chile powder. Let set at room temperature uncovered for 8 hours, until firm, then slice into a 6 x 6 grid to make 36 squares.

Nonstick pan spray

3⅓ **cups (20 ounces/567 grams)** semisweet or bittersweet chocolate chips

1 **14-ounce can (414 ml)** sweetened condensed milk

3 **tablespoons (44 ml)** whole milk

2 **teaspoons** vanilla extract

¼ **teaspoon** chipotle chile powder, plus more for sprinkling (**see Note**)

½ **teaspoon** ground cinnamon, plus more for sprinkling

¼ **teaspoon** kosher salt

2 **teaspoons** raw or turbinado sugar

Note
Pure chipotle chile powder (not to be confused with chili powder, which is a combination of several different spices) is made from dried and ground chipotle chiles. It can be found in the spice section of most well-stocked grocery stores or easily ordered online.

Storage
Cut fudge squares can be stored in an airtight container at room temperature for up to 1 week, or in the freezer for several months. (Just make sure to bring them to room temperature before serving.)

Crunchy Muscovado Meringues

Makes 12 large meringues

These muscovado meringues are the stormy, darkened version of the white cloud–like cookies you know and love (like on page 118). Muscovado sugar is an unrefined cane sugar with an intense caramel flavor, and these cookies are made entirely with it in place of white (granulated) sugar. They're molasses-y, caramel-like, and pleasantly bittersweet. The slightly smoky flavor of the sugar gives the meringues a richer flavor, while an additional sprinkle on top contributes an added layer of crunch. Try crushing them on top of fresh fruit with whipped cream for a quick dessert that hits all the right notes.

01 Preheat the oven to 200°F and set 2 racks at the upper-middle and lower-middle positions. Line 2 baking sheets with parchment paper or nonstick baking mats.

02 In the bowl of a stand mixer fitted with the whisk attachment, combine the egg whites, cream of tartar, salt, and vanilla extract. Mix on medium speed until the cream of tartar is completely dissolved and the eggs are very foamy, 2 to 3 minutes.

03 With the mixer running on medium speed, gradually add ¾ cup (150 grams) of the muscovado sugar 1 tablespoon at a time, waiting until the sugar is completely dissolved before adding the next, 11 to 14 minutes total. You should see no specks of sugar left undissolved in the meringue. Increase the mixer speed to medium-high and whip until the meringue is glossy, very fluffy, and almost tripled in volume, 3 to 4 minutes more. The long, slow whipping makes sure that all the sugar is completely dissolved, so don't rush.

04 Use a large 2⅓-inch (#16) cookie scoop or ¼-cup measure to dollop big mounds of the meringue onto the prepared baking sheets, spacing 1 inch apart (6 per sheet). Sprinkle the tops with the remaining 2 tablespoons (32 grams) muscovado sugar.

05 Transfer the baking sheets to the oven and bake for 3 hours. (Do not open the oven door.) Turn the oven off and let the meringues cool in the oven for an additional 1 hour with the door shut. (Don't be tempted to open the door and check on them. You need the residual heat from the oven to continue cooking the meringues.) Meringues will be slightly soft when taken out of the oven but will crisp up within 10 minutes.

3 large egg whites, room temperature

¾ teaspoon cream of tartar

Pinch of kosher salt

1 teaspoon vanilla extract

¾ cup plus 2 tablespoons (182 grams) muscovado sugar, divided (see Note)

Note

If muscovado sugar is unavailable, you can make these meringues with an equal amount of dark brown sugar instead. The flavor will not be as bold but still delicious.

Storage

The cookies will keep in an airtight container for several days. The centers might become slightly chewy, but they are delicious, nonetheless.

Savory

Cacio e Pepe
Slice-and-Bakes

1¾ **cups** spooned and leveled all-purpose flour
(224 grams)

¾ **cup (about 2 ounces/57 grams)** finely grated
pecorino romano cheese

½ **teaspoon** kosher salt

¾ **teaspoon** garlic powder (optional)

2 **sticks (16 tablespoons/226 grams)** cold unsalted
butter, cut into ½-inch cubes

2 **tablespoons (14 grams)** freshly and coarsely ground
black pepper (see Note)

Note
To quickly grind the black peppercorns, I recommend
using a spice or coffee grinder instead of a pepper mill.
Just make sure to thoroughly wash it afterward so your
coffee isn't spicy.

Make Ahead
The dough logs can be stored in the fridge, tightly
wrapped in plastic, for several days before baking.
If they are too cold to slice easily, let sit out at room
temperature for 15 minutes and try again.

Storage
The cookies will keep in an airtight container for up
to 1 week.

Makes 24 cookies

Cacio e pepe ("cheese and pepper" in Italian)
is a simple Roman pasta dish made with sharp
pecorino romano cheese, black pepper, and
pasta. The simplicity of the dish lets the pepper
shine and shows off its sharp, fruity flavor that
oftentimes gets lost in more complex dishes. This
savory shortbread relies on the same combination
of cheese and pepper to create a savory cocktail
cookie that's much more than the sum of its
parts. Cheesy shortbread dough gets formed into
a log, covered with freshly ground black pepper,
sliced, and baked until golden. These simple little
cookies are wonderful served alongside dips and
cured meats for a perfect pre-dinner snack—or
eaten all by themselves while watching TV.

01 In the bowl of a food processor fitted with the
blade attachment, combine the flour, cheese,
salt, and garlic powder (if using). Process until well
combined, 10 to 15 seconds. Add the diced butter
and process until a smooth, soft dough forms that
pulls away from the sides of the food processor,
35 to 45 seconds. (The dough will have the texture of
a soft sugar cookie dough.)

02 Divide the dough in half and transfer each portion to
a large sheet of plastic wrap. Form each portion into
a 1½-inch-diameter log using your hands and gently
wrap each log in the plastic, twisting the ends tightly
to help form their shape. Chill in the refrigerator for
at least 4 hours and up to overnight.

03 Position a rack in the middle of the oven and preheat
to 350°F. Line a baking sheet with parchment paper
or a nonstick baking mat.

04 Unwrap the dough logs and lightly brush the
outsides with water using a pastry brush. Sprinkle
the outside of each log with the black pepper,
pressing it into the sides to help it stick. Use a thin,
sharp knife to slice each log into ½-inch-thick slices,
rotating it after each slice so it stays round (12 slices
per log). Arrange the slices on the prepared baking
sheet, spacing about 1 inch apart.

05 Bake the cookies until the tops are lightly browned,
16 to 18 minutes. Let them cool completely on the
baking sheet.

Manchego Linzer Cookies with Quince Jam

Makes 24 linzer cookies

Manchego cheese and quince paste are a match made in heaven (a.k.a. Spain). The classic combination is a staple in tapas bars, and these linzer cookies (a type of sandwich cookie from Austria) riff on the magical pairing to create the perfect sweet-savory cookie. Salty manchego butter cookies get sandwiched together with a fruity quince jam made with nothing more than store-bought quince paste and water. It's an impressive cocktail cookie that is perfect served with a glass of Cava or Tempranillo.

2½ **cups** spooned and leveled all-purpose flour (320 grams), plus more for dusting

¾ **cup (about 3 ounces/85 grams)** finely grated manchego cheese

¾ **teaspoon** kosher salt, plus more as needed

½ **teaspoon** paprika, preferably smoked

½ **teaspoon** freshly ground black pepper

2 **sticks (16 tablespoons/226 grams)** cold unsalted butter, cut into ½-inch cubes

3 **large** egg yolks

1 **10-ounce (283 grams)** block quince paste, cut into ½-inch cubes (see Note)

Note
Quince paste (also called membrillo) can be found in the cheese or jam section of most well-stocked grocery stores. If unavailable, guava paste can be used in its place. The flavor will be slightly different but just as delicious.

Make Ahead
The cookies can be baked and then kept at room temperature, stored in an airtight container, for several days before filling with the jam.

Storage
The filled cookies will keep in an airtight container in a single layer for up to 1 week.

(recipe continues)

01   In the bowl of a food processor fitted with the blade attachment, combine the flour, cheese, salt, paprika, and pepper. (If your food processor has a grater attachment, feel free to grate the cheese directly into the bowl before adding the dry ingredients.) Process until well combined and no visible strands of cheese remain, 20 to 25 seconds. Add the diced butter and process until the butter is the size of peas, 20 to 30 seconds. Add the egg yolks and process until a smooth dough forms that pulls away from the sides of the bowl, 35 to 45 seconds.

02   Transfer the dough to a lightly floured work surface and press together into a disc. Wrap in plastic and chill in the fridge for 30 minutes.

03   Line 3 baking sheets (or as many as you have) with parchment paper or nonstick baking mats.

04   Unwrap the dough and transfer to a lightly floured work surface. Dust the top of the dough with flour and roll out to a ⅛-inch-thick sheet. Use a 2½-inch round cookie cutter to stamp out as many circles from the dough as you can, then transfer them to a prepared baking sheet, placing them 1 inch apart. Set the scraps aside. Use a 1-inch round cookie cutter to remove the centers from half of the circles; add the circle cut-outs to the dough scraps. Freeze the cookies on the baking sheet for 15 minutes. While the first batch freezes, lightly flour your work surface and repeat the rolling, cutting out the shapes, and freezing by combining the dough scraps until you have 12 solid circle bases and 12 circle tops with cut-out centers. Discard any remaining dough scraps.

05   Preheat the oven to 350°F and set 2 racks at the upper-middle and lower-middle positions.

06   Leave 1 baking sheet in the freezer and place the 2 baking sheets in the oven, swapping the top sheet to the bottom rack and bottom sheet to the top midway through baking, until the cookies are lightly browned, 15 to 17 minutes. Then bake the remaining baking sheet on either rack. Let cool completely on the baking sheets for at least 45 minutes. (The cookies will be very delicate when warm.) If reusing baking sheets, allow them to cool completely before baking the next batch and leave the unbaked cookies in the freezer.

07   While the cookies are cooling, combine the quince paste, ⅓ cup of water, and a pinch of kosher salt in a small saucepan and cook over medium heat, stirring often, until the paste has completely melted and the mixture is smooth, 6 to 8 minutes.

08   Working quickly, dollop about 2 teaspoons of the jam onto the centers of the cookie bases and spread into an even layer across the entire surface, going all the way to the edges of the cookie. Top with the cut-out circles, using the filling as glue to seal the cookies together. Let the cookies set at least 1 hour before serving.

Everything Bagel Biscotti

Makes 3 dozen biscotti

This recipe crams all the beloved flavors of an everything bagel into crunchy biscotti. They are perfect for serving at breakfast with coffee or as an after-dinner snack. A recipe for homemade everything bagel seasoning is here, but feel free to use your favorite store-bought blend.

4 cups spooned and leveled all-purpose flour (512 grams), plus more for dusting

1½ cups (about 6 ounces/170 grams) finely grated (not shredded) parmesan cheese

2 teaspoons baking powder

½ teaspoon kosher salt

1½ sticks (12 tablespoons/170 grams) cold unsalted butter, cut into ½-inch cubes

1 cup (240 ml) whole milk, plus more for brushing

3 large eggs

¼ cup (48 grams) everything bagel seasoning (recipe follows)

Everything Bagel Seasoning

Makes about ¼ cup (enough for 1 batch of biscotti dough)

1 tablespoon poppy seeds

1 tablespoon black sesame seeds

1 tablespoon white sesame seeds

2 teaspoons dried minced onion

2 teaspoons dried minced garlic

2 teaspoons flaky sea salt

In a small bowl, mix the poppy seeds, black and white sesame seeds, onion, garlic, and salt. The seasoning can be stored in an airtight container at room temperature for several months.

Storage

The biscotti will keep in an airtight container for up to 1 week.

01 Line 2 baking sheets with parchment paper or nonstick baking mats.

02 In a large bowl, whisk together the flour, grated parmesan, baking powder, and salt. Add the butter and use your fingertips to pinch the cubes into the flour mixture, breaking it up until no large clumps remain. The butter should be broken down into pieces that are slightly smaller than peas.

03 Whisk the milk and eggs together in a medium bowl until no streaks of yolk remain. Add to the flour mixture and stir with a rubber spatula until a soft, shaggy dough forms.

04 Transfer the dough to a lightly floured work surface and knead just until the dough comes together. Divide the dough into 2 equal pieces and form each piece into a rough 12-inch-long log. Transfer one log onto each of the prepared baking sheets. Flatten the logs with your hands until they are about 2½ inches wide and ¾ inch tall. Brush the tops and sides of the logs with a thin layer of the milk and sprinkle with the everything bagel seasoning, gently pressing it into the dough so it sticks. Transfer the baking sheets to the fridge and chill the logs for 30 minutes.

05 Preheat the oven to 350°F and set 2 racks at the upper-middle and lower-middle positions.

06 Bake both sheets at the same time, swapping the top sheet to the bottom rack and bottom sheet to the top midway through baking, until the tops of the logs are lightly browned and the logs feel firm when touched, 30 to 35 minutes. Remove the biscotti from the oven and reduce the oven temperature to 300°F. Let the logs cool for 10 minutes.

07 Slice each log diagonally into ½-inch-thick slices on a slight bias using a serrated knife. (If the biscotti start to crumble, lightly brush the tops with warm water and try cutting again.) Transfer the slices, cut side down, back to the baking sheets and bake once more, swapping the top sheet to the bottom rack and bottom sheet to the top midway through baking, until the biscotti are golden brown and crisp, flipping them over halfway through baking, 30 to 35 minutes total. Let cool completely on the baking sheets.

Rosemary–Brown Butter Cookies

These salty brown-butter cookies combine several savory flavors into one bite: spicy black pepper, Parmesan cheese, and fried rosemary. The key to getting that cooked rosemary flavor is to add it to the butter as it browns. As the butter darkens and becomes toasty, the rosemary crisps up, mellows out, and infuses the butter with its herby flavor that perfumes the cookies. Try serving these with slices of apples, quince jam, or hummus. Their subtle cheesy flavor pairs especially well with prosciutto or other cured meats, as well as most sparkling wines.

01 In a small saucepan over medium heat, melt the butter. Once the butter has melted, add the rosemary and continue cooking, stirring often to prevent the milk solids from burning, until the butter foams and then darkens in color slightly and is very fragrant, 3 to 4 minutes. Pour the butter (along with the rosemary and any burnt bits) into a medium heatproof bowl and carefully transfer it to the fridge. Chill for 1 hour, until the butter resolidifies slightly.

02 In the bowl of a food processor fitted with the blade attachment, combine the flour, parmesan cheese, salt, and black pepper. Process until well combined, 10 to 15 seconds. Add the cooled rosemary butter and the heavy cream and process until a smooth, soft dough forms that pulls away from the sides of the bowl, 30 to 40 seconds. (The dough will have the texture of a soft sugar cookie dough.)

03 Transfer the dough to a lightly floured work surface and press together into a ball. Wrap in plastic and chill in the fridge for 1 hour.

04 Position a rack in the middle of the oven and preheat to 350°F. Line a baking sheet with parchment paper or a nonstick baking mat.

05 Unwrap the dough and transfer to a lightly floured work surface. Dust the top of the dough with flour and roll out to a ¼-inch-thick sheet. Using a 2-inch round fluted or classic cookie cutter, cut out cookies and place them on the prepared baking sheet, spacing about 1 inch apart. Press the dough scraps together into a ball and repeat the rolling and cutting process (discard any remaining scraps). Freeze the cookies for 10 minutes.

06 Sprinkle the tops of the cookies with flaky sea salt (if using) and bake until lightly browned, 16 to 18 minutes. Let cool completely on the baking sheet.

1 stick (8 tablespoons/113 grams) unsalted butter, cut into ½-inch cubes

2 tablespoons (6 grams) roughly chopped fresh rosemary leaves

1½ cups spooned and leveled all-purpose flour (192 grams), plus more for dusting

¾ cup (about 2 ounces/57 grams) finely grated parmesan cheese

½ teaspoon kosher salt

½ teaspoon freshly ground black pepper

¼ cup (59 ml) heavy cream

Flaky sea salt, for sprinkling (optional)

Make Ahead
The prepared dough can be stored in the refrigerator for several days before baking if tightly wrapped in plastic.

Storage
The cookies will keep in an airtight container in a single layer for up to 1 week.

Toasted Cheddar Cocktail Cookies

Makes 16 cookies

These cheesy little cocktail cookies are the perfect thing to snack on as a pre-dinner treat. They taste a bit like a cross between a Cheez-It and a shortbread cookie: toasty, savory, and impossibly tender. The trick to getting that rich toasted flavor is to twice-bake the cookies. This helps them take on a robust, caramelized cheddar flavor reminiscent of the "extra toasty" variety of Cheez-It. (My personal favorite.)

01 Arrange a rack in the middle of the oven and preheat to 350°F. Grease an 8 × 8-inch square baking pan with the nonstick pan spray. Line with parchment paper, leaving some overhang on all sides so it's easy to lift out the cookies after baking, and coat once more with the pan spray.

02 In the bowl of a food processor fitted with the blade attachment, combine the flour, grated cheese, paprika, and salt. Process until well combined and no large shreds of cheese remain, 10 to 15 seconds. Add the diced butter and egg yolks and process until a smooth, soft dough forms that pulls away from the sides of the food processor, 35 to 45 seconds. (The dough will have the texture of a soft sugar cookie dough.)

03 Transfer the dough to the prepared baking pan and spread into an even layer using an offset spatula or clean hands. Prick the top several times with a fork and sprinkle the sesame seeds over the top, gently pressing them in so they stick.

04 Bake until very fragrant and the top is just starting to brown slightly, 35 to 40 minutes. Remove the pan from the oven and let cool for 15 minutes. (I leave the oven on.) Meanwhile, line a baking sheet with parchment paper or a nonstick baking mat.

05 Carefully lift the shortbread out of the pan using the parchment paper and transfer to a cutting board. Cut into 16 rectangular pieces by cutting in half, then cutting each half crosswise into 8 bars. Carefully transfer the pieces to the prepared baking sheet, spacing about 1 inch apart. The shortbread will be very delicate at this point, so be gentle and work slowly. I find it easiest to use a thin metal spatula to get under the shortbread and transfer the pieces to the pan one by one.

06 Bake once more until the shortbreads are deep golden brown on all sides, 14 to 16 minutes. Let cool on the baking sheet for at least 1 hour before moving. (The cookies will be very crumbly when warm but will firm up once cooled.)

Nonstick pan spray

2¼ **cups** spooned and leveled all-purpose flour (288 grams)

1 **cup (about 3 ounces/85 grams)** grated sharp cheddar cheese, yellow or white

2 **teaspoons** paprika, preferably smoked

1 **teaspoon** kosher salt

2 **sticks (16 tablespoons/226 grams)** cold unsalted butter, cut into ½-inch cubes

2 **large** egg yolks

1 **teaspoon** white sesame seeds

1 **teaspoon** black sesame seeds

Make Ahead

The dough can be made and pressed into the baking pan the night before you bake the cookies. Just make sure to cover the baking pan very tightly with plastic wrap so the dough doesn't dry out.

Storage

The cookies will keep in an airtight container in a single layer for up to 1 week.

Loaded Shortbread Cookies

Makes 24 cookies

Cheddar cheese, fresh chives, and bacon combine in this savory little cookie that takes full advantage of the beloved baked stuffed-potato flavor combination. Swapping a buttery shortbread base for the standard buttery baked potato makes these cookies just as delicious but in a more snackable package. I like to finish them off with a small dab of sour cream and a sprinkle of chives on top for the perfect bite.

01 Line a plate with paper towels and set aside. Add the chopped bacon to a medium nonstick pan or skillet. Cook over medium heat, stirring often to prevent it from burning, until the bacon is crispy and dark brown, 6 to 9 minutes. Use a slotted spoon to transfer the bacon to the prepared plate and cool for 5 minutes.

02 In the bowl of a food processor fitted with the blade attachment, combine the flour, grated cheese, paprika, and salt. (Feel free to grate the cheese directly into the bowl if your food processor has a grater attachment.) Process until well combined and there are no large strands of cheese left, 10 to 15 seconds. Add the diced butter and egg and process until a smooth, soft dough forms that pulls away from the sides of the bowl, 30 to 40 seconds. (The dough will have the texture of a soft sugar cookie dough.)

03 Transfer the dough to a lightly floured work surface and knead in the chives and cooled bacon. Divide the dough in half (about 1 cup/250 grams per half) and transfer each portion to a large sheet of plastic wrap. Form each portion into a 1½-inch-diameter log that is about 6 inches long. Gently wrap each log in the plastic, twisting the ends tightly to help form a cylinder shape. Chill the logs in the freezer for 1 hour.

04 Arrange a rack in the middle of the oven and preheat to 350°F. Line a baking sheet with parchment paper or a nonstick baking mat.

05 Use a sharp, thin knife to slice each log into ½-inch-thick slices (12 slices per log). Arrange the slices on the prepared baking sheet, spacing them about 1 inch apart.

06 Bake for 18 to 23 minutes, until the tops of the cookies are lightly browned. Let cool completely on the baking sheet.

6 strips (about 6 ounces/170 grams) bacon, finely chopped

1½ cups spooned and leveled all-purpose flour (192 grams), plus more for dusting

1 cup (about 3 ounces/85 grams) grated sharp cheddar cheese, yellow or white

1 teaspoon paprika

¼ teaspoon kosher salt

1 stick (8 tablespoons/116 grams) cold unsalted butter, cut into ½-inch cubes

1 large egg

3 tablespoons (9 grams) finely chopped fresh chives

Make Ahead

The dough logs can be stored in the freezer tightly wrapped in plastic for several weeks. Once you're ready to bake them, let sit at room temperature for 10 minutes to soften slightly.

Storage

The cookies will keep in an airtight container in a single layer for up to 1 week.

Cornbread Madeleines

1 cup spooned and leveled all-purpose flour (128 grams)

½ cup (76 grams) fine yellow cornmeal

1 teaspoon baking powder

½ teaspoon kosher salt

½ teaspoon freshly ground black pepper

⅓ cup (66 grams) granulated sugar

4 large eggs, room temperature

1½ sticks (12 tablespoons/170 grams) unsalted butter, melted and cooled slightly, plus more for brushing the pan

½ cup (70 grams) raw corn kernels, roughly chopped (thawed, if frozen)

3 tablespoons (9 grams) finely chopped fresh chives

Note

For a spicy version, add 1 finely chopped medium jalapeño (with seeds) to the madeleine batter. For a cheesy version, add ½ cup (about 2 ounces/57 grams) shredded sharp cheddar cheese.

Make Ahead

The madeleine batter can be stored in the fridge overnight if tightly wrapped in plastic.

Storage

The madeleines will keep in an airtight container in a single layer for several days.

Honey Butter

To make a quick homemade honey butter, combine 1 stick (8 tablespoons/113 grams) softened unsalted butter with 2 tablespoons (42 grams) honey and a pinch of kosher salt. Stir until smooth and serve at room temperature.

Makes 24 madeleines

Not quite sweet, yet not quite savory, these cakey, cornbread-y madeleines are uniquely delicious. A quick batter made with cornmeal and just enough sugar is speckled with corn and fresh chives, then swirled with melted butter to help keep the madeleines moist. A two-hour rest in the fridge melds the flavors and helps create their signature bump. Baking these in a madeleine pan not only gives them their iconic half-shell shape but also creates crisp edges that contrast with their buttery corn-filled centers. I recommend eating them warm straight from the oven with a drizzle of honey butter (see recipe, below left), served with a bowl of chili, or dipped into tomato soup.

01 In a medium bowl, whisk together the flour, cornmeal, baking powder, salt, and black pepper.

02 In a large bowl, combine the sugar and eggs and whisk until smooth. Add the dry ingredients and mix with a rubber spatula until smooth. Add the melted butter and stir to combine. (It will look like too much butter at first, but don't fret.) Fold in the corn and chives and cover the bowl with plastic wrap. Refrigerate the batter for at least 2 hours, and up to overnight.

03 As the batter chills, brush the molds of a madeleine pan with a thin layer of melted butter and place in the refrigerator to chill as well.

04 Position a rack in the middle of the oven and preheat to 375°F.

05 Remove the chilled madeleine pan from the fridge and immediately fill each mold with 1 rounded tablespoon of the batter. Use a small spoon to evenly spread the batter into the molds and tap the pan on the countertop to evenly distribute in the grooves. (The batter does not need to go all the way up the sides of the molds.) You'll have batter left over; just keep it in the fridge to stay cold. Bake until the madeleines pull away from the sides of the molds slightly and have a small bump in the middle, 10 to 13 minutes. (Don't fret if they don't end up having a bump.) Transfer the pan to a wire rack and let the madeleines cool in the pan for 10 minutes.

06 Remove the madeleines and brush the pan with more melted butter (it's okay if the pan is still slightly warm). Chill the pan in the freezer for 10 minutes, then fill the molds again with batter and repeat the baking process until you run out of batter.

Sesame-Scallion Shortbread Squares

These sesame-scented shortbread squares are delightfully complex with just enough sugar to give them a sweet-and-salty flavor profile that keeps you coming back for more. A tablespoon of toasted sesame oil lends the cookies an earthy nuttiness, making good on the promise that the sesame seed topping offers, while an entire bunch of scallions ups the cookies' savory appeal. Baking them in a pan and then cutting them after they come out of the oven makes them a cinch to throw together, eliminating the need to roll out the dough and fuss with a cookie cutter.

01   Arrange a rack in the middle of the oven and preheat to 350°F. Grease an 8 × 8-inch square baking pan with the nonstick pan spray. Line with parchment paper, leaving some overhang on all sides so it's easy to lift out the cookies after baking, and coat once more with the pan spray.

02   In the bowl of a stand mixer fitted with the paddle attachment, combine the butter, confectioners' sugar, toasted sesame oil, garlic, and salt. (Alternatively, use an electric hand mixer and large bowl.) Beat on medium speed until smooth and fluffy, scraping down the sides and bottom halfway through, 2 to 3 minutes. Turn the mixer off and add the flour. Mix on low speed just until a crumbly dough forms, 1 to 2 minutes. Add the chopped scallions and ½ cup (60 grams) of the sesame seeds and mix just until distributed.

03   Transfer the dough to the prepared baking pan and press into an even layer using an offset spatula or clean hands. Sprinkle the remaining 1 tablespoon sesame seeds over the top and press them in slightly with your hands.

04   Bake until very fragrant and the top of the shortbread is just starting to brown slightly, 45 to 50 minutes. Let cool for 5 minutes.

05   Carefully lift the shortbread out of the pan using the parchment paper and transfer to a cutting board while still warm. (Careful, the pan will still be hot.) Cut into a 4 × 4 grid to make 16 squares. Let cool for at least 1 hour before moving. (Shortbread will be very crumbly when warm but will firm up when cooled.)

Nonstick pan spray

2 sticks (16 tablespoons/226 grams) unsalted butter, softened

1 cup (100 grams) confectioners' sugar

1 tablespoon toasted sesame oil

2 garlic cloves, minced or finely grated

1½ teaspoons kosher salt

3 cups spooned and leveled all-purpose flour (384 grams)

½ cup (60 grams) lightly packed finely chopped scallions (green and white parts; about 1 bunch)

½ cup plus 1 tablespoon (68 grams) toasted white or black sesame seeds, or a combination, divided (see page 18)

Storage

The shortbread will keep in an airtight container in a single layer for up to 1 week.

Savory Thumbprint Cookies with Cream Cheese & Pepper Jelly

Makes 18 cookies

A Ritz cracker smeared with cream cheese and hot pepper jelly is the holy trinity of snacking. The cooling richness of the cream cheese balances the sweet spiciness of the pepper jelly, while the buttery crunch of a Ritz cracker holds it all together. It's the ultimate combination of hot, cold, smooth, and crisp. These festive thumbprint cookies borrow that same flavor profile.

1½ cups spooned and leveled all-purpose flour (192 grams), plus more for dusting

2 cups (235 grams) shredded sharp cheddar cheese, yellow or white

½ teaspoon kosher salt

1 teaspoon paprika

1 stick (8 tablespoons/113 grams) cold unsalted butter, cut into ½-inch cubes

⅓ cup (104 grams) pepper jelly (see Note)

1 large egg

1 sleeve (about 32 crackers/100 grams) Ritz crackers, crushed

6 tablespoons (3 ounces/85 grams) cream cheese, softened

Note
Pepper jelly can be found in the jelly or hot sauce section of most well-stocked grocery stores, including Trader Joe's.

Make Ahead
If wrapped tightly in plastic, the dough can be stored in the refrigerator for several days before baking. If it's too firm to portion, let sit at room temperature for 15 minutes and try again.

Storage
The cookies will keep in an airtight container in the fridge for several days. Let come to room temperature before serving.

01 In the bowl of a food processor fitted with the blade attachment, combine the flour, shredded cheese, salt, and paprika. Process until the cheese is broken down into tiny pieces, 20 to 25 seconds. Add the butter and pulse 15 to 20 times, just until a soft dough forms. (Do not overmix. As soon as it looks moist and starts to stick together, stop mixing.)

02 Transfer the dough to a lightly floured surface and press together into a disc. Wrap in plastic and chill in the fridge for 2 hours.

03 Place the pepper jelly in a small bowl and stir to break up any lumps. Place the egg in a small bowl and stir with a fork until no streak of yolk remains. Place the crushed crackers in a shallow, wide bowl.

04 Preheat the oven to 350°F and set 2 racks at the upper-middle and lower-middle positions. Line 2 baking sheets with parchment paper or nonstick baking mats.

05 Portion out the chilled dough using your hands and roll into balls about 1½ inches in diameter (18 balls total). Working with one ball at a time, dip the ball in the egg, then roll in the crushed crackers to coat it. Place the balls at least 3 inches apart on the prepared baking sheets (9 per sheet). Using the bottom of a teaspoon-sized measuring spoon, press in the center of each ball to create an indentation. If the sides of the balls crack while pressing them, just pinch them back together.

06 Bake both sheets of the unfilled cookies at the same time, until the edges are just starting to brown slightly but the centers are still raw, 10 to 12 minutes. Remove from the oven and let cool for 5 minutes. Use the bottom of the teaspoon to press down on the indentations to flatten them again. Fill each indentation with 1 teaspoon of cream cheese, pressing it into the bottom of the indentation as best you can. Top each filling with about 1 teaspoon of the pepper jelly. Bake once more (swapping the bottom sheet to the top this time) until the cookies are deep golden brown on the sides, 10 to 12 minutes more. Let cool for at least 1 hour on the baking sheets.

Peppery Parmesan Crisps

The distinction between a cracker and a savory cookie is often a blurry one—these crisps are the perfect example. A salty, parmesan-flavored dough gets showered with a generous amount of cracked black peppercorns to give them a spicy kick, then baked until golden brown. The trick to making them so crispy and cracker-esque is to be patient while you bake them. The crisps will look like they're done baking relatively early, but it's important to take them just a tad further. These extra few minutes not only makes them crispier but lends them a wonderful toasted flavor, too.

01 Arrange a rack in the middle of the oven and preheat to 350°F.

02 In the bowl of a food processor fitted with the blade attachment, combine the parmesan, flour, paprika, salt, and baking powder. Process until well combined, 10 to 15 seconds. Add the heavy cream and olive oil and process until the flour is completely moistened and starting to form small clumps, 10 to 15 seconds.

03 Transfer the dough to a large piece of parchment paper and press together into a rough rectangle shape. Top with another piece of parchment paper, then roll out the dough between them to create a rough 12 × 6-inch rectangle that's 1/8 inch thick. Remove the top piece of parchment paper and carefully transfer the rolled-out dough to a baking sheet by lifting it up from the bottom piece of parchment paper. (You will bake the crisps on the bottom piece of parchment paper.)

04 Brush the top of the dough with a thin layer of heavy cream and sprinkle the black pepper evenly over the top.

05 Bake until the top is deep golden brown, 18 to 22 minutes. Immediately cut into 1-inch strips using a pizza cutter and let cool completely on the baking sheet.

½ cup (about 2 ounces/57 grams) finely grated, not shredded, parmesan cheese

¾ **cup** spooned and leveled all-purpose flour (96 grams)

1 teaspoon paprika, preferably smoked

½ teaspoon kosher salt

¼ teaspoon baking powder

¼ cup (59 ml) heavy cream, plus more for brushing

2 tablespoons (30 ml) extra-virgin olive oil

¾ teaspoon freshly ground black pepper

Storage

The crisps will keep in an airtight container in a single layer for up to 1 week.

Parmesan Cheesecake Bars

Cheesecake bars go from the dessert table to appetizer hour with the help of a few unexpected ingredients and a salty, buttery cracker crust. By omitting the sugar and swapping in parmesan and garlic, the bars transform into a savory treat perfect for serving at a soiree. The flavor is reminiscent of a decadent Alfredo sauce or creamy soft cheese, while the texture is just as rich as the sweeter version. I like to dress them up by topping them with an herby salad, but they are just as impressive without.

01 Arrange a rack in the middle of the oven and preheat to 325°F. Grease an 8 × 8-inch square baking pan with the nonstick pan spray. Line with parchment paper, leaving some overhang on all sides so it's easy to lift out the bars after baking, and coat once more with the pan spray.

02 Place the crackers in the bowl of a food processor fitted with the blade attachment. Pulse 20 to 30 times, until the crackers are the texture of coarse sand and no large pieces remain. Add the melted butter and process until the butter is completely absorbed by the cracker crumbs, 15 to 20 seconds.

03 Transfer the mixture to the prepared baking pan and press into an even layer using the bottom of a measuring cup or clean hands. Wipe the food processor out with a paper towel and set it aside. Bake until the crust is light golden brown and very fragrant, 10 to 12 minutes. Let cool slightly. Leave the oven turned on.

04 While the crust is cooling, add the cream cheese, parmesan, sour cream, eggs, milk, garlic, cornstarch, and salt to the empty food processor and process until completely smooth, 25 to 30 seconds. Pour the mixture over the cooled crust and bake until the filling jiggles slightly when moved but the edges are fully set, 38 to 43 minutes. Turn the oven off, open the oven door halfway, and let the cheesecake cool in the open oven for 30 minutes. (This will help prevent the top from cracking.) Refrigerate the bars uncovered for at least 4 hours, up to overnight.

05 When ready to serve, carefully lift out the bars using the parchment paper and transfer to a cutting board. Cut into 16 pieces (a 4 × 4 grid), wiping the knife clean between slices. Garnish the tops with the herbs and greens (if using).

Nonstick pan spray

2 sleeves (64 crackers/212 grams) Ritz crackers

¾ stick (6 tablespoons/85 grams) unsalted butter, melted and cooled slightly

12 ounces (340 grams) cream cheese, softened

1 cup (about 4 ounces/113 grams) grated, not shredded, parmesan cheese

1 cup (235 grams) sour cream

3 large eggs

½ cup (118 ml) whole milk

2 garlic cloves, minced or finely grated

1 tablespoon cornstarch

1 teaspoon kosher salt

Tender herbs and greens, for serving (optional)

Storage
The cheesecake bars will keep in an airtight container in a single layer in the fridge for up to 1 week.

Acknowledgments

Thank you:

To Clarkson Potter, and my editor Raquel Pelzel, for bringing this book to life and taking a chance on me. Working with you has been the most refreshing career experience of my life, and I cannot imagine a more supportive editor to have worked with. Thank you for always being my advocate. And to Bianca Cruz for keeping us organized and on track.

To Robert Diaz and Stephanie Huntwork for creating such a striking, sleek, and timeless book. To Carole Berglie for copyediting the text and making it read so beautifully. And to Mark McCauslin and Kelli Tokos for shepherding the book through production.

To my agent, Jon Michael Darga, for believing in my vision, taking a chance on my proposal, and supporting me every step of the way.

To Danielle DeLott, who introduced me to my agent, provided guidance and support at every step of the process, and cross-tested over half the recipes in the book. You fundamentally helped bring this book to life and I cannot thank you enough.

To Dennis Green, who taste-tested every single cookie in the book and helped me in immeasurable ways. Your influence can be seen on every page of this book, and your loving support is what kept me going.

To Chelsea Kyle, Maeve Sheridan, and Drew Aichele for making the book a true work of art. You are an absolute dream team, and I am honored to have worked with such a talented group of visionaries. To Gabrielle Lakshmi for helping on set and being a hand model. And to Toast, the hardest-working set dog in the business.

To Hello Artists for lending us your studio and supporting the project.

To Ice Sculptures of NY for making us the most gorgeous ice cubes, seen throughout this book.

To my loving family, who baked countless cookies, talked at length about the recipes, and showed endless support: my dad, Anthony Szewczyk; my mom, Lorna Szewczyk; and my sister, Jena Szewczyk.

To all my recipe testers: Ben Weiner, who tested a sizable portion of the book, helped style on set, and has been helping me succeed long before this book; as well as Sara Jerde, James Park, Elazar Sontag, and Vicki Chen.

To Alexis deBoschnek, Eric Kim, Casey Elsass, and Rick Martínez for always being there to answer questions and provide constant support.

To Hannah Wong, who helped translate my vision into a proposal, Megan Hazard for being my personal Uber driver, Elaine Pyles for putting up with my nonsense, and Emily Shwake for supporting my dreams.

And of course, to the countless recipe developers, bakers, authors, and cookie experts who came before me. Your influence is undeniable, and I am forever indebted to the work you have done. No idea starts entirely from scratch, and what follows are just some of the sources I constantly turned to for guidance and inspiration.

Books

America's Test Kitchen. *The Perfect Cookie: Your Ultimate Guide to Foolproof Cookies, Brownies & Bars.* America's Test Kitchen, 2017.

Beranbaum, Rose Levy. *The Cookie Bible.* Houghton Mifflin Harcourt, 2021.

Editors of Martha Stewart Living. *Martha Stewart's Cookie Perfection: 100+ Recipes to Take Your Sweet Treats to the Next Level.* Clarkson Potter, 2019.

Firth, Rebecca. *The Cookie Book: Decadent Bites for Every Occasion.* Page Street Publishing, 2018.

Greenspan, Dorie, and Davide Luciano. *Dorie's Cookies.* Rux Martin/Houghton Mifflin Harcourt, 2016.

Hart Hoffman, Brian. *The Cookie Collection: Artisan Baking for the Cookie Enthusiast.* 83 Press, 2019.

Kieffer, Sarah. *100 Cookies: The Baking Book for Every Kitchen, with Classic Cookies, Novel Treats, Brownies, Bars, and More.* Chronicle Books, 2020.

King Arthur Baking Company. *The King Arthur Baking Company's All-Purpose Baker's Companion.* Revised, updated edition. Countryman Press, 2021.

O'Brady, Tara. *Seven Spoons: My Favorite Recipes for Any and Every Day.* Ten Speed Press, 2015.

Ottolenghi, Yotam, and Helen Goh. *Sweet: Desserts from London's Ottolenghi.* Ten Speed Press, 2017.

Parks, Stella, and J. Kenji López-Alt. *BraveTart: Iconic American Desserts.* W. W. Norton & Company, 2017.

Segal, Mindy, and Kate Leahy. *Cookie Love: More Than 60 Recipes and Techniques for Turning the Ordinary into the Extraordinary.* Ten Speed Press, 2015.

Websites

Bake from Scratch
www.bakefromscratch.com

Butter and Brioche
www.butterandbrioche.com

Cloudy Kitchen
www.cloudykitchen.com

Constellation Inspiration
www.constellationinspiration.com

Hummingbird High
www.hummingbirdhigh.com

Joy the Baker
www.joythebaker.com

King Arthur Baking Company
www.kingarthurbaking.com

My Name is Yeh
www.mynameisyeh.com

Serious Eats
www.seriouseats.com

Smitten Kitchen
www.smittenkitchen.com

The Boy Who Bakes
www.theboywhobakes.co.uk

The Vanilla Bean Blog
www.thevanillabeanblog.com

Index